KEEPING A NATURE JOURNAL

Discover a Whole New Way of Seeing the World Around You

Clare Walker Leslie & Charles E. Roth

Foreword by Edward O. Wilson

Illustrations by Clare Walker Leslie and others

STOREY BOOKS

North Adams, Massachusetts

The mission of Storey Publishing is to serve our customers
by publishing practical information that encourages personal independence
in harmony with the environment.

ilex

Edited by Deborah Balmuth
Cover design by Meredith Maker
Cover illustrations by Clare Walker Leslie
Cover photography by Giles Prett
Text design by Meredith Maker and Mark Tomasi
Production by Erin Lincourt
Indexed by Hagerty & Holloway

Printed in China by C & C Offset Printing
10 9 8 7 6 5 4

A hardcover version of this book was previously published under the title *Nature Journaling: Learning to Observe and Connect with the World Around You* (Storey, 1998, ISBN 1-58017-088-9).

Library of Congress Cataloging-in-Publication Data

Leslie, Clare Walker.
    Keeping a nature journal: discover a whole new way of seeing the world around you / Clare Walker Leslie & Charles E. Roth; foreword by Edward O. Wilson; illustrations by Clare Walker Leslie and others.
        p. cm.
    Previously published as: Nature journaling. c1998.
    Includes bibliographical references (p.).
    ISBN 1-58017-306-3 (pbk.)
        1. Nature. 2. Natural history. 3. Diaries— Authorship.
I. Roth, Charles Edmund, 1934-   . II. Leslie, Clare Walker. Nature journaling.
III. Title.
QH81 .L595 2000
508—dc21

98-14497
CIP

Dedication

This book is dedicated to my daughter, Anna,
because she has been with me throughout the whole process.
It was Anna and her friends who gave me the courage and the support
to find a way through to publication — suggesting exercises, offering
their own drawings, being women naturalists of the future.
Clare Walker Leslie

I would like to dedicate this book to my mentor — naturalist-educator
Charles Mohr, who guided my early ventures into natural history — and
to my five grandchildren, who may each find in these pages a way to
develop their own sense of place in a changing world.
Charles E. Roth

Contents

Part 1: Getting Started

Part 2: Journaling through the Seasons

JOHN BUSBY

Thanks to Our Students

For years students have been badgering us to get into print what they have found to be an extremely useful method for writing, drawing, and reflecting on what lives around them. This book is a truly collaborative effort, containing not only our observations and art, but also the work of some of our students and professional colleagues.

In over twenty-five years of teaching nature drawing and journaling, we have encountered hundreds of students, young and old, in and out of academic situations, and with tremendous ranges of skills in either nature or drawing study, who, in taking on their own nature journals, became their own *learners*. Increasingly, people think that nature is only found in nature reserves and parks. Journaling can help you discover that nature is actually all around. All you need is heightened perception and awareness.

*A*cknowledgments

Both of us would like to acknowledge our debt to the life work of artist-naturalist-teacher Roger Tory Peterson. We trust he would find in these pages an extension of his efforts.

We would also like to thank the many fellow artists, naturalists, and journalists who have shared in the development of this book over the four years of its making. Space does not permit us to list all of you, but we must give special mention to:

Bill Hammond, Hannah Hinchman, Cathy Johnson, John Elder, John Busby, Steve Lindell, Bill Fox, Audrey Nelson, Ron Cisar, John Pitcher, Marcy Marchello, and J. Parker Huber.

We are particularly grateful to those who have supported and piloted the ideas presented here and who believe in this work. We especially thank the teachers of the Hardy School, Tobin School, Caryl School, Massachusetts Audubon Society, Carleton College, Williams College, and many other schools and teaching centers across the country where Clare has taught and is still teaching.

We also thank Lucy Patton, Clare's secretary, who braved many a storm with the calm of a fellow mother, partner, and believer. And we thank Edward O. Wilson, Research Professor at Harvard University, for believing enough in our efforts to take precious time from his own important work with nature to write our foreword.

This book would not be in existence without the commitment, intelligence, and creativity of our editor, Deborah Balmuth, and the creative team at Storey Books. They have made the task of pulling everything together a joy.

We also owe a very special debt of love and gratitude to our respective spouses, David and Sandy, for putting up with the messes in the houses and our mental absences while we struggled to bring order out of a chaos of papers and ideas.

Roger Tory Peterson

Virginia Marie Peterson
July 2, 1995

Foreword

What is natural history? It is virtually the whole world around you. It is the vista of a great forest from a mountaintop, and a swath of weeds growing along a city sidewalk. It is the breaching of a whale, and the protozoans teeming in algae in a drop of pond water. Everywhere the world is alive, awaiting exploration by those who prefer, if only at intervals, real reality to virtual reality. And as to the wonders of modern technology, bear in mind that a sidewalk weed and a protozoan are each more complex than any device yet invented by humanity.

Because humanity evolved in nature over millions of years, there is every reason to expect that we possess an innate capacity to draw deep excitement and pleasure from experiencing it. And because our species has been exquisitely adapted to the razor-thin biosphere covering the planet by this same evolution, our survival depends on understanding and protecting the rest of life. What we most enjoy, including a clean, healthy natural environment, also serves the interest of the human species.

This combination of pleasure and practicality is what makes the kind of illustration promoted in *Keeping a Nature Journal* important. For centuries it has been the mainstay of representing the natural world. For a time many believed that natural history and scientific art would be supplanted by photography and graphs. But these are merely the extremes available to the human eye, bracketing detailed rendition at one end and abstraction of data at the other. In between and just as enduring is natural history illustration, wherein the observer brings out those features thought most important and interesting in settings difficult for photographs and impossible for graphs to attain. Nature journaling is also extremely flexible. It ranges from scientific figures designed for professional publications to creative art whose principal purpose is to convey aesthetic pleasure.

The art of natural history, as *Keeping a Nature Journal* shows very well, serves yet another, equally important function. To a degree greater than photography, it involves the illustrator directly in what he observes. The illustrator *re-creates* what he sees and does not merely record. He expresses what seems important, hence worthy to stress and convey in a single compelling image. He can strengthen his impression with written description and commentary. This creative process is at the heart of natural history observation, and it helps to make the best of experiences also the most lasting in memory for anyone wishing to enjoy it.

Edward O. Wilson
Research Professor, Harvard University
Honorary Curator in Entomology,
Museum of Comparative Zoology

some 60 brant in raw umber field

Preface

When I was young, I played outdoors all the time. Nature was a part of my daily world, as it was for my sisters and our friends. We never knew the specific names of things, but trees were towers to be climbed, bushes were caves, wooded paths were for bicycles, and creek banks were for endless games. Today those woods are gone, but I am the naturalist and artist I am now because of those magical days of play and camaraderie outdoors.

Now I teach and paint and write about the connections between drawing and nature. People ask where I began my study; it is too long a story to tell here, but it goes back to those woods. I left for college and then to teach art and continue my training as a cellist. But the out-of-doors kept distracting me. I tried connecting the teaching of art with teaching about nature. It didn't work. So I quit to learn the path of a naturalist and a painter of nature on my own. One day, canoeing with a friend across a wild stretch of open sea out to an island off the coast of Massachusetts to count migrating shorebirds, I knew I had found my way. A lone peregrine swept over us, swarming up a mass of dunlins that were feeding along the beach. I had my drawing pad and binoculars; I drew wildly in the rocking canoe. And today I still have the print I made from that startling event.

Many of us are self-taught, seeking out courses, books, and mentors where we can. I was fortunate enough to find the teachers and kindly advisers I needed in Eric Ennion of England, John Busby of Scotland, Gunnar Brusewitz of Sweden, and Marie Henry, Libby Darlington, and Don Stokes in this country. To them I owe my drive and desire to bring outdoor field drawing and journaling to this country. It has not been as popular here as in Europe, where it is still part of the traditional method of studying science.

Now, twenty-five years later, with six books published, a marriage, two kids, a double life in rural Vermont and urban Cambridge, and no studio to speak of, I wander throughout this country teaching. I use my own yearly journal as a source of information about and connection with the ongoing pulse of nature. This, in turn, keeps me connected to the rest of life.

In a box on my floor are my journals, back to 1978. I even have the journals I began in the labor and delivery rooms for my children, Eric and Anna.

People ask how I keep so many journals going year upon year. Well, I answer, they have become my job, my source of reverence, my inspiration for books, and my best friends.

I have been developing the ideas in this book over a number of years, but teaching about nature journaling is far easier than writing about it. Chuck Roth, a mentor and professional naturalist-educator, author and artist, agreed to join me in the project and to add his own perspectives when needed. The book has become a moving experience of collaboration and search for a common voice. I am more the artist, he more the scientist. I draw; he writes. I handwrite in pencil; he composes on his computer. But our message comes through our collective beliefs and through those of the students and colleagues gathered in the pages of this book.

Clare Walker Leslie
Cambridge, Massachusetts, 1997

peregrine +
dunlin - Monomoy Island
a blowing September day

I grew up an only child in a relatively rural setting. The world of nature provided my immediate playmates and playthings. They were a most intimate part of my formative years. There were not many adults around me who shared my interests or knew much of anything about the world of nature. I recall being fascinated by the calls of spring peepers, and amazed that none of the adults in my neighborhood could tell me what made those loud noises. I was told variously that the calls came from turtles, snakes, and birds.

I set out to find out for myself. When I first found those tiny, 1-inch frogs with throats blown up like bubble gum, I could hardly believe my eyes or ears. I caught several and brought them home in a jar. My parents at first refused to believe that these little creatures were the real source of such loud choruses of sounds. About ten o'clock that night, however, when the peepers began calling in the jar, they became believers; I was awakened and told to remove that jar from the house — promptly and permanently!

That experience is etched in my memory, and many more as well. But most of the details have long since faded away. I wish I had kept a journal that recorded my childhood discoveries of nature, and people's reactions to them. I made many crude drawings of things I observed, but these have long ago disappeared, probably into a variety of trash containers.

It was in college that I was first encouraged to make detailed field notes about my natural history observations. The style I was taught was quite traditional, formal, and scientific, but in the long run very useful for reviewing a variety of observations. As time passed I learned to add to this formal, scientific approach many informal observations, questions for future observations, philosophical ramblings on the meaning of what I was observing, and other perceptions about the world around me. These journal entries were to serve me well in both later writings and later art projects; indeed, they continue to do so.

My life work has focused mostly on training teachers and youth leaders in natural history and helping foster basic environmental literacy among our citizens. Clare has stimulated hundreds of people to begin keeping nature journals; we have even taught some nature observation workshops jointly in the past. As a journalist I tend to be more writer than artist; for Clare, it's just the reverse. For me the primary task in the field is to observe carefully and intently; later I record my observations and reflect on them in the journals. For Clare the task outdoors is to draw, which helps her focus her observations. She works on the details; I search for the gestalt, the bigger connections, the context in which the objects and events are occurring. These are different ways to approach the same thing —an understanding of the natural world.

Charles E. "Chuck" Roth
Littleton, Massachusetts, 1997

A Man of Place

I am a man of place;
A place in space,
A place in time;
A piece of life
In process of becoming.

I am a man of place;
Low, rounded hills,
Cloaked in forest,
Facing the sea,
Receiving the waves.

I am a man of place.
Fluids bear essences
To build bodies and land
And flush the systems
Of the worn and unwanted.

I am a man of place.
Blood flows through
My aging veins
As streams surge
Through forest and mead.

I am a man of place.
The spirit of the place
Possesses my mind.
I speak with its voice.
We are one being.

I am a man of place.
Though I am but a man
I am also the land,
The sky, the sea,
Fellow creatures are as I.

I am a man of place.
I can be no more,
Nor can I be less.
Our edges are illusions.
I am a man of place.

—Chuck Roth,
in June 1990 journal

PART 1

Getting Started

March 25 — Cambridge   a warm day at last!
                        what it does to spirits and humor!
                        blue skies - sunshine - birds singing

9:30 am -
couldn't resist
drawing my snow drops
at the side walk -
Pushing up through winter's
debris of cigarette butts, trash et al —   5 precious snow drops....

In this 20th century, to stop rushing around, to sit quietly on the grass, to switch off the world and come back to the earth, to allow the eye to see a willow, a bush, a cloud, a leaf . . . I have learned that what I have not drawn I have never really seen.

— FREDERICK FRANCK, *THE ZEN OF SEEING*

It was a cold and dark day
when I went for a walk
in that old abandonned
farm field.
Snow was coming and the
colors were muted — mauve,
                        burnt umber

Then, I saw the hawk-
feathers blowing from the
                        wind —
up in the hickory —
just watching
        the day.

Over me it circled,
eye flashing in the light.
Gone it went into a maze
of trees and houses —
        a suburban denizen.

I continued to collect
winter colors, still caught
by the light in the hawk's eye.

December 4 · 1996
McLeans' fields
Belmont MA

Sunrise = 6:57 am
Sunset = 4:12 pm
    The shortest days
    are with us now.

Clare Walker Leslie

bitternut
hickory leaves
scattered about

partially eaten
hickory nuts

seeds
that feed
the winter-
active
creatures

CHAPTER 1

Discovering Nature Journaling

Many of us are looking for ways to connect better with nature — to learn its patterns, to help protect its inhabitants, to gain an understanding of what makes our own lives tick. Scientists since the dawn of the human mind have sought to know nature better, and to know their own selves better. Many of them went out with pen, parchment, paintbrush, and telescope to record their sightings. The nature journal has been the companion for every man, woman, child, or old sage with an insatiable curiosity about the natural world.

In this book, we offer you a way to join the two of us, our students, our mentors, and our colleagues in a journey of discovery, connection, understanding, and magic. The instruction is simple, the tools minimal, the class size one hundred or one, the environment from the most urban to the most rural, the possibilities for paths traveled infinite, and the test scores nonexistent.

Begin Exploring

Nature journaling is your path into the exploration of the natural world around you, and into your personal connection with it. How you use your journal is entirely up to you. We have made careers from its processes. You can be as involved as is your interest. Are you a classroom teacher, a self-taught and curious

How I would like people to hear . . . the sound of snow falling through the deepening night. . . .

— HAKUIN (SEVENTEENTH-CENTURY ZEN POET)

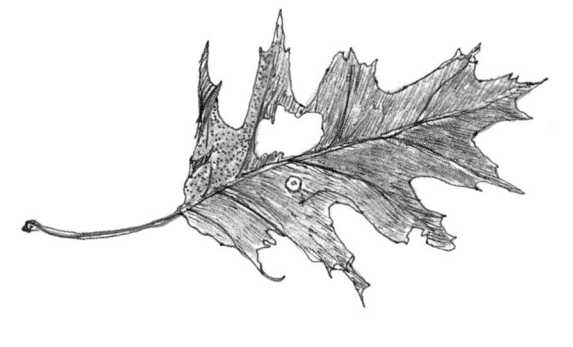

naturalist, an artist who loves nature, a scientist who would love to draw nature, someone who finds in nature a place for healing, meditation, and connection?

Go find a piece of paper; it doesn't matter what type or size. Find any pencil, marker, or drawing tool. Now gather up your eyes, take a deep breath, and ask yourself: "What is happening outdoors, this particular season, this time of day, and in this particular place where I live?" (You can be outdoors, or inside looking out.) Draw a cloud, a bird flying by, a tree branch, ivy vines on a building wall, a potted plant, or garden flower. Don't judge your drawing. You are not an artist yet. You are a scientist, simply recording *what you see,* in this moment in time. Be very quiet, be very still. Slow your breathing and think only "bud," "plant," "bird." After one minute or less, no more, write what you drew and go on to the next sighting, keeping it relevant to season, time of day, and place.

You have begun nature journaling. In chapter 2 you will find suggestions for ways to set up a journal; chapter 3 presents examples of various journaling topics and techniques, and the chapters in Part 3 offer guidance in developing drawing skills and teaching nature journaling to others. As we have found, the advantage of the nature journal is that it is often a personal course that is largely self-taught.

The disadvantage is that there are few people to turn to as resources. As people are seeking new and deeper ways to connect with nature, nature journaling is growing in popularity both as a vital educational tool and a personal course of study. If it suits you, let us know. We offer workshops and provide encouragement by correspondence. But we suggest you turn also to local nature centers, bookstores, libraries, environmental studies departments at colleges, 4-H clubs, and conservation organizations for like-minded people who will say "Yes, I know about cloud patterns"; "I lead nature walks nearby"; "I teach wildflower drawing"; "I, too, feel so much better after taking five to draw a willow, a bush, a cloud, a leaf."

What Is Nature Journaling?

You won't find the word *journaling* in your dictionary. It is a word we created as an action form of the noun *journal.* Simply put, nature journaling is the regular recording of observations, perceptions, and feelings about the natural world around you. That is the essence of the process. The recording can be done in a wide variety of ways, depending on the individual journalist's interests, background, and training. Some people prefer to record in written prose or poetry, some do it through drawing or painting, others with photographs or tape recordings, and still others through musical notation. There are people with the training and inclination to record with mathematical precision and in scientific shorthand. Others like to incorporate the writings and thoughts of others to stimulate their own journaling. Many people use all or a combination of these techniques.

A Flexible Medium

The appeal of the nature journal throughout the course of human history has been its flexibility. People have entered lists of birds seen at certain hours. Some count insects in a square yard of field and record their findings. Others keep moon-phase and weather charts. You can write poems, draw poems, or carefully diagram and draw a dead gull you've come upon on the beach. The journal is yours to use as you wish. This book is not about a prescribed activity that is done in

I have drawn ever since I could remember. Drawing is a piece of paper . . . and rubbing your hand over it the drawing comes up — it's there. Writing is pain, agony, and backache. I certainly could write without drawing, but drawing makes me see so much more. And by the same token, writing and learning makes me see so much more when I draw.

—ANN ZWINGER

California ground squirrel staring at us from stump of ancient oak about 7" long solid · dull brown with some darker spots

7.9.97 2pm
Drawing on the
porch while the
rain pours down +
mists on the notus

....stories unfold as people talk over drawing....

National Wildlife
Federation Summit
Adirondacks · NY
Silver Bay

the same way by everyone; in fact, it is about developing a very personal book of life, one that reflects the life around you — the experiences, encounters, reflections, and observations that you are moved to record, remember, study, and reflect upon.

Be a child. Go outdoors or just look out a window nearby and ask yourself, "What's happening outside today?" Draw the first thing you see. You have begun your nature journal.

When Clare began her first nature journal, the prospect of the blank page and what to draw were daunting. She was out in an Audubon sanctuary with a friend, poking around like blind fools in a park, neither one knowing much about nature but each eager to learn. Twenty years ago, Clare's first drawing was a hesitant description of a golden-rod gall, about which she had asked her friend, "Who made this?" (Her friend today is a prominent naturalist with many books under his belt. But back then he, too, was wondering.)

The two then found a meadow vole's nest, some rabbit droppings, and chewed twigs. A hawk circled above and it began to drizzle. Rain droplets hung on the old raspberry brambles, and for the first time the two amateur naturalists saw the world upside down on the lens of the 1/4-inch watery orbs.

Although years have passed, Clare can return to those early pages from the stack of journals on her shelf and remember the excitement and joy of discovery. In an emergency, those journals go with her first out the door!

A Broad Understanding of Nature

What makes a journal a *nature* journal? What constitutes nature? Is it only birds, animals, plants, and sky? Most people consider a wasp's nest to be natural, as well as a coral reef. But a wasp's nest is made from raw materials that the wasp gathers from its surroundings; a coral reef is limestone that coral polyps have mined from the surrounding waters and formed into a deposit to protect their very fragile bodies. In the same manner, buildings, roads, and manufactured objects are all things made by natural beings — humans.

Our assumption is that people are as natural as other animals and plants. The things people make and use are just as natural as the nests that paper wasps

make or the reefs that coral polyps build. You may not immediately think of people as an integral part of nature, but we are. Human activity offers fertile ground for the observations and reflections of the nature journalist.

It is important to note here that whereas a diary or personal journal records your feelings toward yourself and others, a nature journal primarily records your responses to and reflections about the world of nature around you. A nature journal may not be as private as a personal journal. Often, it is meant to be seen and reviewed by others.

Returning to an Ancient Human Practice

Nature journaling is not new. In fact, it is one of the oldest methods around: People have used it throughout history to record a hunt or battle, the passage of time, the success of an exploration, the sickness in a village. Whether they drew on cave walls, etched marks into sticks, painted stories on vases or tepees, or laboriously inscribed sheepskin manuscripts, nature

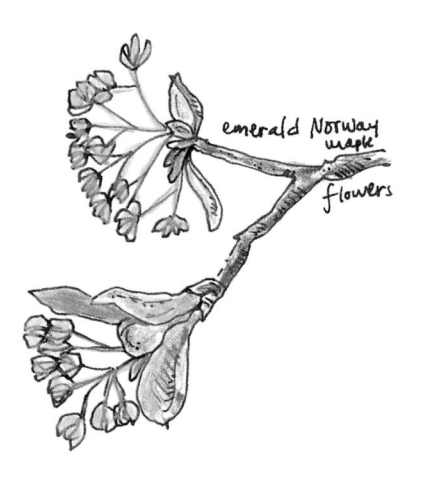

emerald Norway maple flowers

A child's world is fresh and new and beautiful, full of wonder and excitement. It is our misfortune that for most of us that clear-eyed vision, that true instinct for what is beautiful and awe-inspiring, is dimmed and even lost before we reach adulthood.

— RACHEL CARSON, *A SENSE OF WONDER*

Max in the snowy day
2·14·97

It seems only natural that we should value most what we are in contact with every day — local and familiar places, commonplace birds and animals — yet the reverse is often true. We appear to place a higher value on rare animals and plants and spectacular views and far-flung places. Of course both are important because they fulfill different needs. But the everyday places desperately need our attention — partly because they are changing so fast, and not always for the better, and also because tremendous benefit is to be gained from a personal involvement with your own locality.

— THE PARISH MAPS PROJECT,

LONDON, ENGLAND, 1987

red fox

journals have been kept. These records may not have been called nature journals at the time, but nature journals they truly were. Sea captains have kept logs (which are a form of nature journal) noting the weather, constellations, passing birds, human behavior, and other items of interest. How do you think Christopher Columbus convinced Queen Isabella that he had reached the New World? Did he send her e-mail? Did he fax her the information? Did he even have a camera? No, he had his logbook. Many explorers, then and still today, use artist-naturalists on their expeditions. Why do you think they take such people along?

Why do you think President Thomas Jefferson hired explorers Lewis and Clark to lead the expedition on the Missouri River to the Pacific Ocean? Yes, they were skilled exploration leaders, but each also kept meticulous journals containing detailed drawings and writings. Their journals contain some of the best records we have today of their hazardous two-year journey.

In both Europe and America, schoolchildren often made yearly journals of their class observa-

tions about natural and human life in the village or out on the prairie, as a way of learning about where they lived. These journals also served as "basal readers." Students of the next generation became recipients of the knowledge of place gained by an earlier generation.

Today many schools, nature centers, and college environmental studies programs are returning to studies of local backyard habitats, partly in reaction to a previous flood of classroom studies dealing with exotic and far-off habitats, such as the Arctic, rain forest, desert, or ocean. The London-based Parish Maps Project, the National Wildlife Federation's School Yard Habitats program, and the Stories in the Land and Watershed Partnerships programs of the Massachusetts-based Orion Society all support place-based environmental education.

Studies have found many children today consider nature to be somewhere else — on TV, on videos, in *National Geographic* only. The purpose of nature journaling is to study where you live and how you relate to it. Season by season, habitat by habitat.

Becoming a Naturalist

The overwhelming majority of people who become good naturalists don't gain their knowledge from formal schooling. They get it in the field, by devoting themselves to direct observation and spending time with other largely self-taught naturalists. Nature journaling is a process that fosters self-learning, challenging the observer to combine intellect with experience. The word *naturalist* has disappeared from education today. Many of us know about the specialists, the oncologists, dentists, physicists, gerontologists, chemists. But naturalists are considered out with the fossils. No, we do not run around naked, and no, we do not eat just crunchy granola.

We disagree with the current trend towards over-specialization. Naturalists study nature outdoors, everywhere, and every part of it — rocks, volcanoes, buffalo, clouds, tides, earthworms. They are generalists and rank among the oldest of scientific learners. Pliny, Aristotle, Charles Darwin, Linnaeus, Audubon, Pasteur, Thoreau, and Thomas Jefferson were all naturalists.

Who Is Nature Journaling For?

Many of us enjoy journaling as a way of relaxing in nature, experiencing the peace and quiet that can be gained by simply being apart momentarily from the bustle of everyday life. It also increases our awareness of the continued juxtaposition of nature and human life — a dragonfly gliding down a city street; the full moon at a hospital window; a bee lazily poking about a marigold head. We can also have more academic or scientific goals. For example, students on research ships use nature journals to record marine observations that are then used for scientific study. Park rangers use nature journals as a teaching tool to help children focus on their observations in nature by writing, drawing, and studying science. Biologists in the rain forest who cannot collect endangered specimens instead make careful drawings to serve as evidence of plants they find. Senior citizens who cannot get outdoors keep in touch with the outside world by recording the monthly changes observed through their

The naturalist wanders with an inquiring eye, pauses, ponders, notes the bloom of a prairie pasqueflower. It is a tradition that goes back to Aristotle and earlier: observing and identifying earth's myriad life-forms, and discovering the connections that bind them. For those with such interests, said British naturalist Miriam Rothschild, "life can never be long enough."

— AMERICAN NATURALIST-WRITER JOHN HAY, IN *THE CURIOUS NATURALIST*, BY NATIONAL GEOGRAPHIC SOCIETY

People take time off from work to watch phoebes — and are restored. Strangers smile at eachother.

Common birder's stance. field guide braced between legs!

Mt. Auburn Cemetery
Cambridge. MA
5.12
11:30 am
sunny. sunny. sunny
green + green

♂ gray-phase
screech owl
30' up in
same oak I
saw him
in 4.4 -
apparently
a nest of
♀ within

eying
caterpillar

♂ cowbird

♂ oriole

goldfinch
atop
tombstone
black + gold
flash

dogwood
blossoms -
confetti on trees

windows in journals. Families take nature journals on trips to record their activities and observations; together they make sketches, attaching leaves, bark rubbings, or other "artifacts" that will reinforce the memory of their travels and allow them to reexperience their discoveries and feelings years later (more cheaply than by rolls of film or a video camera). Journaling sharpens your enjoyment of experiences as they happen, and creates a "memory record" that you can return to in the future for reflection and reconnection with satisfying moments of your life.

Exploring Different Forms of Expression

Journaling challenges you in the most positive way, by opening up opportunities for you to explore your own creativity and express your own observations and experiences of the world more fully. You may feel you are not creative; you don't know where to look. No one is judging your journal. Anyone can draw clouds. Try it! They change. Now you are learning about weather, as you draw and write. Writing is one of the primary forms of communication used by journalists. The more you write in your journal, the more skilled you will become at developing word pictures in prose and poetry. Sometimes you create simple, prosaic accounts of what has happened; other times you can shape your observations into basic stories or perceptive poems. You may also use the journal as a source for spontaneous well-turned phrases that can be incorporated into more crafted articles, stories, or poems later.

Using the Written Word

Writing, like drawing, is a skill that requires constant practice over time. Many people use the discipline of journal keeping to help improve and sharpen writing skills. Not only do people who stick with this practice learn to observe better, but they also improve their ability to turn those observations into accurate, more sharply turned poetic and prose phrases, or more detailed drawings. Some learn to become more spare with words yet more succinct in meaning; others broaden their vocabulary and use more words precisely to create polished gems of writing.

Focusing through Drawing What You See

In this book, we focus on drawing as a prime record-making tool because drawing and observing are mutually reinforcing activities. If you've ever taken an introductory drawing course, you may know the experience of *really* seeing a tree for the first time by sitting down to draw it. Drawing helps you observe. It demands that you, the observer, focus intently on the object to be drawn, noting such details as shape, texture, surface, and spatial relationships. You can draw a simple diagram of a shell without being a great artist first. Try it and you will see!

However, drawing may also, at times, restrict observation by pushing you to focus too narrowly on only a few objects. In so doing, you may actually not see how the object relates to other objects around it and to the general environment. To avoid this, remember that the context in which an object occurs is a critical part of real observation. If, for example, you are on a beach collecting shells and sea life to draw, take note of the tide height, the makeup of the beach (is it

lengthening shadows on oak and sweet gum

And if you sit quietly a while the sounds come in and so do the birds

10 minutes only listening can be a Zen koan

sandy, rocky, narrow, wide?), and the weather, along with nearby birds, smells, sounds, distant views of waves or boats or clouds, even your own random thoughts or moods.

Drawing adds an element to journaling that is different from other techniques. Many people find it to be a useful form of shorthand that takes less time and is less linear than writing. But drawing is like all other skills: It improves with practice and training. It takes practice to become a good basketball player or golfer; so, too, with drawing. Your early

rhododendrons happy in the rain

a very wet squirrel with white ear tufts

darts into rhodie from tree

Nature offers us a thousand simple pleasures — plays of light and color, fragrances in the air, the sun's warmth on skin and muscle, the audible rhythm of life's stir and push — for the price of merely paying attention. What joy! But how unwilling or unable many of us are to pay this price in an age when manufactured sources of stimulation and pleasure are everywhere at hand. For me, enjoying nature's pleasures takes a conscious choice, a choice to slow down to seed time or rock time, to still the clamoring ego, to set aside plans and busyness, and simply to be present in my body, to offer myself up.

LORRAINE ANDERSON, *SISTERS OF THE EARTH*

drawings may seem crude to you, but as you do more and more, you will be amazed at how your skills improve. A group of ninth-grade biology students found it faster to draw a squirrel jumping from one branch to another than to write out the full description of the squirrel's actions.

The Benefits of Nature Journaling

Spending time in the world, observing and responding to what you see using the simple tool of a journal, is a relatively easy way to reestablish contact with nature. A journal offers a great excuse to simply "mess about" in nature, noting the day, the weather, and signs of the season. Silence and stillness will come on once you open yourself up to the experience. By setting aside a bit of time each day to become absorbed in just being — in the present moment, alone with yourself in nature — you will find yourself refreshed, refocused, and better able to approach the rest of your day. As one eight-year-old said after an outdoor session of nature journaling, "Boy, I have seen the day."

Many nature journalists find, after a while without journal time, that they miss it and, like a hunger, begin searching for a space in the week to sit — or walk — and draw. One student, an emergency medical technician, carried with her in the ambulance Clare's published journal *Notes from a Naturalist's Sketchbook*. When she felt panicky or stressed, the student would pull out the book and feel eased looking at the journal entries about a world beyond the ambulance. She wanted now to find that ease by her own journal drawing and writing.

Making Time to Slow Down

Making the space and time to slow down, observe, and appreciate each day to its fullest is not easy in today's busy world. Journaling opens up the opportunity (and gives us an excuse!) to make the time — whether it's ten minutes a day or an hour every weekend — to fully take in the world and reflect on our own lives. It also gives us a structure within which to carefully observe our own lives, as well as all the life that surrounds us, both human and nonhuman. The knowledge gained by such observation is highly satisfying, as we are able to bring greater insight and interest to the world we see each day.

Clare will sometimes collect several objects while on a walk — leaves, some seedpods, an interesting top of a wild plant, a stray feather. Often unable to draw when outdoors, she will put them in her pocket. Later, indoors, laid out on a side table, the natural objects wait until she finds ten–fifteen minutes to draw them. They become her evening assignment, much like the laundry, dishes, or paperwork. But, fortunately, they can be sketched while talking with family, watching TV, or even talking on the telephone. How many of us say we do not have time? We do, if we want it! Try blocking out on your calendar little bits of time when you'll be able to draw those collected objects, the night sky, a vase of flowers, your child's sleeping head, or your dog. It can be 9 to 9:15 P.M. Tuesday or 5:30 to 6:45 Thursday. This will give you a moment of silence in your week! Drawing a shell, for instance, very concentratedly also offers you listening, meditation, a time with yourself.

Skills and Knowledge Fostered by Nature Journaling

- Scientific and aesthetic observation

- Creative and technical writing

- Layout and presentation of ideas and observations

- Perception and analysis

- Questioning, inventiveness, synthesis

- Reflection, silence

- Meditation, focus, personal healing

- Greater appreciation of nature and place

- Shared family experiences

- Finding your own voice, learning to open yourself to new experiences

- Self-confidence and the ability to express yourself

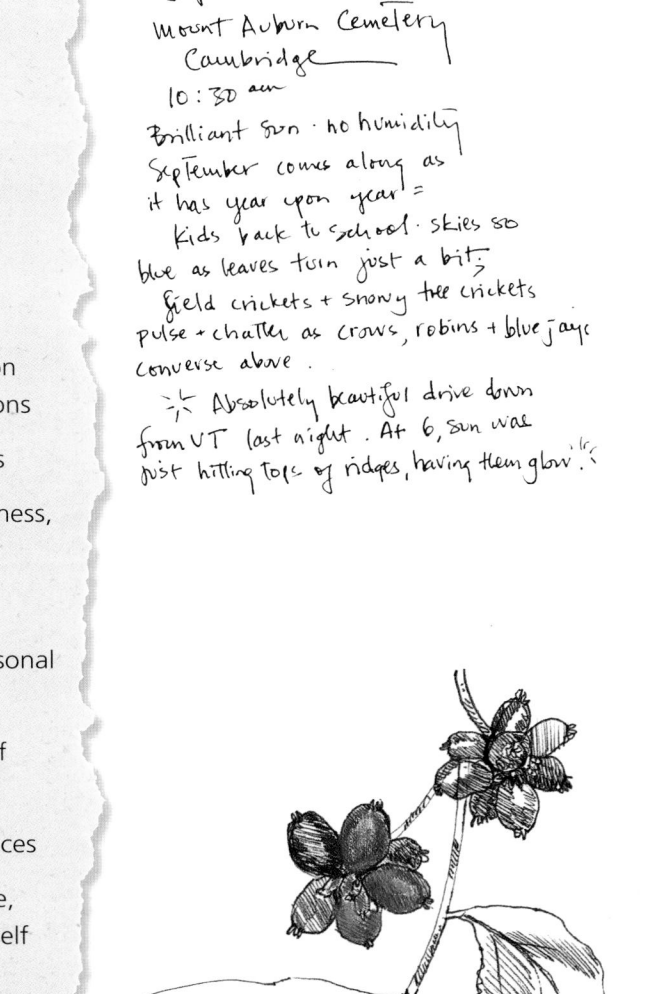

September 13
Mount Auburn Cemetery
    Cambridge
10:30 am
Brilliant sun · no humidity
September comes along as
it has year upon year —
    Kids back to school · skies so
blue as leaves turn just a bit;
    field crickets + snowy tree crickets
pulse + chatter as crows, robins + blue jays
converse above .

☀ Absolutely beautiful drive down
from VT last night . At 6, sun was
just hitting tops of ridges, having them glow .

Clare's Connection to Mount Auburn Cemetery

Many of Clare's drawings in this book were done at Mount Auburn Cemetery, which was founded in 1831 by members of the newly organized Massachusetts Horticultural Society. This place is noted to be America's first garden cemetery, encompassing 172 acres of dells, glades, woods, and ponds. The combination of a cemetery (which is still active) and a premier arboretum located close to bustling Harvard Square in Cambridge, Massachusetts, offers a sanctuary for birds, wildlife, and humans.

Clare says, "For many years I have come to this gem of cultivated wildness for meditation, for my work with nature journal drawing, and for keeping in touch with the pulse of life as it clocks through the seasons, year upon year. Vital for me, I can be within realms of secluded quiet in no more than six minutes from our Cambridge home. Garden spiders looping webs, catbirds vocally guarding territories, raccoons lolling in tree holes, resident red-tailed hawks soaring near enough to sketch, and of course, the famous parade of warblers fluttering through every spring are some of what keeps me coming back for more.

"Like a pilgrim going to church, I go to this outdoor place for the prayer that drawing and observing the nature here offer me."

For further reading on a sense of place see: *The Geography of Childhood* by Gary Nabham, *The Sense of Wonder* by Rachel Carson, and *Children's Special Places* by David Sobel (see Suggested Reading).

Developing a Personal Sense of Place

Nature journaling helps you develop a real sense of a place and your role in that place. In today's world, people are transient, moving from place to place often without much thought or knowledge about the actual landscape they live in — how it was formed, what other creatures live there besides humans, who lived there in earlier times, and what makes it the place that it is. Many of us live in urban areas, where it is easy to forget that this environment, too, is part of nature. We forget to look up at the sky, to feel the warmth of the sunshine, or to really notice the birds on the roofs. Even those of us living in rural locations or visiting there often spend much of our time racing to and from the car, forgetting to take the time to just be and observe the world around us.

A house wren — warbling! How unused I am of their song—after a summer of canyon · cactus + Carolina wrens...

November 3   Monday   10:30 am
                      mount Auburn Cemetery
Aefter Samhain
Rains of weekend break forth
into a gorgeously sparkling day
of mild + sun

*There is a great deal of talk
these days about saving the
environment. We must, for the
environment sustains our bodies.
But as humans we also require
support for our spirits, and
this is what certain kinds of
places provide.*

*A place is a piece of the whole
environment that has been claimed
by feelings. Viewed simply as a
life-support system, the earth is an
environment. Viewed as a resource
that sustains our humanity, the
earth is a collection of places.
We are homesick for places, we are
reminded of places, it is the sounds
and smells and sights of places
which haunt us and against which
we often measure our present.*

— ALAN GUSSOW, *A SENSE OF PLACE*

racha . racha . cha . cha .
of Kingbird fisher
across pond

mockingbird lands
to display striking
tail shadow on
tombstone

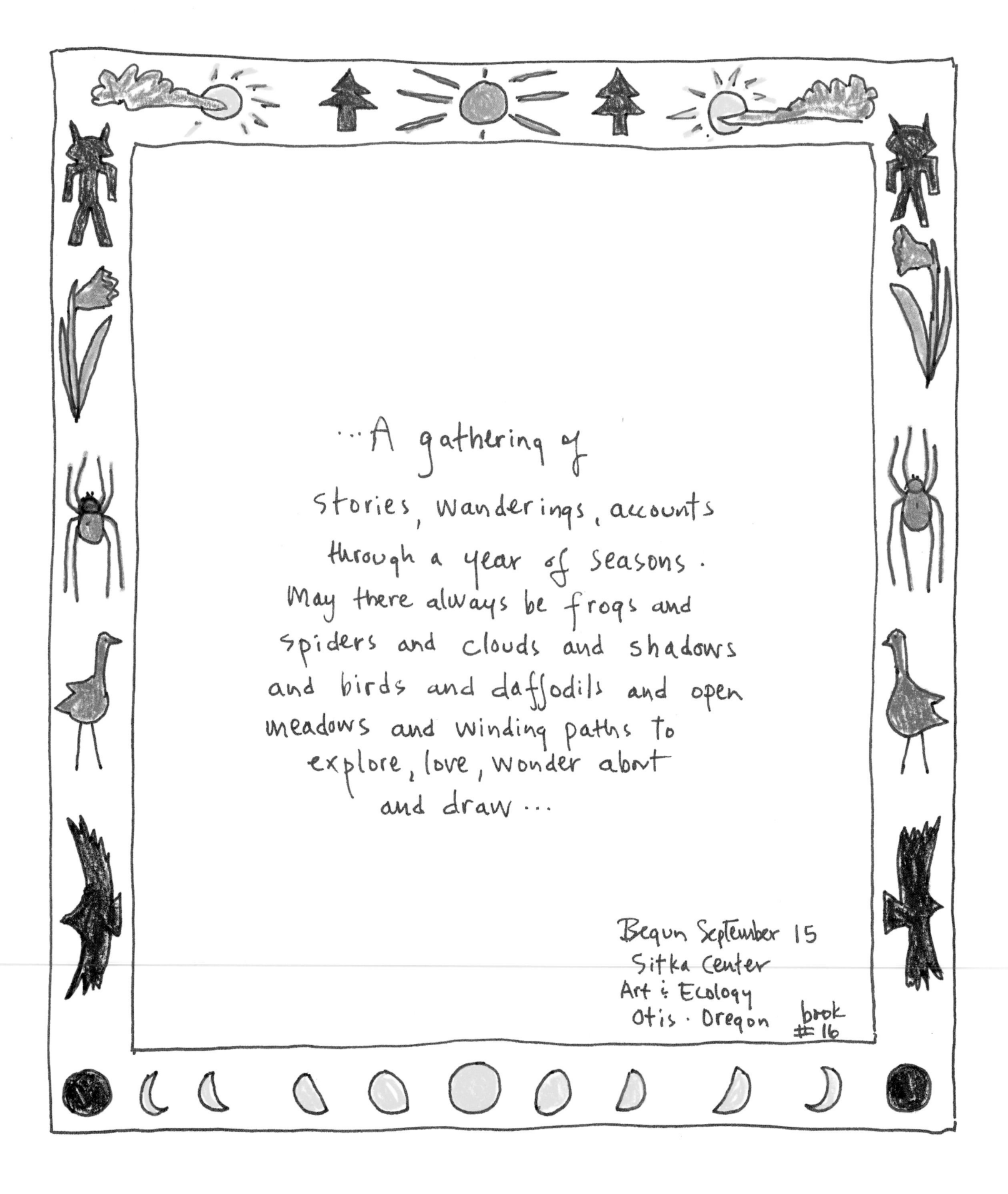

...A gathering of
stories, wanderings, accounts
through a year of seasons.
May there always be frogs and
spiders and clouds and shadows
and birds and daffodils and open
meadows and winding paths to
explore, love, wonder abont
and draw...

Begun September 15
Sitka Center
Art & Ecology
Otis · Oregon   book
#16

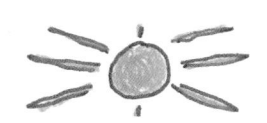

Beginning Your Journal

The type of journal you use and how you choose to use it are matters for personal decision. Your supplies can be as simple or fancy as you like, or your budget allows. If you are doing a lot of sketching, you may want to buy a small hardbound sketchbook that has smooth, unlined paper. These are available in a range of sizes at art and stationery shops. If you are inclined toward writing as your primary means of observation, and don't mind lines going through your additional sketches, you may want lined paper, in either a hardbound or a spiral notebook. If you're not ready yet to commit to a hardbound book, or if you're working with a group, individual loose sheets of paper attached to a clipboard or held onto a piece of stiff cardboard with paper clips is fine. Just be careful to keep the completed journal entries in a folder or loose-leaf notebook, organized sequentially by date, so you can refer back to them easily and trace the evolution of your knowledge and style of recording, as well as the ongoing changes of the seasons outdoors.

Nature-Journaling Equipment, Simplified

The type of book you select for your journal is related to the way you prefer to organize your journals — something you may not know as you start out. Stores are

In the pages of the journal . . . we can get better at reading the body language of the world. The overall expression of a season, the measure of stress, or of . . . vibrancy in a landscape, a garden, a cat, the psychic atmosphere of a city street, the meaning of the robin distress calls in the backyard. . .

— HANNAH HINCHMAN, *A TRAIL THROUGH LEAVES*

full of enticing journals, beautifully designed and often with pithy quotes lining the pages. We suggest you go for the simplest — and cheapest — journal. Make your own beautiful cover and add your own inspiring quotes. Many schoolchildren are launched into journal keeping these days; it is a valuable way to get them writing regularly. Sadly, many of these journals come home in June with only a few entries. With curriculums jammed, teachers forget that journals need to be used. You will need to use your journal, or the blank pages will only stare hungrily at you!

Clare prefers to use a blank book (8½ by 11 inches and roughly ninety-two pages) for her seasonal journals, completing one each year. (These stack nicely together and, after twenty years, are a most treasured storehouse of insights, experiences, and valued information constantly referred to for teaching, drawing, and book writing.) For shorter trips, or for family journals, she experiments with different-size books, ranging from 2 by 3 inches to 7½ by 8½, 6 by 9, or 11 by 14.

Chuck is a more casual journalist who keeps journals on a project basis — a particular natural history study, some trips with a similar focus or an in-depth investigation of some challenging idea. Sometimes he uses separate books for each purpose, sometimes he has several projects running simultaneously in one book. Like Clare, he tends to use bound books: either plain-paper sketch books or lined writing books.

Equipment for the BEGINNING NATURE JOURNAL : for early and older ages

Until you are sure what kind of journal you want to keep, 8"x 11" smooth, white copy paper is good to use. Keep student drawings in individual folders which they can decorate, sign, take home. Vary according to age, subject, amount of time.

Generally, for younger ages:

• 2/3 sheets of 8"x 11" smooth, white copy paper. Generally, it comes in packs of 500 sheets and is inexpensive.

• Firm backing to support drawing papers. This can be anything from cardboard to classroom books to clipboards. Attach with paper clips.

• Pencils (carry along extra as they get dropped.) Ball-point and felt-tipped pens are fine too.

• Collecting bags for objects to draw and study indoors. Collect only fallen objects; pull no roots; collect only when permission is given.

• Suitable clothing for the season — raincoats, warm jackets, boots etc.

If you are really going to use your journal for any length of time, it will get jammed in a backpack, dropped in the snow, left at a friend's house, or even catch an occasional splash of spaghetti or coffee. Some people even experiment with different-colored papers, taping them into their journal as supplementary pages, or draw on other pages and then cut out and tape these into their journals. You can do a journal in many ways. But, an empty journal is — an empty journal.

Clare carries in her pocketbook a 3-by-5 pad of notepaper. If the moment arises to sketch a bird flying past a friend's window, or a child spying a frog on the path, she pulls out the paper; she then tapes the sketches into her journal when she gets back home with the date and place added.

Pens and Pencils

Some people have a favorite pen or pencil that makes their writing and drawing most enjoyable. Experiment until you find the instrument that has just the right weight in your hand, has the type of tip and thickness of line you like best, and moves along the paper surface smoothly. Pens, as well as pencils, respond differently to different kinds of paper and to different kinds of people. So, what works for us may not work for you the same way.

Pencils come in many types: HB (hard, firm lines for plants), 2B (softer graphite for plants and birds), 3B (softer still for birds and animals), 4B, 5B, and 6B (very dark

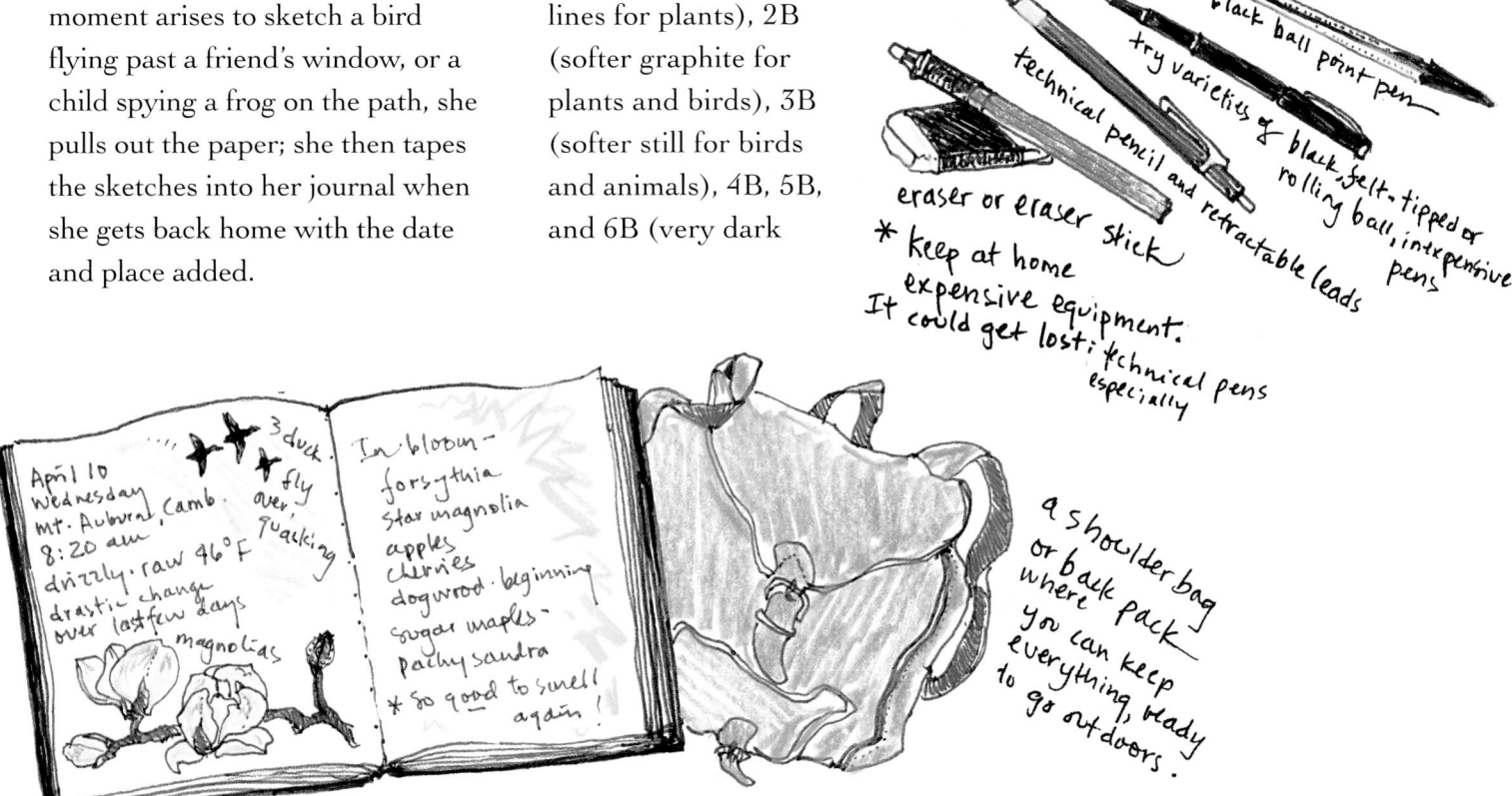

for COLOR —
try Venus Spectracolor
or Berol Prismacolor
colored pencils.
Also try the Derwent
water colour pencils. With a
brush and some water, they create
a nice water color wash.

Knife for clipping
branches + sharpening
pencils — or metal
sharpener

black ball point pen

try varieties of black felt, tipped or
rolling ball, inexpensive
pens

technical pencil and
retractable leads

eraser or eraser stick

* keep at home
expensive equipment.
It could get lost; technical pens
especially

April 10
Wednesday
Mt. Auburn, Camb.
8:20 am
drizzly· raw 46°F
drastic change
over last few days
magnolias

3 duck
fly
over
quacking

In bloom —
forsythia
star magnolia
apples
cherries
dogwood· beginning
sugar maples—
pachysandra
* so good to smell
again!

a shoulder bag
or back pack
where
you can keep
everything ready
to go outdoors.

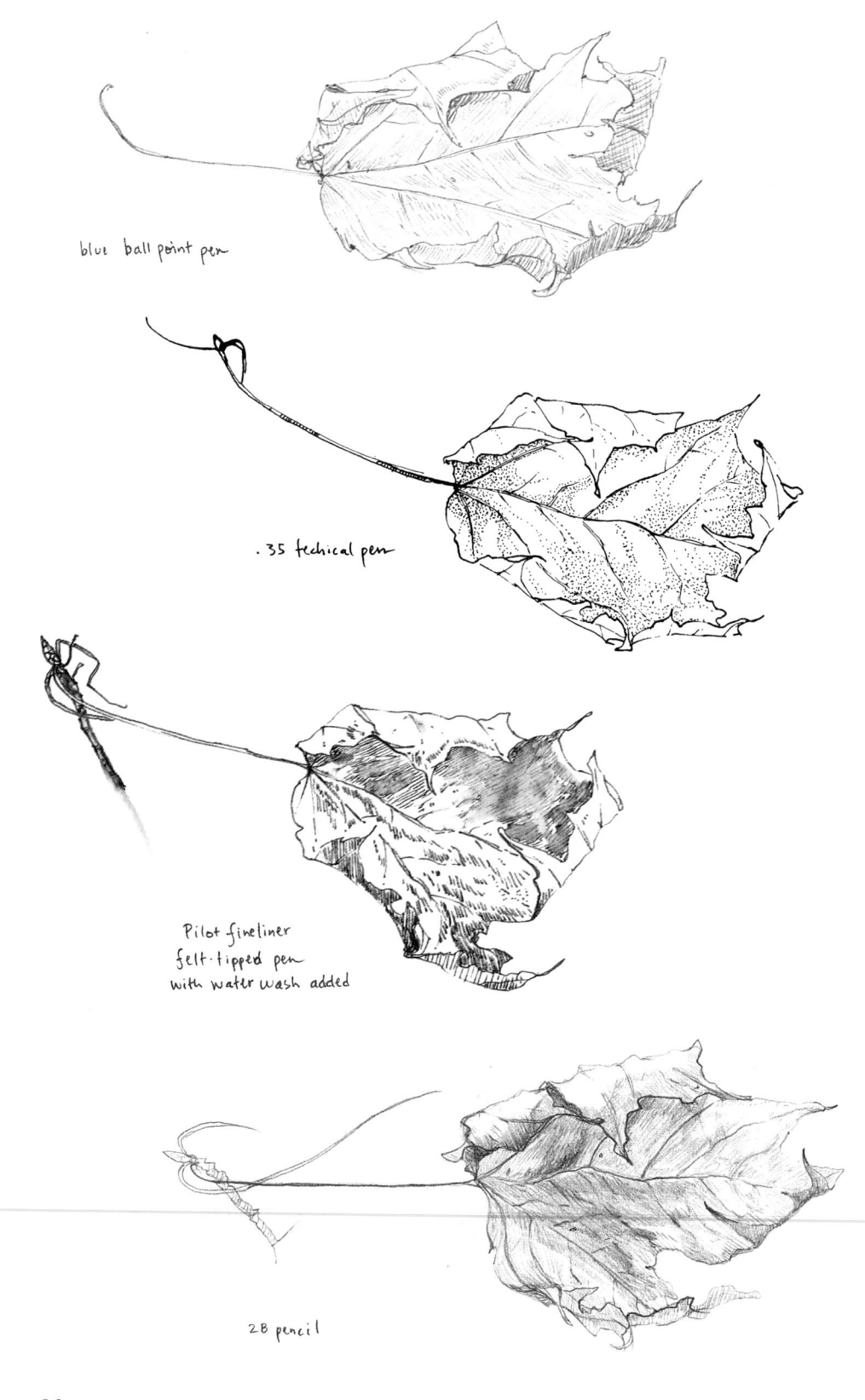

blue ball point pen

.35 techical pen

Pilot fineliner
felt-tipped pen
with water wash added

2B pencil

and soft for landscapes and tonalities, but they smudge and need to be sprayed with a fixative). If you're using a pencil, you'll also need a good eraser or eraser stick.

Sharpeners vary in quality. The best is either a knife or a battery-run motorized pencil sharpener. Technical drawing (automatic) pencils work well for outdoor drawing (leads 2B and 3B preferred). These leads don't need sharpening, do not break in a packet, and are ready with a sharp point if a hawk flaps past.

The First Page of Your Journal

It is useful to establish a stated reason why you want to start a nature journal. You may have no other purpose than to learn about where you live, or to observe and record the daily weather, or to document the inhabitants and activity in a local wetlands. The more you use your journal, the more these purposes will change and unfold. In our years of teaching, we've found that every new journalist has begun and developed her nature journals in a slightly different way, yet her purpose has always remained the same throughout — to study nature, to have fun, and to feel pleased with her own learning style.

If you have fears about beginning your drawing and recording, however, it may help you to follow a journal-entry format we have developed. The format is used by a wide range of age groups, from six-year-olds to ninety-year-olds. We encourage you to try the sequence, which you'll find on page 22; it may help you put something down on your paper right away, reduce any writing or drawing block, and jump-start your thinking process. Given the time constraints many of us work within, this journal-entry exercise is designed to take about forty-five minutes: ten to fifteen minutes spent indoors, and thirty to thirty-five minutes outdoors.

Observation can be done alone or in a group. Of course, you'll have more time to spend reflecting on your entries if you are journaling alone. But in a group you'll have fun comparing the differing objects everyone has chosen to draw and respond to.

When it comes to the journal-entry format's drawings, remember, you are a scientist right now, recording simple line drawings.

No one has taught you yet *how* to draw. The artist in you will come out as you practice. (Remember, too, though, that learning to do anything — drawing, playing the piano, reading, driving a car — takes instruction, not just meaningful effort. You'll find exercises in drawing in chapter 9.) For now, just do a page and see what happens. Many of the drawings reproduced here are first efforts.

Under the clouds,
across meadows and woods
and city streets
and inside the homes
of harried house people,
and along the trails
of adventuresome folk —
these stories
travel.

They are not finished stories, nor are they "art" stories. They are just accounts of one year's curiosity.

Begun August 6. 1996
Sitka Center for
Art & Ecology
OTIS · OREGON

1. Sam Austin

2. October 5

3. Brown elementary School

   Reading, MA

4. 9:30 am

5. Cloudy, cool
   a little wind
   around 55° F

   Waxing moon
   Sunrise = 6:40 am
   Sunset = 4:38 pm

6. leaves turning color
   fall flowers
   insects — crickets
                flies
                ants
   birds
   Squirrels
   fall seeds, nuts, fruits

   I hear:
      leaves
      wind
      bird
      people's feet
      car

7.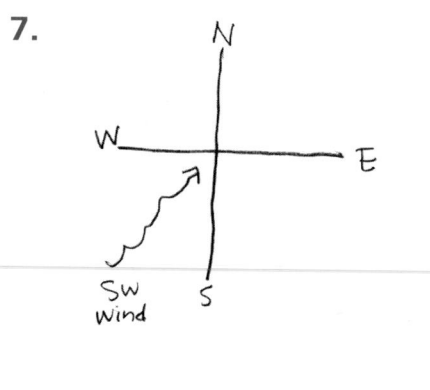

   SW wind

8.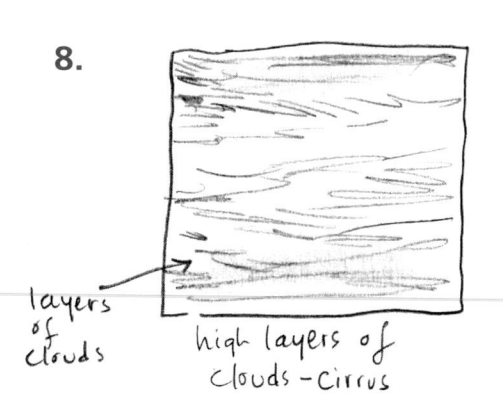

   layers of clouds

   high layers of clouds — cirrus

Entering Observations

You are ready to begin recording your observations. Although there are numerous ways to format a journal, the following is one that we use.

I. Basic Information

In either the upper right- or the upper left-hand corner of your page record the following, using both written word and illustration, as appropriate and desired:

1. Name. If you don't already have it written on the outside of your bound book, or you are using loose pages, add your name.

2. Date. This establishes the season and month in relation to the year. How would things look outdoors in spring? In winter?

3. Place. What town and state do you live in? Compare habitats to get a sense of place or home. How is this place like someplace else where a relative or friend lives? How does this place differ from other places you have traveled or seen pictures of?

4. Time. This does not have to be accurate clock time; it can be simply "early afternoon," "late morning," or the like. Animals and plants respond to light conditions. What would be happening outdoors at 2 A.M., as distinct from 2 P.M., or 6 A.M. and 6 P.M.?

5. Weather. Weather conditions affect the activity of most living things. Record such things as *temperature,* which affects animal activity and plant growth; *barometric pressure,* which affects animal behavior and activity, and the movement of air masses that generate weather; and *moon phase and daily sunrise and sunset,* which can be found in local newspapers or *The Olde Farmer's Almanac.* Recording this data helps keep you aware of monthly and annual astronomical cycles. Some plants bloom only with long daylight periods, for instance, and others with short daylight periods. Goldenrod blooms only in the late summer, and daffodils only bloom in early spring. The time of year birds and animals court is determined not only by weather conditions, but also by the amount and quality of light.

6. First Impressions. Once you're outdoors or beginning your walk, take a few moments of silence to orient yourself. Listen. Write what you hear. This helps acclimate you to what you may be observing and drawing. Brainstorm mentally, or on paper, what you might expect to find out here to observe and draw — new flowers, insects, birds you hear singing.

7. Wind direction. Locate and draw the points of the compass. Then add wind direction by looking at which way flags or even your hair is blowing.

8. Cloud patterns and cloud cover. Cloud patterns can be drawn; cloud cover can be recorded by drawing a small box and adding an illustration of the clouds or the kind of sky you see. Write a description of the sky below the box. Add the names of the cloud types, if you know them: stratus (layered); nimbostratus (rain clouds); stratocumulus (puffy layers); cumulus (puffy, large). Put the moon in, if you see it. (*A Field Guide to the Atmosphere* by Vincent Shaefer is a good reference. See Suggested Reading.)

II. Begin Drawing

To get started, you may find this sequence of observations helpful; they get you looking at different distances from where you are standing or sitting. This pattern gets you in the habit of observing all around you.

9. Ground Observations. Anywhere there is ground, even if partially paved, look around. Get close to individual objects, where you can readily examine a leaf, flower, insect, rock, or earthworm "casting." Try to draw everything actual size. Draw two or three objects and move on. Label each item if you know what it is. Take no more than five minutes per drawing. Give size measurements. Estimate using your knowledge of your own body parts: "The last joint of my thumb is about 1 inch, my forearm is about 17 inches," and so forth. For further learning, try writing down one question about each object: How did it get there? Where does it go in winter? Can it also be found in other habitats?

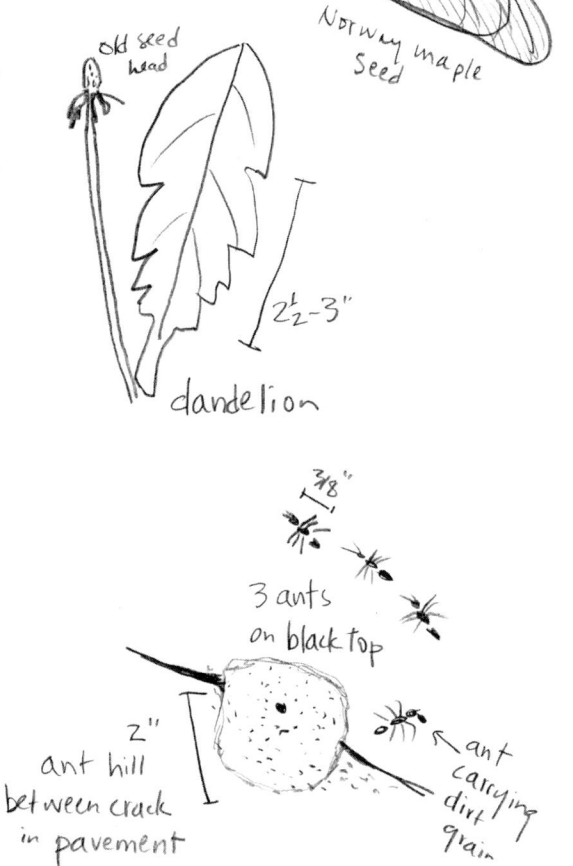

9.

clover leaf — white?
in school yard

Norway maple
seed

Old seed
head

dandelion

2½–3"

3 ants
on black top

ant hill
between crack
in pavement

2"

⅜"

ant carrying dirt grain

10.

detail of fading flowers
$\frac{1}{4}$" yellow

4' goldenrod
no leaf stems

dog wood leaf turning red
red fruit

yellow jacket on ripe crab apple

10. Eye-Level Observations. Standing up so you are free to move around, draw what comes into view at eye level — particular leaves, tall plants, shrubs, low nests, insects on surfaces, birds. Don't worry about your ability to render the objects realistically at this point. Label the object and describe what it's doing or is part of.

11. Overhead Observations. Look up. Choose a tree to draw — deciduous or evergreen. The sky is an ever-changing show. Record the colors you see. Illustrate any objects, such as birds, insects, planes, or snow, flying or drifting through the sky. Draw the clouds and how their shapes are changing. Indicate the moon, if it's visible, and what phase it's in. Write some words about how viewing the sky makes you feel.

12. Whole-Landscape Observations. Landscape drawing can be overwhelming; it helps if you divide the landscape into simple shapes and label what is there. (See pages 148–149 for tips on drawing landscapes.) Keep your shapes simple, like pictograms. Label the elements so that you, and others, will know what you have drawn.

11.

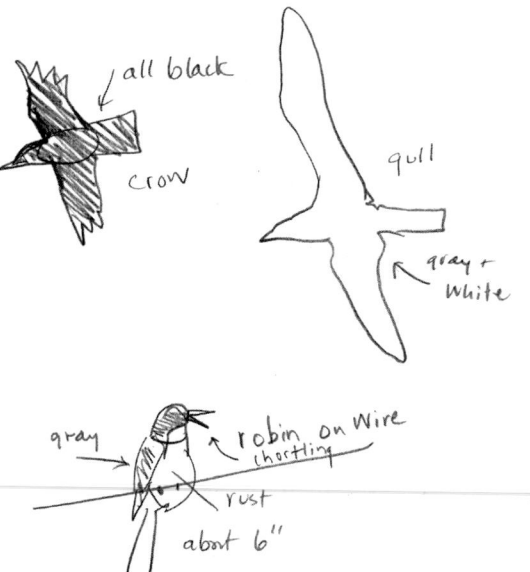

all black
crow
gull
gray + white
gray
robin on wire throstling
rust
about 6"

12.

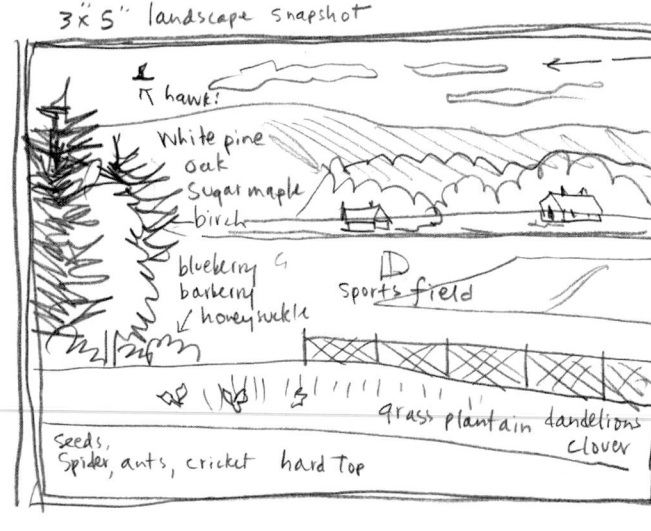

3" x 5" landscape snapshot
small cirrus clouds
hawk!
White pine
oak
Sugar maple
birch
blueberry
barberry
honeysuckle
Sports field
grass plantain dandelions clover
seeds, Spider, ants, cricket hard Top
View NW to town + low hills

Getting Focused

Before you even move outdoors, you can get yourself in the mood to observe, record, and reflect with some simple context-setting activities. Here are several suggestions:

- Focus for a few minutes, either privately or in discussion with others, on what a naturalist is. Think about what you want to achieve with your own nature journaling, and how it may relate to other personal goals you have.

- Develop a flow chart or webbing (showing an interconnected range of topics, see page 165 for example) that illustrates what you imagine you will find once you get outside — what kinds of trees, shrubs, flowers, clouds, bugs, birds, and weather you will encounter.

- Think of the nature journal as a treasure hunt. Ask yourself, "What's out there beyond the doorstep? What treasures will I find?" You will be amazed when you actually get outside at all the things there are to draw or write about.

- Remind yourself that you are keeping the journal to learn to observe, record, and fully appreciate. This is not an art exercise or any kind of test. You are doing this for yourself, and your own enjoyment.

- Focus on the purposes of your journaling. Think about becoming more aware of where you live, and how you might want to share this awareness with others. Regular immersion in your surroundings helps the earth flourish, as well as yourself. As you develop your understanding of nature and the earth, you also grow in your ability to speak knowledgeably and passionately for its preservation.

Continue Observing

If you have more time, keep observing/drawing. Follow your own curiosity. You will find things to draw — other leaf shapes, another insect, a new seed pod, a bird on a branch, an unexpected animal track. As one student said, "Boy, I had no idea that there was so much nature out here. I need more and more paper to keep up with all this drawing." You'll find that to be true, too!

widgeon

20 common mergansers

red-breasted mergansers

hooded mergansers

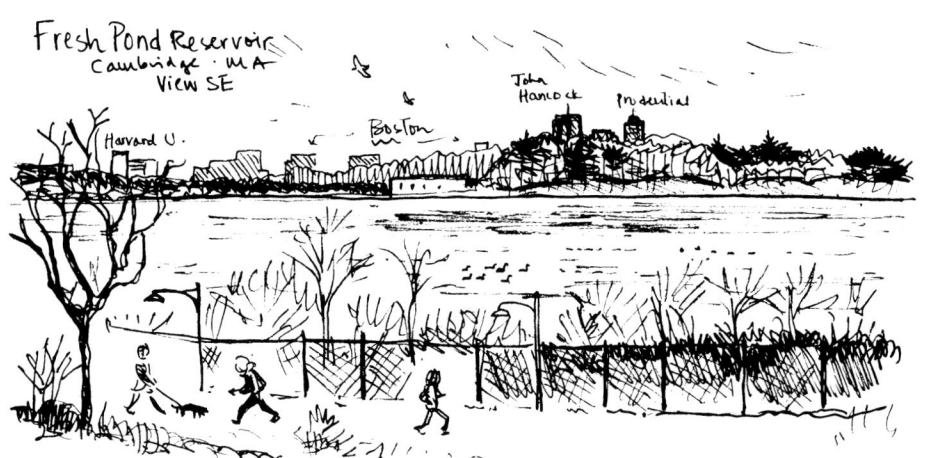

Fresh Pond Reservoir, Cambridge · MA, View SE

Seeing and drawing can become one, can become SEEING/DRAWING. . . No longer do I 'look' at a leaf, but enter into direct contact with its life.

FREDERICK FRANCK, *THE ZEN OF SEEING*

FALL SIGNS:

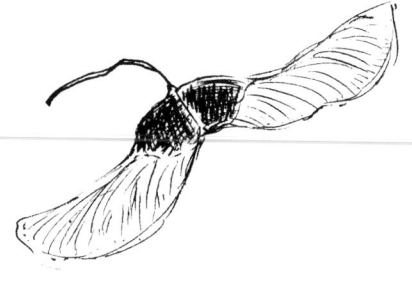

black oak acorn

umbrellas twisting through the blue

Learning to Truly Observe

Observation is at the heart of nature journaling. You cannot record what you have not observed. True, you can imagine things and record them, but observation deals with using all your senses and perceiving the reality of what they reveal to you. Observing expands your world; the more you see, hear, feel, smell, and taste, the more you know and understand. You become attuned to the context of objects you previously thought of as isolated; you find they are connected to other objects and events. Discovering these connections is great fun, but it also takes a conscious and concerted effort to fully engage your senses and your mind.

The more you practice focusing in and observing, the more you will see. Chuck suggests beginning by observing still, natural objects, looking for indirect clues of animal presence and the activity of minuscule or previous life in that habitat. Listen for the songs or calls of birds or insects that indicate their presence even though you may have trouble sighting them. Some of the signs you may notice through close observation are:

- The molted feathers of a bird
- Patches of fur from a mammal
- Seedlings of trees or other plants where no mature individual can be seen
- Holes chewed in leaves by some insect
- The tracks of animals in dust, mud, or snow

As you observe an event in nature, allow yourself to fully enter into it, paying attention to every detail. Some of the questions you might ask yourself include:

- Who is doing what to whom?
- How often are various actions being repeated?
- What are the reactions of each party in an activity to the actions of the others?
- How long does each action take; how long the reaction?
- Over how much area or distance does the event take place?
- What is the context in which the event is taking place?

nipped twigs

Overcoming Fears of Drawing

Some people panic at the thought of making sketches in their journals. If you believe you can't draw, now is the time to lay that fear aside. Everyone can draw at some degree of competency by simply making lines that correspond with what is observed.

Clare once accompanied a class of students and their teacher outdoors to set up journal pages. The teacher, Mrs. Jay, said she preferred not to draw because she was "no good." Teachers are obvious role models to students, so Clare encouraged her to try. (Students *like* to see their teacher struggling with what they might do more easily.) Seeing how engaged her students were in drawing, and feeling the safety of Clare's support, Mrs. Jay, giggling, joined her class and drew the November oak tree in their school yard. The class discussed tree branching, an exposed summer squirrel nest, afternoon shadows across the tree's bark. They guessed at the tree's height. The sixth-graders were involved, curious, proud to show their drawings. And Mrs. Jay, carried by the mood, admitted, "This is the best tree I have ever drawn!" She had leaped off the cliff of fear — and found she could draw. (Clare is still working in this school, and Mrs. Jay is still drawing.)

Remember the first time you tried riding a bike, baking a cake, hitting a tennis ball, writing your name? How overwhelming it seemed then — and how easy it is now.

American Beech — Mt. A.
10·14·93 11 am

As a person without any drawing experience, contour drawing has been satisfying and encouraging; I feel like I'm able to see the essence of a plant. If I start to draw without doing a contour drawing first, I stiffen up and quickly get bogged down in details. Often I like my contour drawings better than my extended drawings — they feel more alive.

— GAIL GUSTAFSON

Practice

Whether you think you are good or bad at drawing is not the issue. No one is particularly good at anything unless they have practiced, and had some instruction. Yes, somewhere back in third grade you used to draw. But maybe someone told you that you weren't good at it, or your friends laughed at it. And so, you quit. If you still draw like a third-grader and you are forty-five years old, don't worry. That was probably the last time you drew!

With practice, good observation, and instruction in a few simple drawing techniques, you will improve more quickly than you might think. We really encourage you to try. This is just one more way nature journaling offers you a chance to grow personally and broaden your skills for living.

Beginning Drawing Exercise

Whether you are drawing indoors or out, the following warm-up exercise is useful in getting anyone, of any age or ability, feeling relaxed about drawing as part of the process of careful observation. When you first try these drawings, you may find yourself laughing, feeling clumsy or slow or unable to make a "good" picture right away — but you will also discover how a form works. This is right-brain, not left-brain, work, so just let your creative side lead the way. Don't try to overrule it with your logical side.

For complete instructions on these exercises, turn to chapter 9, pages 141 to 143.

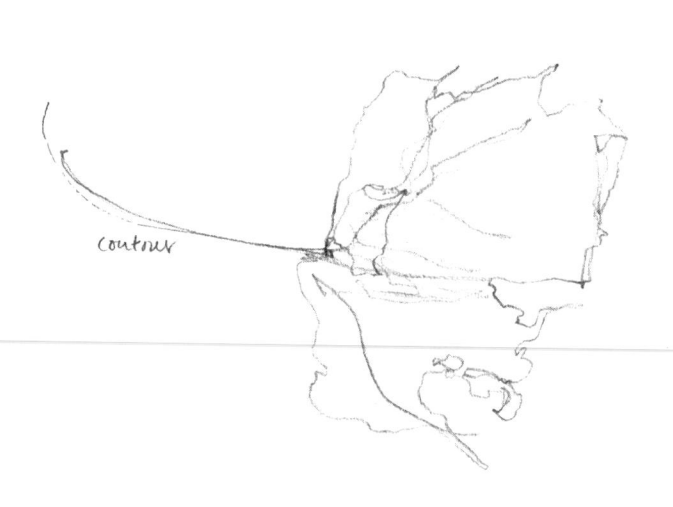

contour

1. Blind contours, done in one continuous line without ever looking at your paper, are very good for capturing moving animals that may leave at any moment.

2. Modified contours allow you to peek a bit at your paper, while still moving your pencil in one continuous line. This technique helps you capture the form of any plant or animal.

3. Quick gestures are sketches of the complete form, done as quickly as possible. This style is used a lot by field artists because much of what they draw moves quickly!

4. Diagrammatic drawing involves much detail of a particular specimen. This technique is useful when you need to identify something.

5. The finished drawing is used when you wish to produce a more completed work; it takes from ten minutes to ten hours!

3.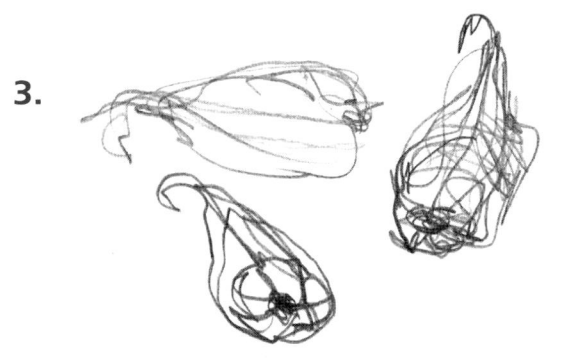

1.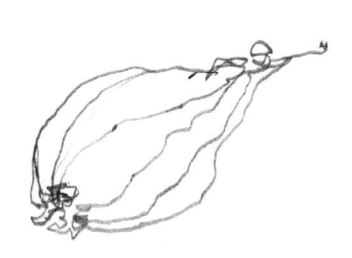

2.

4.

stem

rattles when shaken!

8 grooves

dark brown

Found in garden of art museum in Williamstown MA 1.24.97

3¼"

? lily seed pod

seed head

5.

Monhegan Island 6·17-97
little island studies:
teaching studies:

perspective:
above horizon ↑
below horizon ↓

island spruce

repeated, close lines for evergreens

where did you fly in from?

house perspective

see geometries

see egg in gull shape. quick gestures

keep horizon line water flat

ways to draw rocks - angle your lines along plane of rock face

waves - draw contours of wave pattern, direction, shape

Support and Nurture Your Own Creativity

As you begin to integrate drawing into your journal, you may be encountering fears of incompetency, inadequacy, or inability. As we get older, we often fear trying new skills or facing our own creative obstacles. Don't be afraid to seek support and create a nurturing environment for yourself as you explore this dimension of yourself, which you may not have tapped into since childhood. If you're working with students, you may find that — young and old — those with certain learning difficulties often rise to the occasion and love to draw.

Clare once held a weekend workshop on an island off the coast of Maine. One student, a woman in her early sixties, came because her husband loved to draw and kept a journal. When telling Clare her frustrations with drawing, the woman became increasingly agitated and emotional. Some art teacher long ago had told her she couldn't draw; that she should spend her time in math, science, and sports. Although she came from a creative family, she stopped drawing completely, and whenever she'd tried it since then, she felt humiliated by not knowing what would make a good picture.

She challenged Clare to help her overcome her fifty-plus years of feelings! Clare praised everything she drew and gave her lots of specific instruction. They laughed, cried, and drew together. They shared family stories while hiking and eating clams. The woman made many, many drawings and her ability blossomed until, by Sunday, she had to be pried off the island. She drew plants, waves, rocks, water, lighthouses, lobster pots — and very well. Why? She found a supportive place with people who praised her, helped her, made mistakes with her, and shared her deep love of the out-of-doors.

She and her husband recently told Clare they were off on a weeklong Elderhostel walking trip to the coast of France. Both were taking their journals and were so happy to now share this creative experience together. With a twinkle in his eye, her husband said, "We'll send you Xeroxes when we return."

Varying Your Focus

As you intensify your observation of natural objects and events, you may well encounter one of the dangers of such a practice — focusing too narrowly on the object and missing what surrounds it. The best way to compensate for this is to develop the ability to perform *intermittent differential focusing*. Begin by looking at the object close up for a few seconds. Then refocus your attention to the middle distance surrounding the object, and with which it may be quietly interact-

ing. After a few seconds at this level, take even a broader perspective of the general scene that includes the object and its near surroundings. Now refocus on the object for a few seconds, and repeat, observing large circles of influence. In this way you can observe much more; the broader understanding you gain will be reflected in what you enter into your journal.

Chuck once spent a day observing animals at a refuse dump in the woods of Maine. Squirrels and chipmunks were there, as were several female black bears and their cubs. It was fun to focus on the bear cubs and their antics, Chuck found, but it was also informative to keep track of all that was going on at the dump. For example, chipmunks would be very busy for a while; then suddenly they would disappear. Usually before long one of the female

Monarch of the Dump
Katahdin 1957
CR

closer. A refocus on the bears saw them silently herding the cubs into the brush. The squirrels and chipmunks returned; then they, too, quietly disappeared.

Within moments, a huge male bear scrambled into the dump and began to forage. All around, the forest was quiet. Only after the male had finished eating and drifted away did the sounds of the forest return; after them came the smaller animals, and finally the mothers and cubs. Chuck's use of intermittent differential focusing helped him understand what was really happening. And he can retell this story now because many years ago he recorded it all in his journal.

As this example shows, good observation may involve what you are *not* currently observing as well as what you are. The moving silence foretold some large object moving about, frightening the singing birds and calling chipmunks. In spring marshes, too, the sudden silencing of frog choruses may alert you to something prowling about. In any woods or field, you may become as concerned by what you don't find but feel should be there as by what you do find.

bears would appear at the same location with her cubs in tow. By backing off his focus from the bears, Chuck could also take in the sounds of birds singing. Squirrels chirring. Wind in the trees. Then he'd go back to watching the bears, particularly the cubs.

In one of his backing-off observations, Chuck noted that in one direction the surrounding forest had become silent. In fact, the silence seemed to be moving toward the dump. When he turned back to the bears, Chuck found that the mothers appeared to be tense, testing the wind while the cubs played; so he backed up to the broader environment again, and found the silence spreading and growing

Where to Roam with Your Journal

Nature journaling can be done just about anywhere, indoors or out. Wherever there is something living, you can begin to observe. You may feel, "How can I begin observing nature? I don't know answers to these questions. I don't even know what questions to ask." We were all once beginners, barely knowing a robin from a sparrow. Your beginning questions may be very basic ones, such as "What season is it?" Curiosity will lead you to answers. If you want to learn more about nature in your area, seek out others who might have answers, check out books in your local library, and enroll in courses and workshops at your local nature or educational centers. (See Resources, page 175.)

Following are a few places you likely have easy access to where you can begin honing your observational skills and developing a new sense of the place you call home. As you sit amidst each of these spots, ask yourself: What plants grow here? What trees? What things affect their growth here? What insects can you find? What birds use the plants and trees? What other nonhuman creatures live here? Can you see them, or only evidence of their presence? What creatures can you see here during the day; what others are only active at dawn or dusk, or perhaps at night? What kind of interactions occur among these creatures? What human activities go on in relationship to this place? How has human activity influenced the appearance of this place? What light, colors, shapes, and patterns do you notice? How do these elements change throughout the day, from day to day, and from month to month? How do you imagine this place looked fifty, 100, or 200 years ago? How has the plant and animal life changed over time?

- The back yard
- The school yard
- Gardens
- Bird feeders
- The sky
- The river, stream, lake, or pond nearby
- The seacoast or rocky shore
- A nearby meadow or farmer's field
- Parks or nature centers
- City streets
- Inside your home

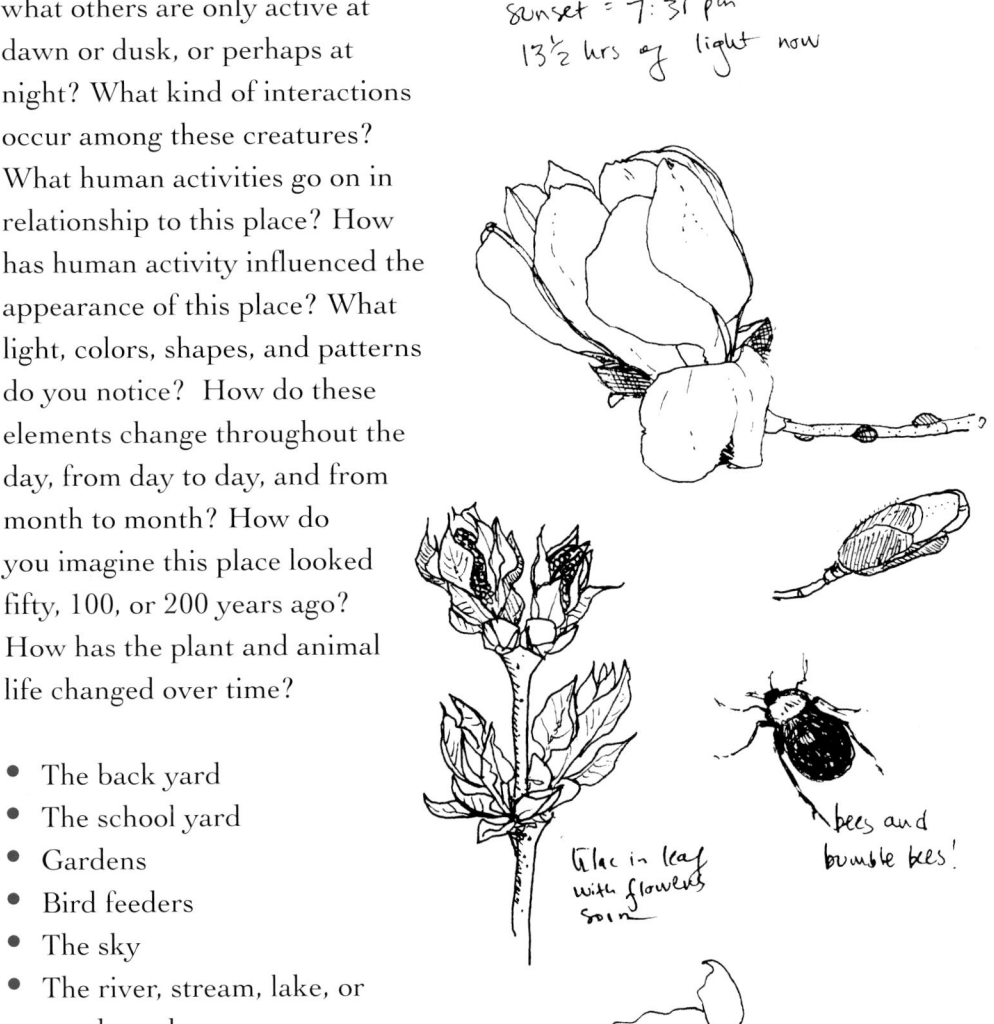

April 19 —
mount Auburn Cemetery · Camb.
Sunny · high 50°'s
SPRING REALLY COMING
Sunrise = 5:56 am
Sunset = 7:31 pm
13½ hrs of light now

Lilac in leaf with flowers soon

bees and bumble bees!

tiny bee fly on petal

Journal keeping often begins with a short-term project and grows into a lifetime habit. To get started, try creating a record of one of the following activities:

- A vacation trip

- Visits to local parks, nature centers, wildlife refuges, or beaches

- Monthly changes in your yard or neighborhood

- Changes in a particular tree you can readily observe

- The bird activity at your nearby bird feeder

- Observations and thoughts from a special meditation spot in your yard or home

- Changes in school yard habitats throughout the year

These are, of course, only openers for the curious observer. You can move in many directions from here. At various places throughout this book are suggestions for other kinds of observations you can focus on as you develop your ongoing commitment to keeping a nature journal.

Fine-Tuning Your Journaling Skills

Once you've started journaling using this format and simple drawing techniques, there are many ways to expand and fine-tune your skills. You may want to expand the scope of your journal, keeping records of a broader range of observations, insights, and questions. Here are a few directions you might go in to expand your observational and drawing studies.

February 21
Antioch / New England
Keene NH
12:45 pm

Wind
N
W — E
S

Sunrise = 6:18 am
Sunset = 5:35 pm

We have 2 hrs 15 min. more of light than Dec. 21!

Cold · Windy · Clear
mid 30°'s but
Wind chill drops it down

FIELD JOURNALING
with 14 graduate students / environmental educators;
in railroad yards behind the school = Soil much disturbed over time

WINTER TREE SILHOUETTES

← green gray bark

quaking aspen about 30'

weeping branches turning yellow already

weeping Willow about 60'

3/4" buds swelling + showing some florets

tansy

old leaf on snow

leaf petiole twisted so it shakes in wind

← flat → this way
← flat ↑ this way

Draw and Write

With journal and pen in hand, try exploring the following questions:

• What are the trees in my neighborhood? When do they bloom? What do their fruits and seeds look like? What insects use the trees? When do they shed their leaves? How do their seeds get to new sites to grow?

• How does the shape of the moon appear to change over a two-month period? What path does the moon follow across the heavens? At what time of day does the moon rise and set? How does the appearance of the moon affect the activity level of night creatures?

• How does the daily path of the sun affect the shape and length of shadows of the buildings in my neighborhood? Do the shadows affect the microclimates around the buildings? How does this affect the distribution of plants, insects, and other life around the buildings?

• What birds live in my neighborhood? Which ones visit local bird feeders, mine or a neighbor's? What times of day do various birds visit? How do different species of birds interact at the feeders? Which birds prefer which foods in the neighborhood?

• What are the human activity patterns in my neighborhood? What seems to be affecting these activity patterns: commuting, weather, friendships, time of day?

• What is the flowering sequence of local flowers? When does the first bloom of each species appear? When are half of the flowers of a species in bloom? When does the last flower of each species bloom? Are some species found growing together more often than others? What does the dead plant look like in winter?

• What reptiles or amphibians might live near me? Can I draw and write about the ones I see and the ones I haven't seen yet?

• What kinds of insects gather around the light at my doorway each night throughout the year?

• When and where do mushroom species appear in my neighborhood or regular visiting spot?

• What changes can I observe in a selected tree, perhaps a maple or oak, throughout the year? Who lives in that tree, and when?

• From a given vantage point, what changes in the landscape can I see throughout the year?

• How do the patterns of clouds and light change over a period of weeks? What things are happening around me that seem to be affected by the changes in the sky?

Journaling might well be thought of as a form of journeying — through the seasons outdoors as well as through your own inner seasons. As we journey through life our journals become a record of where we have been, what we have seen and attended to, what we have felt as we interacted with our world, what we sure of, and what we are puzzled by. The thrill of a used journal is that it enables you to go back over its pages and reflect on, process, and marvel at where you have been, what you have thought, what you have seen. A nature journal may get shelved for months, or even years. But when you pull it out again, we guarantee that the life within its pages will spring out at you. It was you who was there recording, no one else.

Journaling as Meditation

This visitor to Garden in the Woods, a sanctuary in Framingham, Massachusetts, came to this spot tired after a day at a high-pressure job. Making time in the evening to be quiet, draw, and reconnect with nature offers a wonderful way to relax, release the stress of the day, and maintain balance in your life.

May 22
Garden · in · The · Woods · Framingham MA
   5:50 pm
raw · damp · dark
black flies a biten'
warblers
orioles
tufted tit.
red · winged blackbird

A Sampling of Journaling Styles

If you're new to nature journaling, it can be helpful to look at styles that other nature journalists use. We encourage you to explore the written and drawn journals kept throughout history by scientists and explorers, as well as writers and artists (see Resources for suggestions), for ideas on how to develop your own style. Although a nature journal focuses on nature observation, travel experiences, family events, personal observations, and town or regional happenings can be intermingled, depending on your purposes.

This chapter highlights some of the different styles contemporary nature journalists have chosen, with examples from their journal pages.

Journalist Bill Hammond says about his own style, "When beginning a new journal, I sit quietly and absorb my location. On the left page, I create a color image in some fashion; the image may be abstract or realistic. It is something specific about the time and place — and reflects some insights that flow from the nature around me. It may begin in the mountains, at a beach, in the city, or in my yard at home — it can be anywhere outside that takes on a special meaning to me.

"On the right hand page, I write in a stream of consciousness mode. I record what flows from my mind at that time and place.

"The journal then becomes the journal of that place or time.

"Hands-on experience at the critical time, not systematic knowledge, is what counts in the making of a naturalist. Better to be an untutored savage for a while, not to know the names or anatomical detail. Better to spend stretches of time just searching and dreaming."

— EDWARD O. WILSON, *NATURALIST*

Observe and Record

Far and away the most common purpose of journaling is simply to observe and record. That is the point where almost everyone begins. (The word *journal* comes from the Old English — not Latin — word *journal*, meaning "daily.") The "everyday" journalist keeps an ongoing record of aspects of day-to-day living, whether it be by sketching, list making, writing, photographing, or collecting specimens. The journal is a way to keep an ongoing connection with the flow of life, day upon day, year upon year.

In Your Own Backyard

Oregon artist-naturalist Laurie Troon Mintz observes and records the changing seasons as seen in her own backyard. She says of her work, "Keeping a journal of nature's details seen around me is what lends clarity and brings a focal point to the passing days. Trying to capture these unique details on paper brings great pleasure and I find with each page my sense of connection to and wonder in the natural world is renewed. The artist and scientist within are happily joined — the products of this union being a tangible record of fleeting moments, new knowledge, and personal growth."

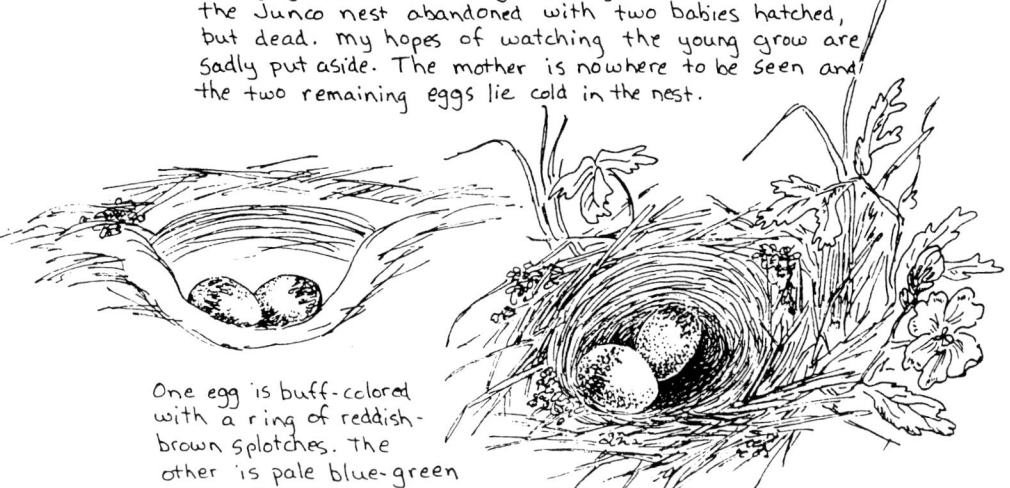

April 29th:
Stormy grey clouds once again hang overhead. I found the Junco nest abandoned with two babies hatched, but dead. My hopes of watching the young grow are sadly put aside. The mother is nowhere to be seen and the two remaining eggs lie cold in the nest.

One egg is buff-colored with a ring of reddish-brown splotches. The other is pale blue-green with splotches on one end. The chicks have tiny down on their heads and skin so thin I can see the backbone.

April 30th: Rainy
The day is cool and windy, with sunbreaks between brief showers. Camellia blossoms fall like pieces of perfection from the bushes, too soon parted. Buds on the Siberian Iris come up, also tall panicles of buds on Jacob's Ladder. Starling eggs have hatched.

Studies for Later Reference

The accomplished British wildlife artist John Busby keeps field journals in which he records observations he can later use to improve or clarify the figures in his studio paintings. These pen and watercolor-wash studies show three bird species he observed on an expedition to Spain. Note how he has tried to capture the essence of different behavioral poses. Such poses will add liveliness and reality when translated into his more formal paintings. Journals are the perfect medium for recording quick word or drawn sketches that can later be refined into finished poems, essays, drawings, or paintings.

Learning About a New Place

Steve Lindell, a research chemist in Great Britain and former student of Clare's, observes and records around his home and when traveling, detailing both the objects themselves and the context in which they occur. Steve writes, "I have kept a regular nature journal since 1980 (when I attended your class), and find it the best way to learn about places I visit and things I see. For example, the act of drawing a plant reveals details I would otherwise have missed and helps me to better understand its structure. I use a felt-tipped pen and an 8½" x 12" hardbound sketchbook which I carry with me whenever I go anywhere new or interesting."

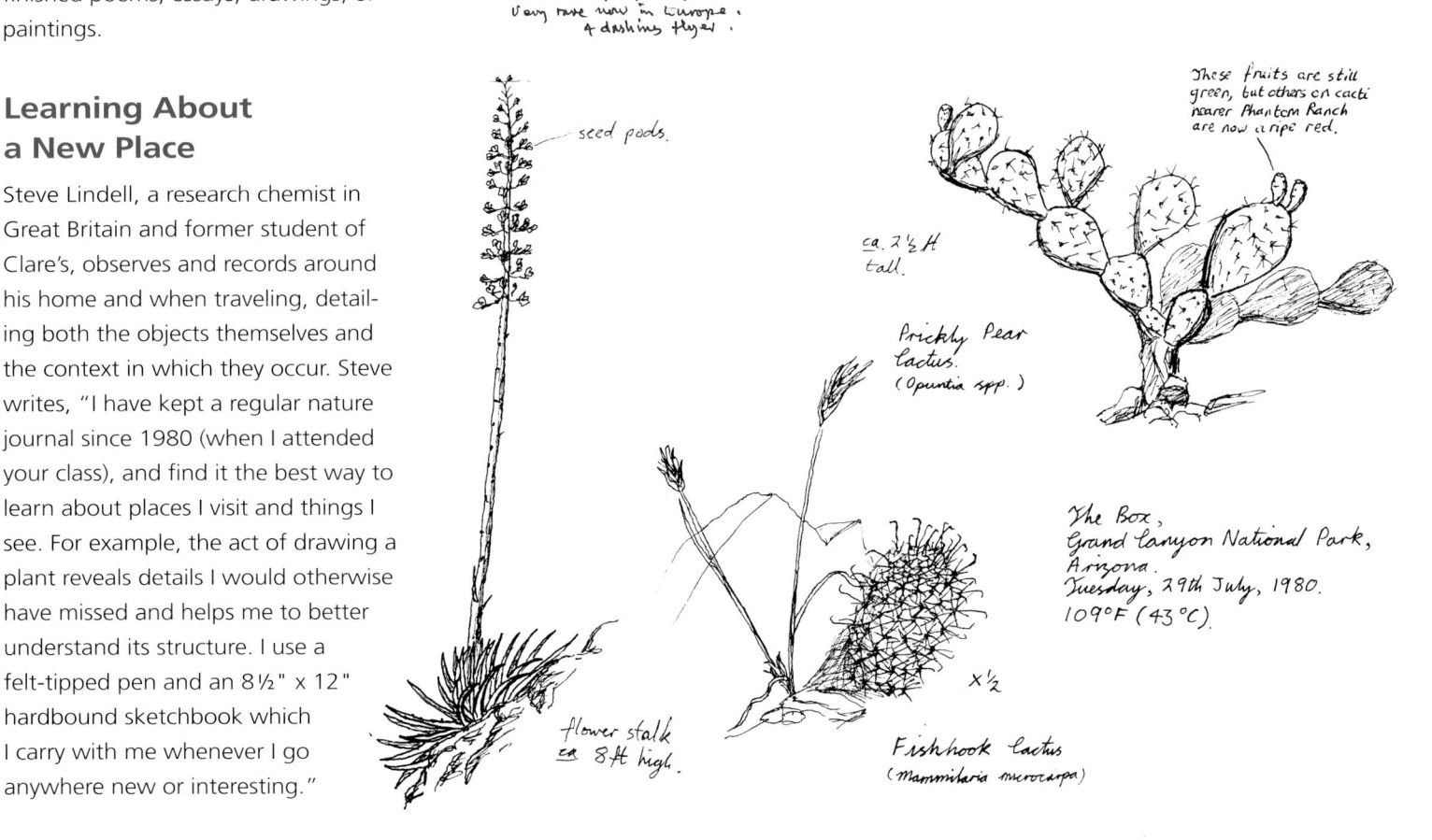

Azure-winged Magpies
Very common round the Trujca & throughout Extremadura. 2·10·94
excitable characters, gregarious & noisy. Jet black heads contrast with soft pink/brown bodies & blue wings.

Bonelli's eagle
One of the highlights of Extremadura. Very rare now in Europe. A dashing flyer.

Little Bustards: males displaying.

These fruits are still green, but others on cacti nearer Phantom Ranch are now a ripe red.

seed pods.

ca. 2½ ft tall.

Prickly Pear cactus. (Opuntia spp.)

The Box, Grand Canyon National Park, Arizona. Tuesday, 29th July, 1980. 109°F (43°C).

flower stalk ca. 8 ft high.

x ½

Fishhook cactus (Mammilaria microcarpa)

Combining Text and Visuals

John Elder, professor of environmental studies at Middlebury College, finds that combining sketching with his writing adds another dimension to his words. In this example, Elder enters his handwritten account of seeing a mountain ash, illegible to most, on one side of his journal and draws his visual account on the other side. John notes that "Drawing has helped my journal practice become more centered. I tend to stay with a given observation much longer now, as eye perceives and hand records the details of form and texture. A more concrete, immediate quality has also come into my written entries since I was introduced to drawing, not primarily as a way to make pictures, but rather as a mode of paying attention."

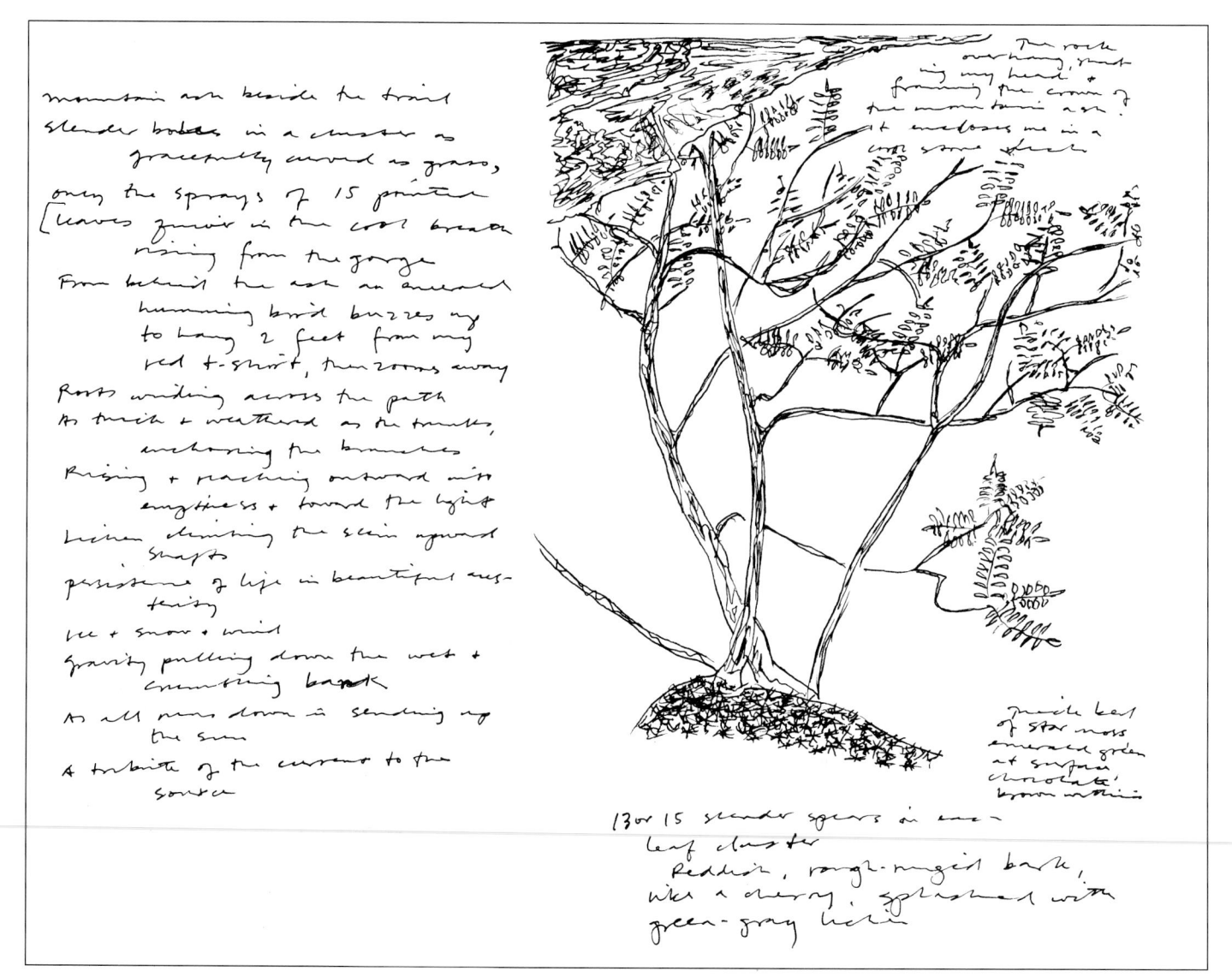

Setting Up a Nature Study

Not all your detailed observations need to be made outdoors. You may want to collect objects that have some immediate appeal and bring them home. You can then set them up for study in more ideal conditions and draw or describe them in detail in your journal.

Careful and detailed drawings of dead creatures you might find that have flown into windows or clashed with cars can be part of your science education. Handle the creatures carefully, if at all. To avoid getting possible animal parasites on your hands, handling with gloves may be advisable, and always wash your hands afterward.

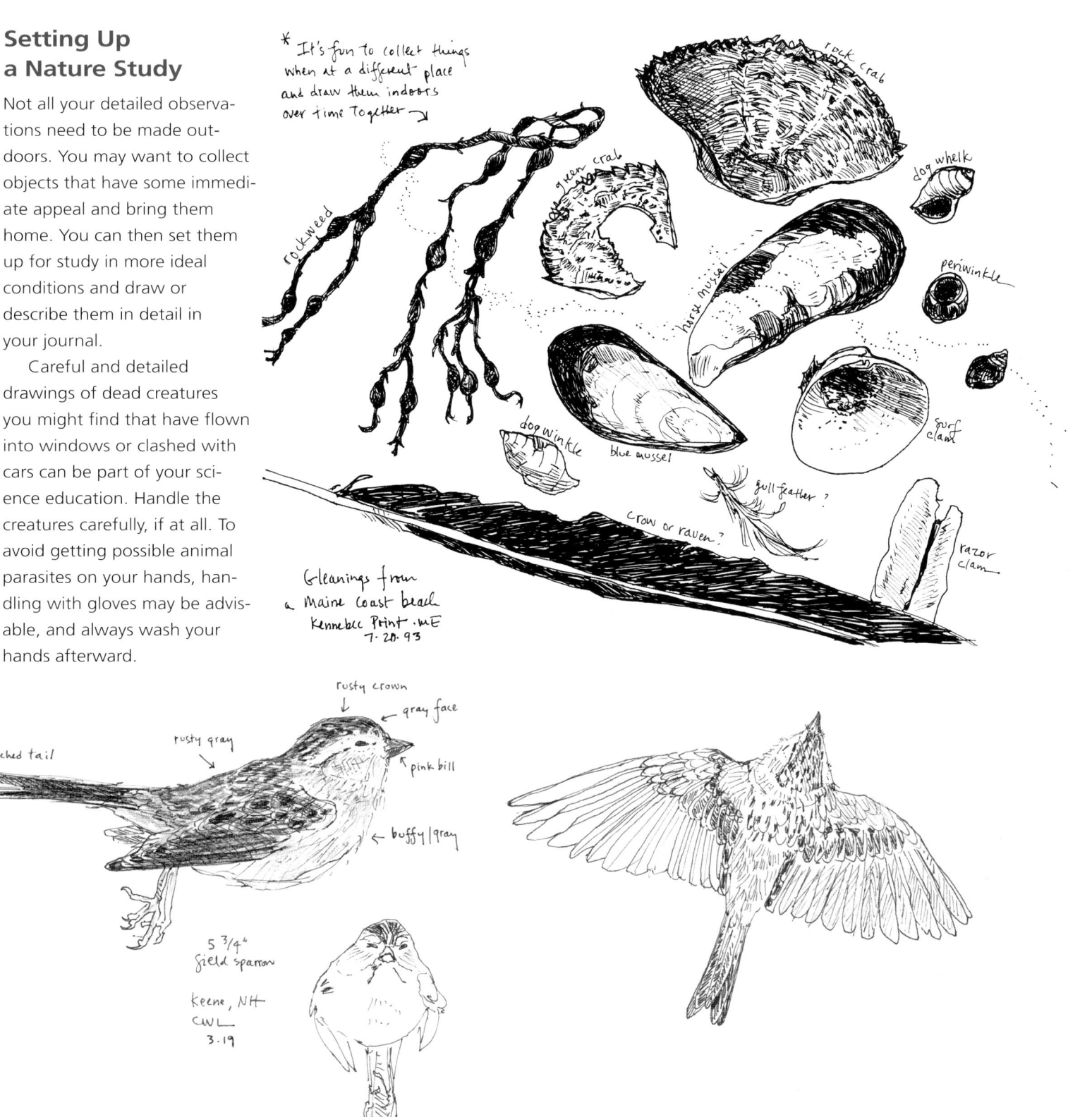

* It's fun to collect things when at a different place and draw them indoors over time together →

rock crab

green crab

dog whelk

rockweed

horse mussel

periwinkle

dog winkle

blue mussel

surf clam

gull feather?

crow or raven?

razor clam

Gleanings from a Maine coast beach Kennebec Point. ME 7. 20. 93

rusty crown

gray face

rusty gray

pink bill

notched tail

buffy/gray

5 3/4"
field sparrow

Keene, NH
CWL
3.19

Working from Indoors

You don't need to go far afield to make great observations. You don't even have to go outside. You can use the nearest window as an observation post and record the many things you see going on beyond the glass. This can be a great opportunity for those restricted by disabilities or illness or just by inclement weather.

NATURE in the CITY =

Oxford St. looking S. towards Lesley Col. Harvard U. Agassiz School neighborhood

hazy sun

silver maple

Agassiz elementary

Norway maples

ash

sugar maple

yellow leaves

yews + hemlocks

lilacs

privet + lilac

marigolds + old petunias

playground

junipers + barberry

honey locusts

honey locust — hot ash leaves

few American elms left

Silver maple

Nov. 14 11 am overcast

pigeons

starlings

black ring

gray

gray

great black-backed gull

black

herring gull

gray

pink

yellow

plus all the various gray phase immature gulls!

ring-billed gull (smaller)

*drawing gull species through the windshield of my parked car — freezing cold!

February 11
Porter Square shopping mall
Cambridge
Sunny but biting wind
6° at 8 am

If you look only at the gulls circling overhead, it is easy to imagine they are spiraling over some rocky seacoast headland — instead of a cluttered city parking lot!

yellowing willows

buds red on silver maples

DUNKIN' DONUTS

McDonald's

COMMAND PERFORMANCE STYLING SALONS

Connecting with Nature

Carolyn Duckworth, a teacher and naturalist-artist living in Gardiner, Montana, writes of her experiences journaling: "From my earliest memory, I have soaked in colors and shapes and images and feelings of the world. I remember always drawing, coloring, and writing — and I remember the time that these three things first combined with science, in my sixth grade class. We were told to draw what we saw on a field trip to an estuary. I can still see that pink and orange crab I drew, though that journal is long lost.

"I've become convinced," Carolyn continues, "that if you want to understand and become connected to your environment, keeping a field journal is one of the fastest ways to accomplish this goal. One simple, periodical act — that of marking where the sun rises and sets on your horizon each day — provides a sense of your place on this earth and in this solar system. Noting when the rain falls — or doesn't — sets up another rhythmic connection. Making quick sketches of one or two critters you observe on a walk — another connection. Stopping to smell, hear, and feel the wind, and then describing each sensation — these simple acts begin making your field observations personal and unique."

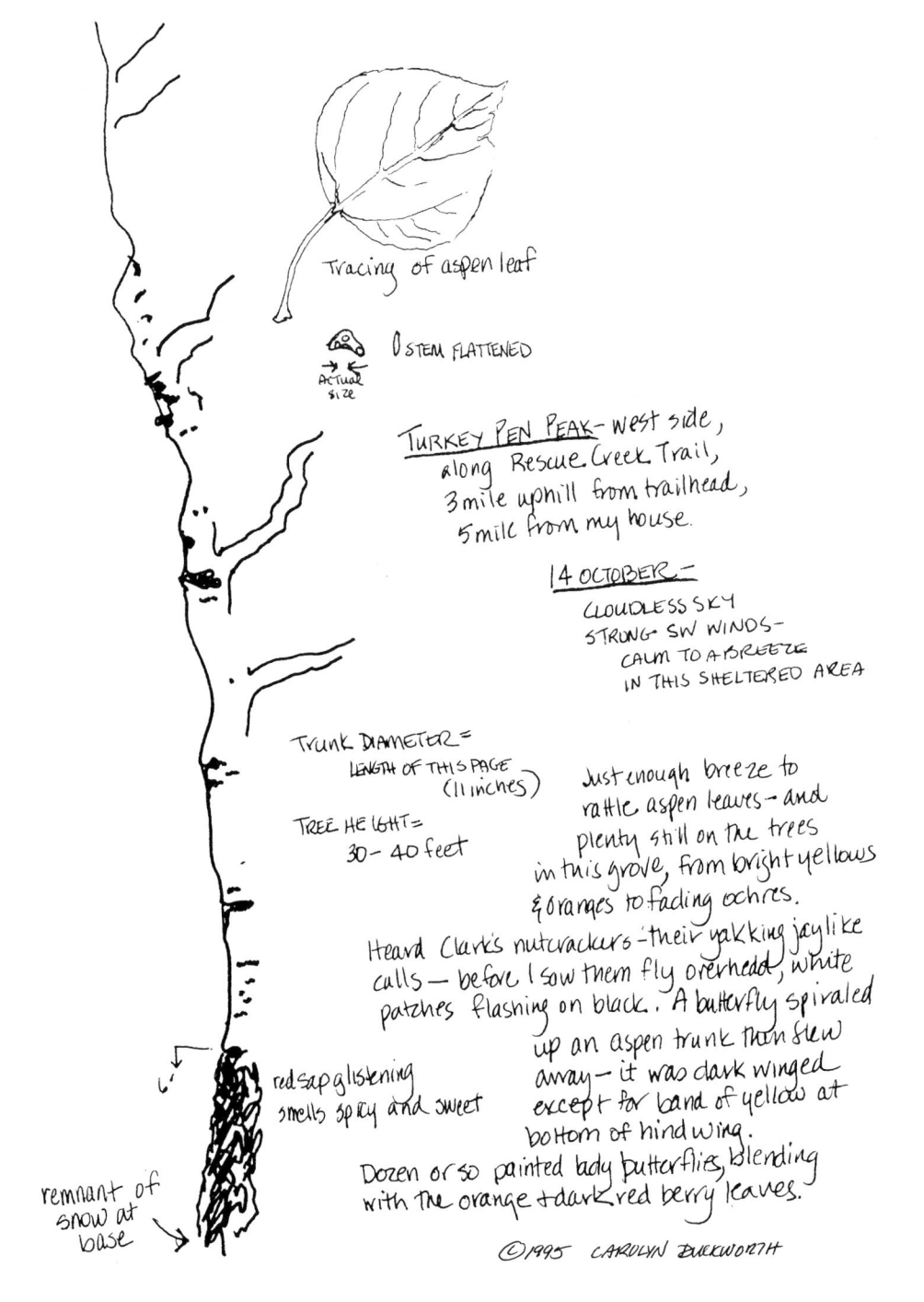

Tracing of aspen leaf

STEM FLATTENED

ACTUAL SIZE

TURKEY PEN PEAK— west side, along Rescue Creek Trail, 3 mile uphill from trailhead, 5 mile from my house.

14 OCTOBER —
CLOUDLESS SKY
STRONG SW WINDS—
CALM TO A BREEZE
IN THIS SHELTERED AREA

TRUNK DIAMETER =
LENGTH OF THIS PAGE
(11 inches)

TREE HEIGHT =
30 - 40 feet

Just enough breeze to rattle aspen leaves — and plenty still on the trees in this grove, from bright yellows & oranges to fading ochres.

Heard Clark's nutcrackers — their yakking jaylike calls — before I saw them fly overhead, white patches flashing on black. A butterfly spiraled up an aspen trunk then flew away — it was dark winged except for band of yellow at bottom of hind wing.

Dozen or so painted lady butterflies, blending with the orange + dark red berry leaves.

© 1995 CAROLYN DUCKWORTH

red sap glistening smells spicy and sweet

remnant of snow at base

Systematic Record Keeping

Journaling is best when it is an ongoing process. One way to get into the habit of journaling regularly is to set up some regular system for recording. This can be as simple as deciding that you will record the temperature every morning and evening, or make a list of the birds at your feeder each day. As you gain experience, you will most likely develop other standard record-keeping systems and formats to structure your observations. Depending on how systematic a person you are, you may eventually decide to set up all your journal pages in a similar format, or to set up several journals to record different types of observations.

You might also try setting up journaling times and writing them into your calendar so you have a "date" with yourself and your journal. It can be anywhere from ten minutes to a full day long.

Using a Series of Field Journals

Vermont naturalist and professional wildlife artist John Pitcher writes, "Because my professional life as an artist and my work as a naturalist have co-evolved, I have come to use several systems or 'tools' for learning, recording and connecting with nature. By combining the results of Field Journals, Species Account Books, Sketchbooks, and personal reference photos taken on location, I have the raw materials for making finished studio paintings.

"The style of the Field Journal I use is rooted in science and fills my needs as a naturalist to record my observations. The Journal is chronological and the layout is formalized so that the information can be retrieved and used long after the observations were made. . . . Small sketches/paintings in my Sketchbooks and photographs taken are all cross-referenced in the left margins with the symbol 'D' for drawings and 'P' for photographs taken. Within the text I write, parenthetically, the sketchbook the drawing was made in. The text is mostly diary-like but I also list plants and animals of interest in a given location.

"My Species Account Book is not a field book. It stays in the studio and like the field journal is a loose-leaf three-ring notebook. This is where I record more lengthy descriptions of a

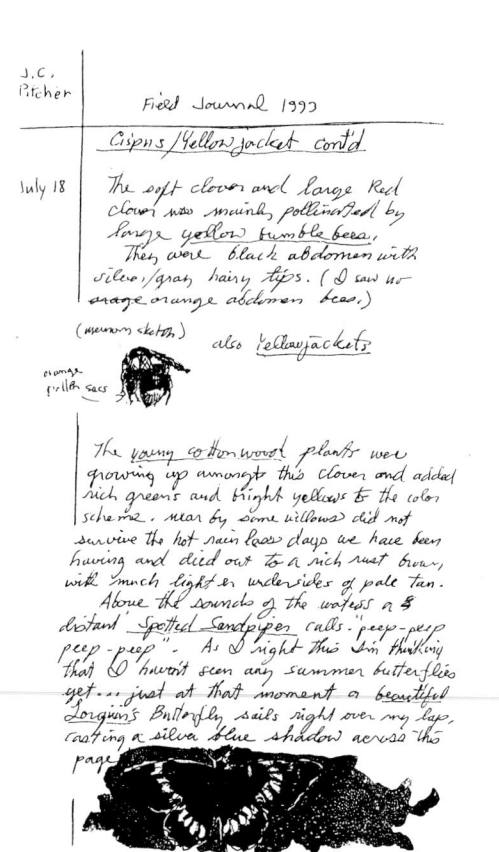

single species made in the field or later from memory. The format of the page differs from that of the Field Journal in that it is headed with the species name and filed phylogenetically.

"My Field Sketchbooks are not strictly chronological. I put drawings from different days and locations on the same page, plus I carry three different Sketchbooks afield with different types of paper for different drawing/painting needs.

"Because each sketchbook is coded and each sketch is dated and cross-referenced in the Journal, the written/sketched information of an observation is easily retrieved. My Sketchbooks exhibit several kinds of sketches and I employ various drawing techniques but the one I use most is a kind of modified gestural drawing."

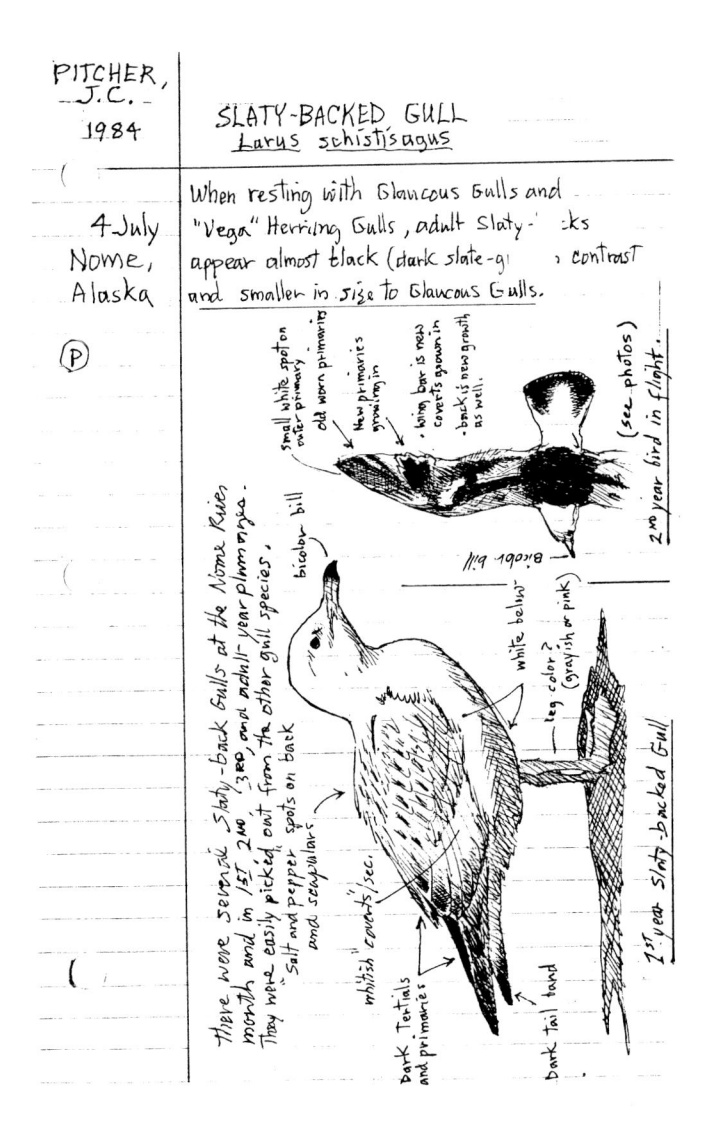

Regardless of your recording style, the heart of nature journaling lies not in the objects and events you respond to, but in the connections you see among them and the contexts in which they appear. As you become more experienced at journal keeping, context and connection become ever more apparent. Creativity and richness deepen, and the journal becomes an invaluable tool for personal growth, teaching you how to look for connections and interactions. As you observe and write or draw, then, ask yourself the following questions:

• Can you correlate what you have observed to other observations you have made?

• Can you perceive patterns — visual, behavioral, temporal — among your observations?

• Can you find obvious, or subtle, connections among the objects and events you have observed?

• Can you determine how the things observed work? How do seeds move away from their parents, for instance? Do insects fly the same way birds do?

Journaling for Scientific Study

Massachusetts artist-naturalist Marcy Marchello combines writing and sketching to make a series of detailed observations, such as this one of heron behavior in a breeding colony.

"I love keeping a nature journal because it's such a dynamic, creative fusion of my passions for writing, drawing, and nature. I actually keep three different active journals. One is exclusively for reflection in my personal growth, essentially a diary. Another is for daily written notations about birds and animals that I observe. And the third, my sketch journal, is where I focus on drawing, combined with field writing which often includes my immediate personal responses. I've been a journaler in one form or another since adolescence and cherish the ongoing discovery process that journaling both is and supports. It's a natural expressive process for me. I love tracking myself and the natural world through many seasons of change, often reading past entries to compare to current observations and thoughts. This process keeps me in tune with myself and nature to the depth that I need, that feeds my spirit. And best of all, there's always more to discover."

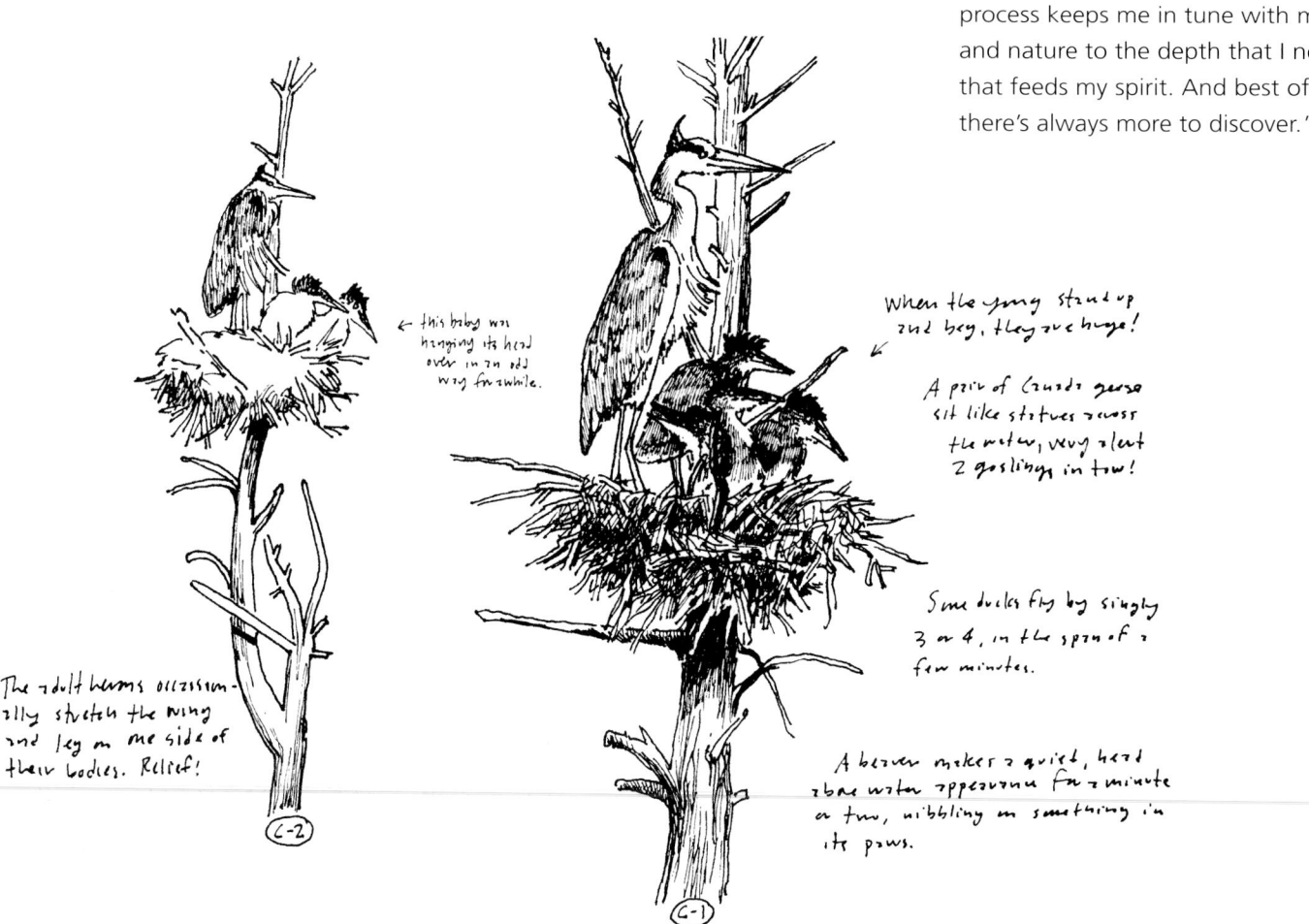

Red Squirrel scolds while shredding a new white pine cone

← this baby was hanging its head over in an odd way for awhile.

The adult herons occasionally stretch the wing and leg on one side of their bodies. Relief!

When the young stand up and beg, they are huge!

A pair of Canada geese sit like statues across the water, very alert 2 goslings in tow!

Some ducks fly by singly 3 or 4, in the span of a few minutes.

A beaver makes a quiet, hard to see water appearance for a minute or two, nibbling on something in its paws.

C-2

C-1

Conducting a
Biology Research Project

Ron Cisar, a high school honors biology teacher in Omaha, Nebraska, has his students keep a weeklong journal of their observations. The calendar is one of the simplest organizing systems for students to try. Excerpts from these journals are published and circulated within the school, offering students a chance to gain an awareness of how others organize items similarly or differently from their own techniques.

October 10-14

Its about 6:00p.m on a Monday evening. The wind is blowing, the trees are swaying, and the sun is shining. I watch the leaves fall from the trees. As you may notice, the tree is almost bare.

Wednesday - October 12th 7:00 A.M
Last night it rained. So this morning I observe a drop of rain hanging off a leaf.

Week: January 23-29 By: Lorelei King

Monday: Today, it was very cold and windy. No animals or birds spotted. Abandoned nest seen.

Tuesday: Today, was like yesterday, only without the wind. Crows spotted in distance.

Wednesday: Today, it was warmer, but still a little cool. Squirrel spotted.

Thursday: Today, the sun came out. I saw some crows again. The snow is gradually melting, but it is still here.

Friday: It rained this morning, but we didn't get any more snow. I saw a raccoon by Spring Lake.

Saturday: The streets were very icy from yesterdays rain, but the birds didn't care all to much. I see more and more every day now.

Sunday: Eventhough it's Super Bowl Sunday, the animals have decided to come out and play. I saw a fox, I'm not sure if it was a baby, on the Spring Lake Golf Course. It was very cute!

Tues - October 11th. 6:30 p.m.
Today I observe the sky, and I watch some birds fly south. They're in a perfect V shape of ten. I was unable to see what species they were.

Thurs. October 13th 5:45
Today I saw some weird kind of cocoon on a tree. It was gray and fuzzy.

Friday October 14th 7:30 p.m
In a near by tree, I watched a spider in its web. Five minutes later, a bug got caught in the web.

Kara Vasquez

Review and Reflection

The natural urge to ask questions, look for connections among observations, and reflect on what you saw and what was in your mind at an earlier point takes the journal to another level. Recognizing patterns in your observations can lead to a better understanding of the world around you. Some naturalists use their journals over and over for factual reference, as well as for sources of ideas and creative material for other writing or sketching.

Reflecting On the Fragility of the Environment

Clare recorded these studies while attending an environmental educators' conference on Sanibel Island in Florida. While the island is naturally exotic, exquisite, and full of varied bird and animal life, it is fast facing the onslaught of human development. The conference was held in a large and luxurious hotel, complete with air-conditioning and sealed windows. Conferees were dependent on all the advances in telecommunications and computer technology. Although the conference discussion focused on waking students up to environmental awareness, Clare wondered, "Are we conscious enough of our own presence on this fragile outpost?" As she drew what lived on this beach, she reflected on these things, not clear in her own conscience.

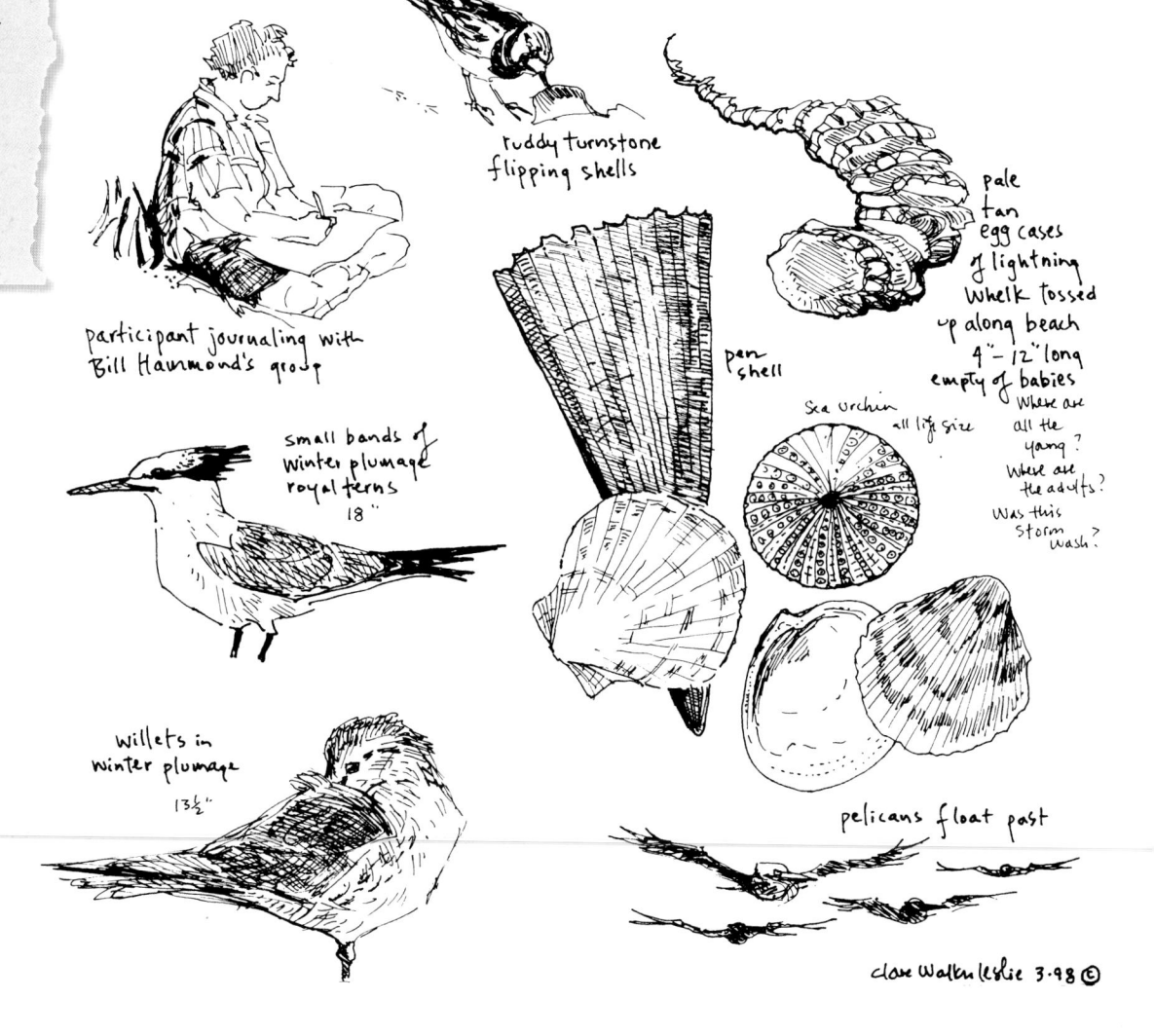

Sanibel Island · Florida
March 7
NAAEE at FGCU
6:30 am beach walk
hot · sunny · muggy 70's
- Sounds of rolling · slurrying waves
- squeaks of shorebirds
- blowing palms + sea grasses

The beach we lived beside at the Sundial Hotel:
"We teach about how we are connected to the world." David Orr 3.6

participant journaling with Bill Hammond's group

ruddy turnstone flipping shells

pale tan egg cases of lightning whelk tossed up along beach 4"-12" long empty of babies Where are all the young? Where are the adults? Was this storm wash?

pen shell

Sea urchin all life size

small bands of winter plumage royal terns 18"

willets in winter plumage 13½"

pelicans float past

clare Walker leslie 3.98 ©

Reflecting On One Place Over Time

Return often to your journal entries to revisit your feelings; consider if they remain the same, or if they have changed with new experiences. Check out the questions that you raised. Do they provide ideas for new studies and observations you can undertake? You may even want to create special reflection pages where you pull together the questions raised in the separate entries: Why do there seem to be fewer blue jays this year? How does the water flow out of this creek? If a new shopping mall is built near this marsh, how will the ecosystem change here? How has your own life changed since the last time you visited?

You must walk sometimes perfectly free, not prying nor inquisitive, not bent on seeing things. Throw away a whole day for a single expansion, a single inspiration of air. . . .
You must walk so gently as to hear the finest sounds, the faculties being in repose. . . . Nature will bear the closest inspection. She invites us to lay our eye level with her smallest leaf, and take an insect view of its plain.

— HENRY DAVID THOREAU

I draw the Cucumber tree over my parents' marker and watch Betsy sleeping.

September 28
3:45 pm
Mount Auburn Cemetery
Sunny · lovely · blue skies
green · green
high 60°'s
Sunrise = 6:38
Sunset = 6:32
length of day =
11 hrs 57 min.

many robins

Squirrels about

Two years ago today my mother died - in the morning. The light was the same - the colors of leaves and pulse of crickets the same. Where have I've been since then?
I sit and watch the lengthening afternoon shadows slide across ground, trees and stones. What metaphor was the car crash? What do I need to learn?

*Betsy arrives from Japan last night at 11pm! Here until Oct. 11

ROBERT MILLER WALKER
. . . . . .
ALICE SMITH WALKER
. . . . . .

May 11
Saturday 1pm
Downtown Minneapolis
Driving along one of
their busy connector
roads, I spy a
Woodchuck spying
us under an
underpass!

Minnehaha
95

Allie 7 CWL

The woodchuck
had an air of
authority, as
he/she surveyed
his backyard property—
even if it was an
asphalted highway!

Travel Journaling

Some people only journal when traveling, recording anything from short weekend hikes to month- or yearlong journeys around the globe. It is nice to have more than photos to take home. Your travel journal can expand your vision beyond what you see in simple snapshots. Try to really observe the habitat by describing the place, sketching animals and plants observed, and labeling everything to help you remember details of what you saw. In essence, these are pages of memories that you can return to long after your journey is over.

Travel journals are often done in the evening around a campfire or in a motel room after the day's journey has ended. But you can also journal at periodic points throughout the day as you travel, even when you're moving. On one trip to Minneapolis, Clare spotted a woodchuck alongside the road near an overpass. As her sister drove, she made a sketch with a felt-tip pen to capture the moment.

Group Journaling

If you're traveling with a family or close group of friends, try keeping a group journal. Each person can contribute observations in his individual style, which are then shared or combined into one book. This often enriches the traveling experience for everyone. Maps can add a great dimension to such travel journals, reminding you later of just where you had those fine experiences.

When our family traveled across the country, some of us kept drawing journals, some of us written journals, and some of us took photographs.

my journal hardbound 6 × 9"

my 9 year old daughter's hardbound lined paper 5 × 8"

my 14 year old son's spiral unlined 9" × 6"

Eric drew maps of our drive.

Involving Children

Encourage kids to keep journal pages of things they do and see on a trip that they can later share with other family members who weren't along. At age ten Clare's daughter, Anna, accompanied her to the National Wildlife Federation's Conservation Summit at Rocky Mountain National Park. While Clare taught her class, Anna joined a group of thirteen kids about her age to learn about nature there. They all did some nature journaling, and Anna was able to share some of her observations later.

They all did some Nature Journaling:

Estes Park, CO July, 3, 95 cold and cloudy, 50° 8:50 AM

View looking west – Rockies

Elk scat

Barn Swallow

orange

Black Blue

Rock

3/4 inch nichill

4 inch Ponderosa

Baby Pinecone

anna Leslie

The orange-red mesas, buttes and spires of Monument Valley viewed from just south of Mexican Hat, Utah on route 163 (above). Many of these sandstone monoliths tower as much as 1000 ft above the valley floor, which is covered by clumpy desert shrubs and occasional stunted trees. Navajo nomads first entered the area perhaps in the 1600's, the original occupants having abandoned the valley in the 1300's. Since then the Navajo people have herded their sheep and other livestock and raised small quantities of crops in this hot and arid environment.

Monument Valley,
Utah - Arizona
Monday, 28th July, 1980.
Midday, brilliant sunshine.

West Mitten Butte and East Mitten Butte,
Monument Valley Navajo Tribal Park.

Better Than a Photo

These examples from Steven Lindell's trips to Monument Valley (left) and Anne Gamble's trip to the Galapagos Islands (below) are great examples of how you can use sketches to remember your experiences. Often sketches let you capture things that photos cannot. They bring a different kind of authenticity to your observations.

Drawing helps me to see better, because I have to really notice what I am looking at. I took a journal with me to the Galapagos and drew everything I saw and I can still vividly recall so many details of the trip. I know that keeping a journal consistently has made this clear memory possible, even years later.

— ANNE GAMBLE,
A NATURE JOURNALING STUDENT

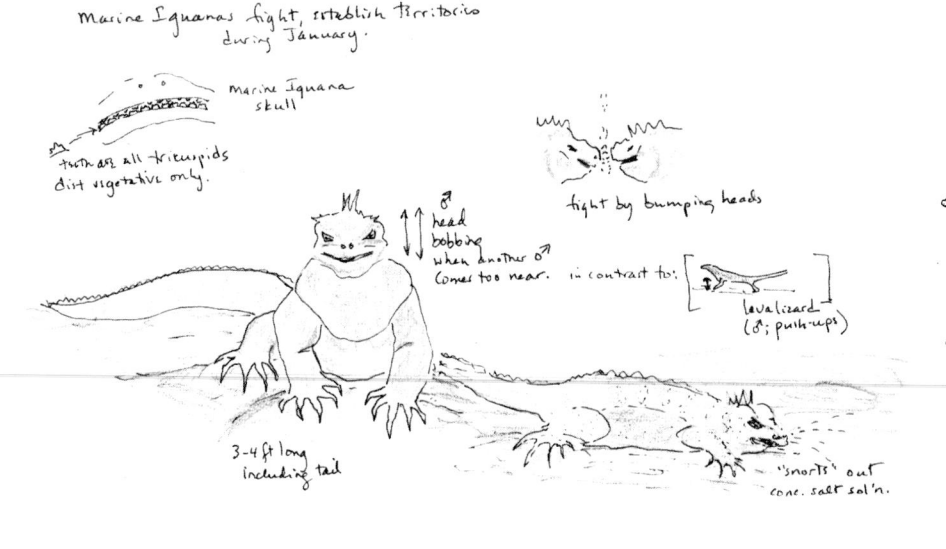

Journaling While Hiking

Journaling on hikes is a great focusing activity and gives you a good excuse to take frequent breath-catching breaks, along with the opportunity to reflect on the places you are visiting. Another good time to journal is while you are picnicking. You can write and draw and tell good stories.

If hiking, you might want to write in your base information before you get started (see page 22). Then, once you're walking, stop and draw what first catches your attention that is less than 3 inches in size. Then draw objects from different levels: ground, waist-high, treetop, or sky levels. The time you take for each level will depend upon who is accompanying you on the hike.

You may want to just group lots of little sketches on one page, setting them in frames, the way Jeannine Reese, a North Carolina artist, records these plants she wants to remember.

At right is Clare's system of listing elements noticed on a hike up a trail in New Hampshire. Drawings can be done later from a field guide and added to the journal entry.

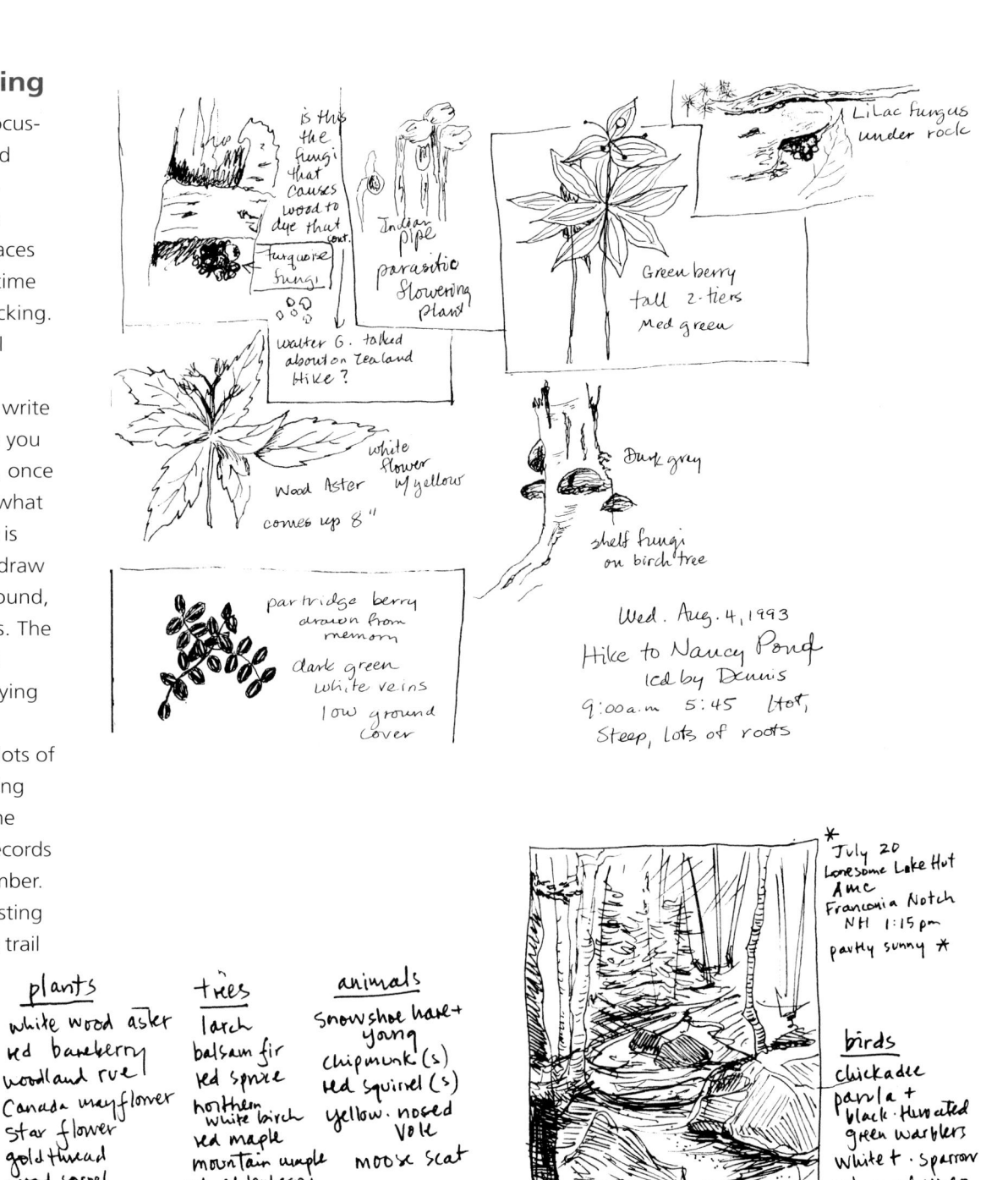

is this the fungi that causes wood to dye that color.

turquoise fungi

Indian Pipe
parasitic flowering plant

Lilac fungus under rock

Green berry tall 2-tiers med green

water G. talked about on Zealand Hike?

white flower w/ yellow
Wood Aster comes up 8"

Dark grey

shelf fungi on birch tree

partridge berry drawn from memory
dark green white veins
low ground cover

Wed. Aug. 4, 1993
Hike to Nancy Pond
led by Dennis
9:00 a.m. 5:45 Hot,
Steep, lots of roots

* July 20
Lonesome Lake Hut
AMC
Franconia Notch
NH 1:15 pm
partly sunny *

plants
white wood aster
red baneberry
woodland rue
Canada mayflower
star flower
goldthread
wood sorrel
bunchberry
painted trillium
hellebore / Indian poke

shrubs
sheep laurel
labrador tea
sweet gale
mountain holly
swamp alder
meadowsweet
Lapland rosebay?
swamp honeysuckle?
hobblebush viburnum

trees
larch
balsam fir
red spruce
northern white birch
red maple
mountain maple
red elderberry
mountain ash

animals
snowshoe hare + young
chipmunk (s)
red squirrel (s)
yellow-nosed vole
moose scat

birds
chickadee
parula + black-throated green warblers
white t. sparrow
red-eyed vireo
solitary vireo
winter wren
Swainson's thrush
raven
spotted sandpiper
hawk? merlin?

When Drawing Isn't Practical

Barbara Turley lives in Alaska, where she and her family are frequent mountain climbers and sea kayakers. This selection from her self-published *Journal of an Arctic Odyssey* shows how photography and prose can be used to record observations. Photography is a good alternative when time and weather conditions just are not conducive to field sketching. The camera allows for a quick recording of events that can be elaborated on in writing or drawing later. The process of framing a photo through the camera's viewfinder involves selecting, focusing on, and observing your subject carefully.

June 14. . . *Even unencumbered with sleds, the eight-hour hike we did today was difficult. Sometimes we were in big, loose rocks with moss-covered pit traps between them. Three-foot-tall tangles of willows obstructed our progress in draws between the rock piles. When we moved a little farther away from the steep hillsides and out into the valley, we had wet tussocks to pick our way through. As we got into the mountains, rushing, boulder-filled creeks poured off the slopes. The stepping-stones we crossed on were barely close enough together. Admittedly, there were some stretches of very nice walking, too, over short plants that almost seemed like a lawn; soft, springy moss, and smooth, packed sand near a channel of the river. We took breaks, taking our packs off and sitting down to nibble on some food every hour and a half or so. All in all, I guess it wasn't too bad.*

We saw our first bull caribou of the trip today. Even in the velvet, their antlers look very big. We could instantly distinguish them from the cows. Unlike many deer species, both the male and female caribou have antlers. The bulls drop theirs just after the rut in October. By now, as they are arriving on the North Slope, their new antlers seem to be about half grown. The pregnant cows haven't lost their antlers from last year yet. They keep them so they can out-compete the bulls and barren cows for forage during the winter, and to provide weapons against predators during the calving season. The cows' antlers are much smaller and lighter weight than the bulls'. They seem to come in many shapes, but most look a lot like a small elk antler. We see quite a few of the cows' old antlers on the ground. Only the bulls have the big, forward-pointing shovel on the brow tine that gives caribou and reindeer their classic appearance.

The groups of caribou with the bulls didn't have new calves with them. These groups allowed us to approach much more closely before they ran. They also seemed more curious about us. They would only run a short distance, then trot back toward us for another look. Watching them run, backlit by the low sun, their hooves splashing up golden fans of water from the wet tundra, was a beautiful sight.

The bull caribou seemed curious about us.

Sketch Roughly

Your sketch may almost be like a doodle, as happened here. Clare drew on the page while talking to a friend and waiting for a cake to bake.

View from our porch looking West; kids playing running bases

A Record of Family Holidays, Stories, and Precious Moments

Keeping track of the little pleasures of family and neighborhood life and the treasures of seasonal celebrations is what drives some journalists. You need not travel very far to keep a journal. You can "catch a sketch" in your journal of any particular moment you want to remember. Keep your journal handy — on the kitchen counter, on your desk, or even in your car — and you will use it more often.

Share the Experience

When you stop to journal, the practice often rubs off on other family members: Start writing or drawing and the kids want to do the same. So put family stories into the journals. Family activity is a part of the nature of your life and belongs in the nature journal that can be shared with others. Do not generally include more highly emotionally charged family concerns, however. These are more appropriate for your personal journal, which you do not show others but which contains material you want to personally remember and reflect upon.

Granville—
Vermont
December 13

7:30 pm
dark
dark-dark
snow blowing
wildly outdoors

When I sit down to draw, I right off have two children on each knee — also drawing

Drawn from reflection in overhead, angled window...

Remembering Holidays

Record images from your various holidays. Take your journal to family events and draw or describe images you want to remember. Journaling on a holiday can provide some moments of quiet and reflection during an otherwise highly charged day or evening.

Seasonal Celebrations:

Original Thanksgiving: Plimouth October 6.1621

November 23
Duxbury
Thanksgiving

Lochlins · Leslies + Icelandic folks

home of Original Thanksgiving

Plymouth Manomet

Thanks for family
Thanks for friends
Thanks for warmth + good food

Thanks for beach + sea beauty

Thanks for silly dogs

Cold grey. Windy
Walk along the beach
I have always loved

Pies of apple · mince + pumpkin

my father's empty chair

Gone are the parents; but now are my sister + family...

my mother's empty desk

pulled curtains dark at 5:40!

Meditating on Small Bits of Life

California artist Richard Gayton, whose sketches are shown here, often uses his nature journal "to discover the life of a place." He will sit for long hours slowly following the lines of flower, leaf, stem, or bee with his pencil or pen. Out of this, he notes, comes deep meditation.

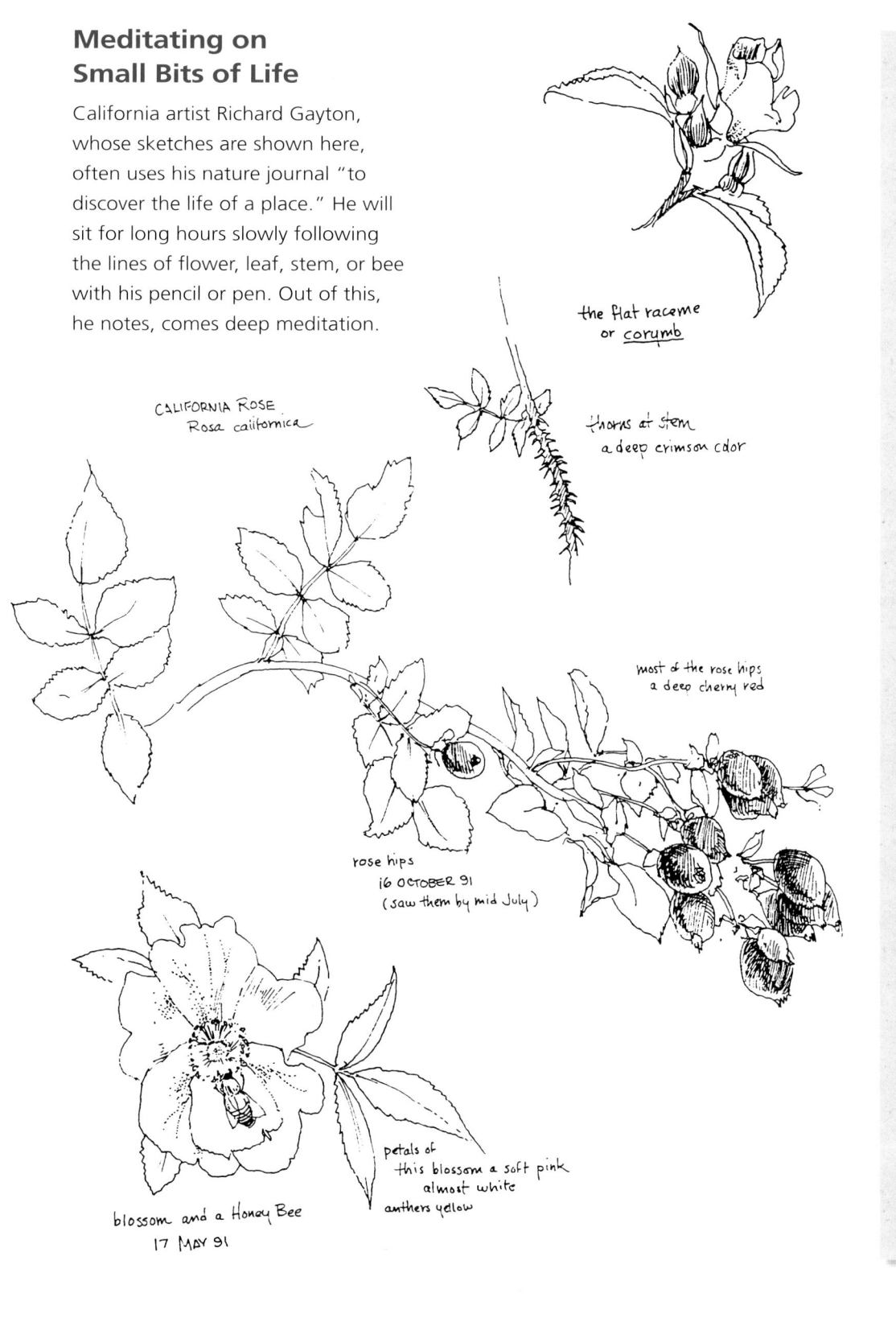

the flat raceme or corymb

thorns at stem a deep crimson color

CALIFORNIA ROSE
Rosa californica

most of the rose hips a deep cherry red

rose hips
16 OCTOBER 91
(saw them by mid July)

petals of this blossom a soft pink almost white
anthers yellow

blossom and a Honey Bee
17 MAY 91

A Place for Meditation and Healing

The meditative journal may focus more on descriptions of feelings, moods, and aesthetics than more scientific description. It may give more weight to the subjective than the objective. The key is to jot down your feelings of connectedness to the world around you. What attitudes do you feel? How do these change with time and context? The journaling process can provide a vast amount of emotional healing through internal dialogue and reconnection with the natural world. The journal offers a place to record perceptions, feelings, and sensations using drawings, poetry, and prose. Later you may return to the journals to further meditate on what you created there and gain an even deeper understanding of nature. Journaling can also occupy your mind at times when more negative thoughts might try to crowd in to nurture illness. Nature can be a healer for any age.

Stories of the Land   May 10-12

Orion Society Colloquium at
Breadloaf / Middlebury College
Ripton VT

Fri night - rain - fog dense · earth greening up

Mitch Thomashon · "Finding what's ordinary
in the extraordinary"

① What do I know about the place where I live?
Who are your neighbors? What is the water source?
Where is your habitat?
What

② Where do things come from and where do they go?

③ How do I connect w/ the earth?

④ What is my responsibility to the earth?

Barry Lopez -
create a campus
naturalist

Sunday -
"Education of Place"
9 am snowing,
raw · raw · raw!

"For us as teachers, what are our
central goals?"
"You can't be a teacher w/out being real"
"students need to feel before they can care,
to see   can make a difference"
to experience

"How can we practice what we preach in places
where we teach?"   Walk the Talk
How much time in woods vs time in school today?

raindroplets
on
honeysuckle   OUTDOOR WONDERS =

drawing
raindroplets
outdoors - upside down
suspended tree images

Here it is
still winter -
snow falling on
a wild turkey's back

Happy
Mother's Day
rose breasted
grosbeak at
our feeders!
a gift

no
gardening today!

Reflecting on the Words of Others

Keeping a nature journal for meditation may go well beyond recording your contemplations on natural objects and events. You may want to try jotting down quotes from poems and nature writing to reread and reflect upon later, even as you focus on sky or sea or babbling brook. Inspiring classes, lectures, and conferences are all places to record words and images you wish to remember for later reflection.

Appreciating the Gifts of Each Day

Journaling can also be healing, allowing you to move away from excessive dwelling on difficult emotional situations. Clare says, "When my mother was dying, I found it releasing to turn to my journal to note some of the positive things that were going on in my world at the same time. These are things I call spiritual blessings, or daily exceptional images. They help me connect with the larger world when I'm grounded in human worries. The images can be beautiful, funny, wicked, or sudden, but all are nature related."

Look for one exceptional image a day, simple or complex. Hold it in your mind until you can draw or write about it. Holding it like a talisman in your mind (and in your heart) can give you strength and calm. Then, when you do have a moment to record the memory in your journal, you can gather new energy from that moment with the recorded image.

DAILY EXCEPTIONAL IMAGES - Begun Aug 1 Granville
(Drawn/written from memory, at day's ending) As a daily ritual, pacing me through the coming tough days of my mother's dying. I cling to these like a fulcrum balance!

8·16 - Jeweled raindrops hanging upside down on a pine beside food store. In drawing/seeing I can breathe again evenly!

8·17 - Heard odd "cheeping" - sounds from back room in post office Rochester! ! ! Asked - A large box of almost 50 chicks arrived from Pennsylvania for Valerie Brown's chicken farm! Chirps sent us all laughing...

8·18 - As I drove home from teaching in Woodstock, a broad-winged hawk flapped down to pluck out from road edge what seemed like a vole. So close I caught glint in its eye! What does it know of life?

8·19 - ♀ bluebird alighted on top of wood lawn chair over at Boread loaf. Terry Tempest Williams + I were talking of losing mothers and hard pain, when along came this spark of blue and momentarily set us afire.

8·20 - Raining off + on. muggy. dense cricket sounds. Roads awash in puddles. Today I learned my mother has terminal cancer and the weeks are few left. What do I look for to hang onto today? Mists washing low gray over darkened mountains — ah, a lone raven circles. High over mists below.

8·23 - ☽ Waxing summer moon rises to E over highway and MacDonalds where we eat on way back from hospital. Later, a bat winks past car as we pull into driveway.

8·24 - Eric + Anna fall asleep. I can't. Sit on steps listening to deep throb of meadow crickets. Even pulse joins my breathing. Coyotes barking.

8·27 - What was the image today? Anna chose it. A crimson rose, so sweet smelling, down in Molly + Bobbi's garden. My mother's favored perfume.

8·28 - Talk with my mother over the phone as the moon full is rising over our ridge. She asks what it looks like. I describe the image and we both know the years we have watched that rising orb together - and will keep watching for many years more...

Breaking the Mold

In many places in this book we focus on particular journal formats — which can be very helpful when you're just starting your journaling adventure. However, these same formats can become blocks to creativity as you gain experience and grow in your journaling skills. Don't feel hemmed in by the suggested formats. Following are some samples from journalists who have ignored the "rules" and played with different creative formats to better express what is on their minds.

Varying Your Layout

Generally the nature journalist mixes writing and drawing, but you can focus some pages just on writing or just on drawing — as Wyoming artist, writer, and naturalist Hannah Hinchman has done here with drawings of deer. Hannah also likes to play with ways to mix her drawings with her observational text to create interesting designs. See her most recent book, *A Trail through Leaves: The Journal as a Path to Place,* for many more examples (see Suggested Reading).

Twenty deer and two magpies

December 5

Drawing Maps and Adding Clippings

Observations can be described through diagrammatic maps that help create context as well as describing. You might also find newspaper articles or almanac reports that highlight activity in the natural world at a particular time. These can be taped right onto a journal page. (Article reprinted courtesy of *The Boston Globe;* Almanac courtesy of Alan MacRobert.)

Birds in flight; moose in love

By Tom Long
GLOBE STAFF

September is a month of migration as millions of birds soar south toward warmer climes and greener pastures. But birds aren't the only animals that head south for the winter. One of the most remarkable migrants is the monarch butterfly, the orange and black denizen of milkweed patches that flutters 3,000 miles south on tissue-thin wings to a stand of oyamel fir trees in Sierra Chincua, Mexico. It's an incredible journey made by more than 100 million of the fragile insects that brave daunting winds and weather, trains, planes and automobiles to answer the instinctive call of Mexico. Nobody knows the reason for this remarkable journey, but they've been doing it for more than 30,000 years. Next May, the females head north and lay their eggs so the next generation can continue the cycle.

Nature Watch

Sept. 1: As the sun sets, the drone of crickets, the song of September, fills the night air.

Sept. 2: It's mushroom season in the woodlands as the pale-capped fungi push up through the decaying leaf litter on the forest floor.

Sept. 4: It's mating season for moose. You can expect the stilt-legged twig-eaters to show up in unlikely places when young moose go looking for love in all the wrong places.

Sept. 5: Out in the Berkshires a turkey is spooked by a noisy hiker. The 50-pound tom can run from 15 to 20 miles per hour for short distances when startled.

Sept. 7: As acorns ripen and fall, gray squirrels skitter and scramble to reap the bounty and bury the nuts for midwinter munching.

Sept. 9: The height of hay fever season. This year should be particularly uncomfortable for those affected because numerous thunderstorms have created ideal conditions for ragweed.

Sept. 10: A skunk circles a honeybee nest. The aggressive omnivore will eat even the bees as it fattens up for winter.

Sept. 12: Broad-winged and sharp-shinned hawks ride the ther-

mals above hills and ridges as they slowly make their way south.

Sept. 15: Black ducks begin to arrive at their wintering grounds on Dorchester Bay after summering at inland lakes and ponds.

Sept 19: Full moon, the harvest moon. Before the invention of the electric light, farmers made hay in the moonshine.

Sept. 21: The great hurricane of 1938 swept in from the sea, flooding downtown Providence with 13½ feet of water before roaring up the Connecticut River Valley. Its 100 m.p.h. winds snapped and uprooted millions of trees throughout

Sept. 23: Autum a.m.

Sept. 25: Asters tected thickets.

Sept. 28: The fi rives about now.

Sept. 29: On a snapping turtles er buried in the mud the safety of the w

Sept. 30: Marsh as the trees start to in preparation drought.

showers and thunderstorms. Humid. Highs in the upper 60s.

New Hampshire: Becoming mostly cloudy with afternoon showers. Highs in the upper 60s. Tonight: showers. Lows 60 to 64. Tomorrow: continued cloudy with scattered showers. Humid. Highs in the upper 60s.

Vermont: Becoming mostly cloudy with scattered showers in the afternoon. Highs 64 to 68. Tonight: showers. Lows 50 to 55. Tomorrow: continued cloudy with showers likely. Highs in the 60s.

EXTENDED FORECASTS

Massachusetts, Rhode Island, Connecticut: Friday: partly sunny and cooler. Highs 65 to 75. Saturday: mostly sunny, continued cool. Highs in the mid 60s.

Maine, New Hampshire, Vermont: Friday: partly cloudy and noticeably cooler. Highs in the 60s. Saturday: mostly sunny and continued dry. Highs in the 60s.

ULTRAVIOLET INDEX

▶ Today's forecast of ultraviolet intensity: Low. People with fair complexions will be safe in the sun for 15 to 20 minutes without protection; those with more protective skin types will be safe for 75 to 9stat0 minutes.

POLLEN COUNT

▶ Yesterday's mold spore count: 10; and pollen count: 9 (on a scale where 0-3 is mild, 4-6 is moderate and 7-10 is severe) according to the New England Allergy and Immunology Corp.

AIR QUALITY

▶ Today's air quality forecast: Good statewide, according to the American Lung Association and the Massachusetts Department of Environmental Protection.

Forecasts © 1994
Weather Services Corp.

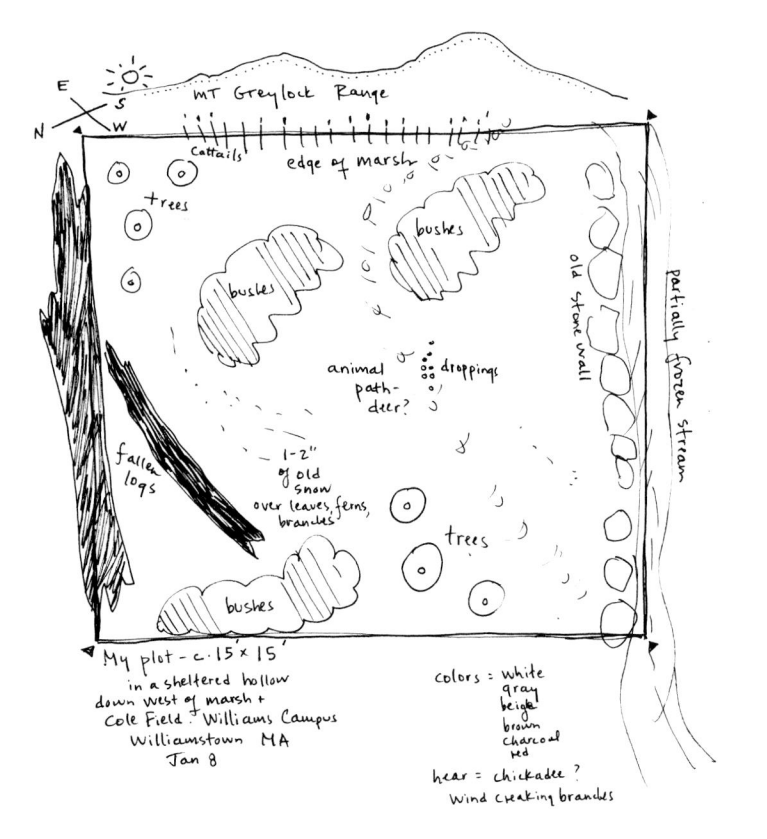

ALMANAC
Wednesday, August 31, 1994 (EDT)

Sunrise 6:08 Moonrise 12:44 A.M.
Sunset 7:20 Moonset 3:48 P.M.
Length of day 13:12
Day of year 243

	A.M.	P.M.
HIGH TIDE	7:26	7:42
Hgt. of tide	8.2	9.3
LOW TIDE	1:11	1:23
Hgt. of low tide	1.6	2.0

MOON'S PHASES
First — Full — Last — New
Sept 12 — Sept 19 — Sept 27 — Sept 5

STARS AND PLANETS AT TWILIGHT
Look low in the southwest as daylight fades; the bright "star" there is the planet Jupiter. Down to its lower right is Venus. Use binoculars to spot the fainter star Spica barely to Venus's upper right.

SOURCE: Alan MacRobert

The Stuff of Journals

The journals of some of our most seasoned nature journalists show the richness and versatility of this practice. Stephen Trimble, in the introduction to *Words from the Land*, describes his visit with writer-naturalist John Hay.

"I stayed with John Hay for a night at his apartment in Hanover, New Hampshire, where he was teaching his annual fall term at Dartmouth. Just before he went upstairs to bed he brought out a box for me to look at, bundles and stacks of pocket-sized spiral notebooks and tiny bound black books, in a carton left over from a University of Chicago book order. These were the field notes for his book about terns, *Spirit of Survival*.

"I looked through his scrawled notes and found what I would expect to find in any nature writer's raw archives. A stream of ideas, questions, journal citations; book titles; anecdotes about nudists Hay surprised on the beach; bird observations; addresses of people met on walks; Ojibwa and Micmac names for terns; drafts of poems; sketches of waves, yellowlegs posturing, circling and landing eider ducks, directions, sensory canals in the inner ear; comments on weather; and the following fragments of writing:

- 'Nature — only beside us not with us or within us?
- love of place is love of familiarity
- "keery, keery" when carrying fish — an announcement of having
- sky courting, loud passionate "cutta chea"
- Fish size relate to the season?
- ANTS
- Kik kik (crossed out) kikik
- We are desperately concerned, consciously or otherwise, about whether the universe will accept us — the aberrant arrival. It might be better to wonder whether we have the guts to accept the universe.
- April 30 — terns very far out from island
- Roseates modest about copulating in the open
- Dreams are an outline that have to be filled in
- Curiosity, hope, anger, love, irritation, gluttony, speed, slow time, confusion.'"

Rte 12 N
The road to
Keene NH

11.17.95
3pm
darkening
late fall

PART 2

Journaling through the Seasons

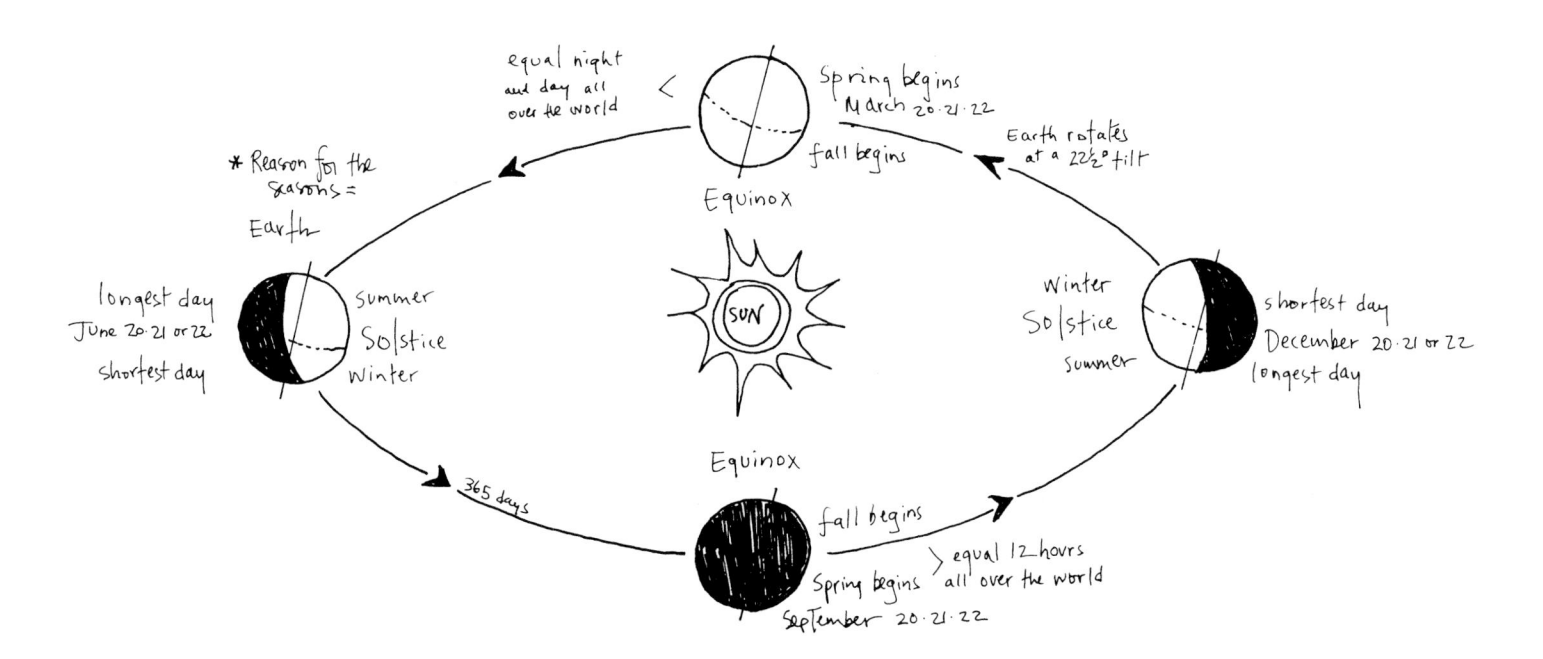

equal night and day all over the world

Spring begins March 20·21·22

fall begins

Earth rotates at a 22½° tilt

Equinox

* Reason for the Seasons =

Earth

longest day June 20·21 or 22 shortest day

summer Solstice Winter

SUN

Winter Solstice summer

shortest day December 20·21 or 22 longest day

365 days

Equinox

fall begins

Spring begins September 20·21·22

equal 12 hours all over the world

There is one quality that characterizes all of us who deal with the science of the earth and its life — we are never bored. We can't be. There is always something new to be investigated. Every mystery solved brings us to the threshold of a greater one.

— RACHEL CARSON

September 18
Cambridge · MA
Avon Hill St.
        9:30 am

Sunny + pleasant
low 70°'s + breezy
humidity gone
hear = airplane
        Wind in leaves
        1 cicada
        1 cricket

The year seems to
begin afresh in September,
with kids back in
School. The body
stretches out again...

✱ A neighborhood walk reveals many signs of fall.

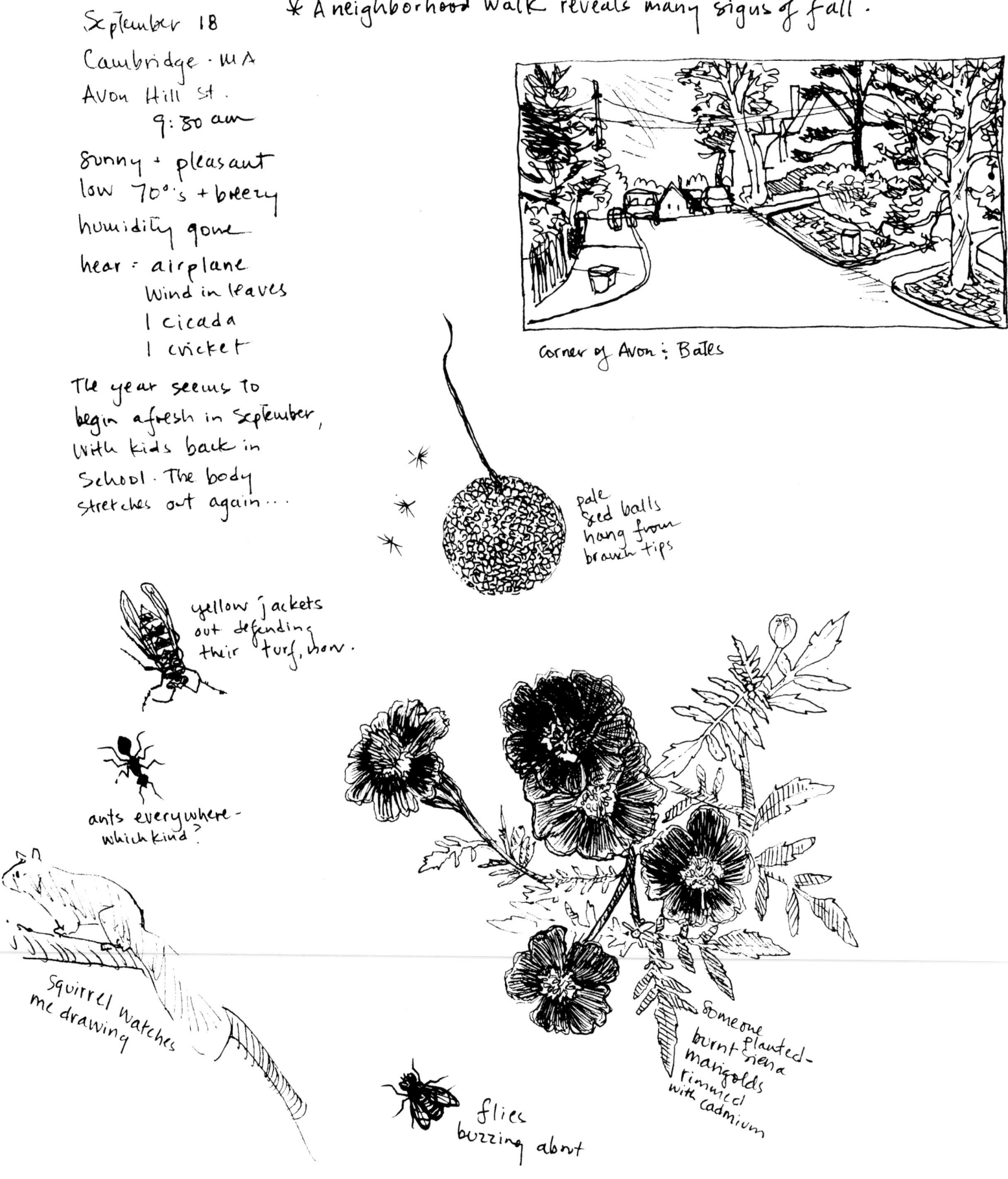

Corner of Avon : Bates

pale
seed balls
hang from
branch tips

yellow jackets
out defending
their turf, now.

ants everywhere-
which kind?

Squirrel watches
me drawing

Someone planted-
burnt-siena
marigolds
rimmed
with cadmium

flies
buzzing about

The Ongoing Journal

To get the most out of journaling, try to integrate the practice into your life, day to day and year to year. Understandably, this is hard for all of us to do since nature journaling is usually not part of our job, school, or even family life. But, you may find, as we have, that the nature journal becomes the connecting force between all the elements in your life, giving you hours of joy, relaxation, calm, increased knowledge, and a feeling of connectedness with the natural world. As one friend of Clare's says, "I get restless, on edge and nudgy if I haven't gotten out with my journal for a while." We can't place a monetary value on nature journaling — the value is measured only by the soul.

A relatively easy way to make it part of your daily routine is to have a project or theme you want to develop in your journals. This commitment to exploring a particular theme or focusing on a particular place or object offers a motivation for getting outside regularly to observe and record seasonal events.

Select a theme that is general enough to help guide your perceptions as you observe and record the world around you without being restrictive: "the place where I live," "my natural neighbors," or "interactions with my world throughout the changing seasons." Journaling encourages you to journey to the core of every place you visit. It helps you develop a much deeper, richer perception

jay calling from Sycamore — why?

Why do people keep journals? Well, we just do. Some people keep track reading the daily newspaper. Some keep track with the evening news. Some call their neighbors, or chat at work. I keep my place by putting my connection on paper.

—CLARE WALKER LESLIE

and understanding of the world than when you were just the average passerby.

By exploring your natural neighborhood, you will learn about not only the people who surround you, but all your neighboring living things, plants, and animals as well. These nonhuman neighbors are key features of the environment that contribute to the distinctive sense of that place. Try drawing portraits of your natural neighbors and chronicling each one's activities and interactions with your own life in your journal.

You can study your interactions with the world around you (whether you live in a rural, urban, or suburban locale.) As you pursue the common human endeavors of seeking food, water, shelter, recreation, companionship, and inspiration from those around you, you encounter all aspects of nature — (other people, other living things, objects, and events. These are all grist for long-term journaling.)

Keeping a Seasonal Journal

"The changing seasons" is perhaps the most obvious theme conducive to keeping an ongoing nature journal. (The advantage of) keeping a journal through a full year is that you can bear witness to how much, in fact, the outdoors changes and unfolds month by month through a full cycle — and then begins again, with the same pattern but different details.

The keys to keeping the journal going and growing are to choose objects or places that are bound to go through regular change, and to set a goal of recording the changes regularly and faithfully. This can be as simple as watching a tree in your neighborhood and noting all the ways it changes through a year, as well as the creatures that visit it and how they interact with it for food, shelter, nesting, or denning.

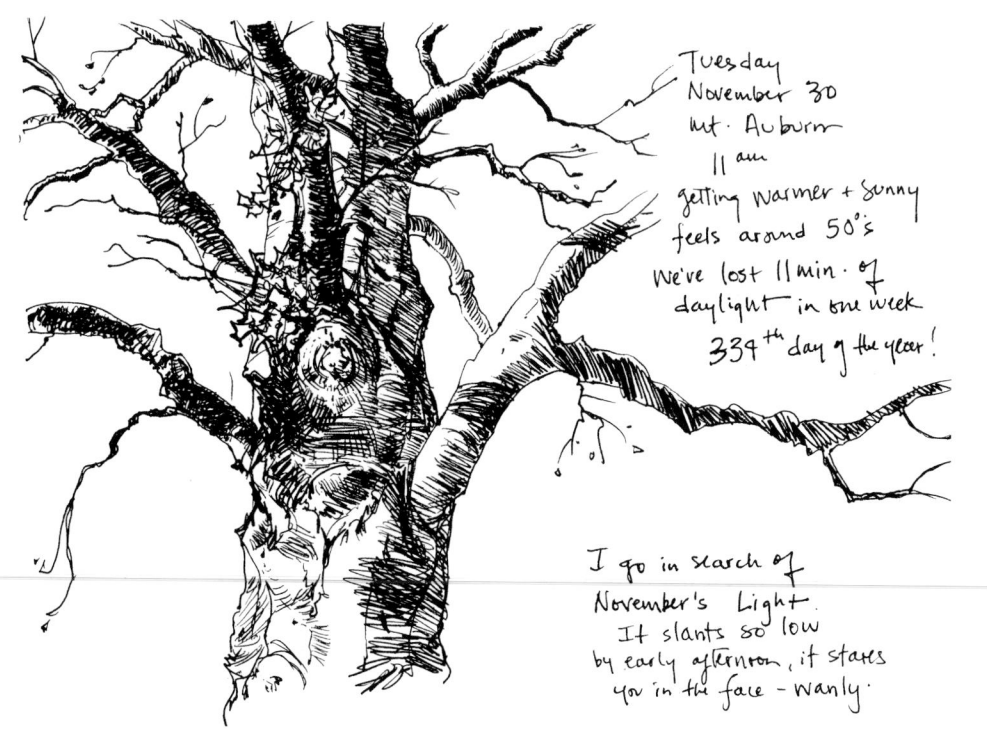

Tuesday
November 30
Mt. Auburn
11 am
getting warmer + sunny
feels around 50's
We've lost 11 min. of
daylight in one week
334th day of the year!

I go in search of November's Light. It slants so low by early afternoon, it stares you in the face - wanly.

Focusing Your Seasonal Observations

Here are a few suggestions for focusing your observations on objects and living things that change — some dramatically from moment to moment, others more subtly, almost imperceptibly — with the seasonal changes in temperature and light.

Watch the moon. From almost anywhere on earth you can observe the brightest object in the night sky — the moon.

Pick an easily observed park or street corner. Who visits it? When? What are they doing there? How do humans and other creatures interact at this place? How do you feel about what you see going on? If you don't like the changes, is there any way you could talk with others about preventing or slowing those changes?

Keep track of the sky. What colors do you see? How do these colors change over short and long periods of time? Observe and sketch cloud formations. Can you correlate cloud patterns with weather changes? How does the state of the sky affect your moods? What objects, natural and man made, do you observe in the sky above?

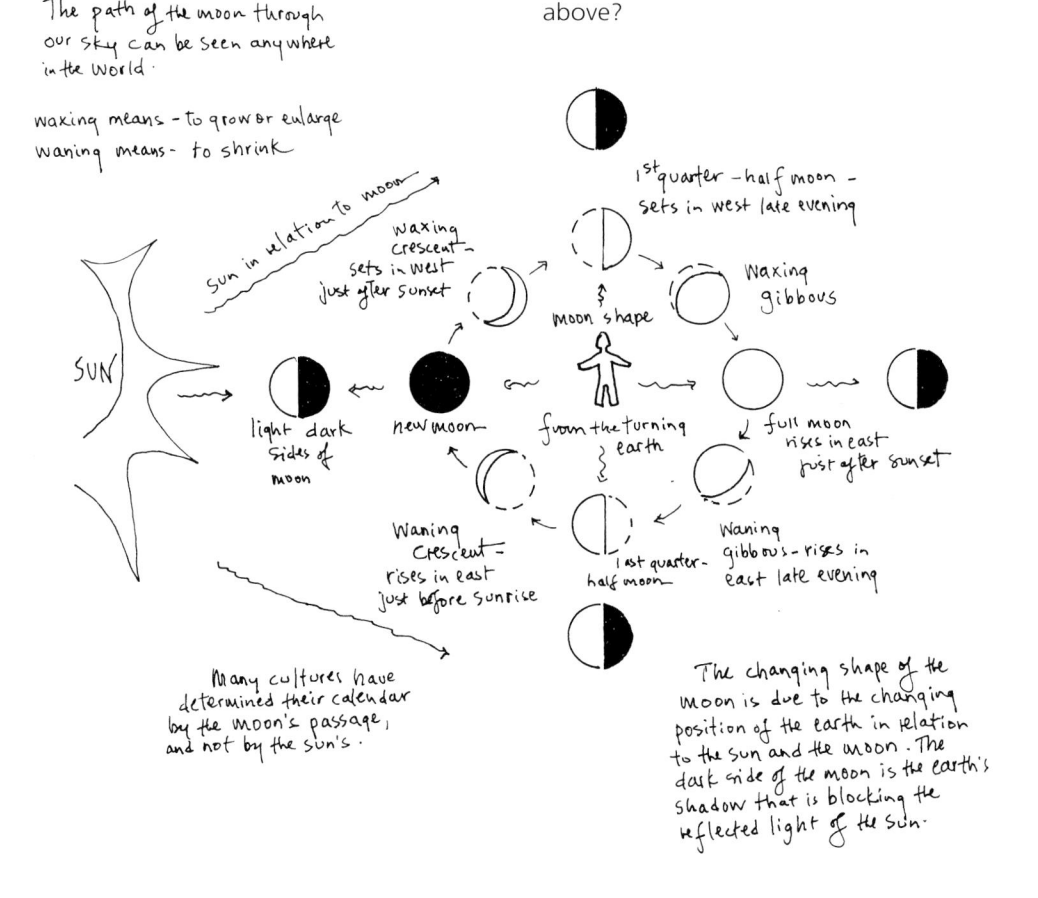

The path of the moon through our sky can be seen anywhere in the world.

waking means - to grow or enlarge
waning means - to shrink

sun in relation to moon

Waxing crescent - sets in west just after sunset

1st quarter - half moon - sets in west late evening

Waxing gibbous

moon shape

SUN

light dark sides of moon

new moon

from the turning earth

full moon rises in east just after sunset

Waning crescent - rises in east just before sunrise

last quarter - half moon

Waning gibbous - rises in east late evening

Many cultures have determined their calendar by the moon's passage, and not by the sun's.

The changing shape of the moon is due to the changing position of the earth in relation to the sun and the moon. The dark side of the moon is the earth's shadow that is blocking the reflected light of the sun.

The Reason for Seasons

Because our planet is tilted on its axis, the amount of sunlight available to any one spot on earth varies with the season, as does the intensity of its energy. This has a strong impact on the activity of living things at different times of the year.

The earth is continually rotating around its axis, 360 degrees a day. During the rotation each section of the earth is first exposed to, then removed from, the rays of the sun, causing day and night. The earth is also continuously, but slowly, circling around the sun without changing its 23½-degree axis. The complete annual journey around the sun takes about 365 days.

The earth's tilt means that different parts of the earth get differing amounts of daylight as the annual journey progresses. This results in the seasons we know as winter, spring, summer, and autumn, or fall. The tilt also is the reason these seasons are reversed in the Southern Hemisphere.

Seasonal Guideposts

A seasonal journal is essentially your personal record of riding the planet earth through one annual journey around the sun. That journey takes us past four key marker points — the two solstices and two equinoxes.

Within each of these periods, there are many natural objects

Subjects to Observe, Draw, Record throughout the Seasons

SEASON	BIRDS	ANIMALS	
AUTUMN	• Observe change in activity and preparations for winter or migrations south among starlings, hawks, geese, shorebirds. • What fruits are robins, mockingbirds, and sparrows eating?	• Look for signs of winter preparations, including butterfly migration, and dragonfly migration, and changes in cricket, cicada, and grasshopper calls. • Salamanders, slugs, spiders, sowbugs, and fish head for dark places.	
WINTER	• What birds stay through winter and where can you find them? • Observe the habits of feeder birds: cardinals, house sparrows, mourning doves, blue jays. • Look for wilder birds: owls, hawks, turkeys, ducks, vultures, crows.	• What creatures stay active? • What do they eat? • What creatures disappear to hibernate or die? • Observe animals that are active: houseflies, spiders, centipedes, rabbbits, red and gray squirrels, foxes, raccoons, deer, elk, and moose. • Look for tracks in the mud or snow.	
SPRING	• Watch for the first birds returning from the south: bay and sea ducks, warblers, sparrows. • Observe activities of nearby nesting birds: starlings, house sparrows, crows, robins, cardinals.	• Focus on the birth, awakening, or return of butterflies, earthworms, chipmunks, insects, frogs and toads, salmon, herring, caribou, dall sheep.	
SUMMER	• Learn to identify birds by their calls and habitats. • Read bird guidebooks and practice drawing bird shapes: blue jay, chickadee, magpie, red-tailed hawk, song sparrow, mallard duck, herring gull, common loon.	• This is the height of productivity for frogs, toads, snakes, salamanders, turtles, spiders, and earthworms. Document who is doing what. • Focus on night sounds: crickets, owls, mice. • Learn your local animals and draw them, learning about their habits.	

and events to observe and record. See the box below for some ideas of natural activities, objects, and changes to study at various points in the year. These are just a starting point; you may want to change the questions and focuses depending on where you live and what your interests are.

PLANTS AND TREES	WEATHER, SKY, LANDSCAPES	SEASONAL CELEBRATIONS
• Which plants bloom the latest: asters, goldenrod, chicory, marigolds, or butter-and-eggs? • What trees and shrubs lose their leaves, turn colors? • Observe and draw the varieties of tree seeds, nuts, and fruits.	• Watch for weather changes. • Draw cloud shapes, sunsets, rain patterns. • What sounds in nature are changing? • Days are noticeably shorter after September 22. • Draw a little landscape scene showing tree shapes and color changes.	• Autumnal equinox • Sukkot • Halloween • Thanksgiving Day • Fall festivals • Year's End in Celtic calendar
• Draw silhouetttes of winter trees. • Observe the twig, leaf, and flower bud shapes on deciduous trees. • Observe the seeds and cones of evergreens. • Observe the leaves and buds of broad-leaved evergreen.	• Focus on weather changes. • Draw snowflake shapes. • Observe rain patterns. • Record moon phases. • Draw constellation shapes. • Days get longer after December 22. • Draw a little landscape scene showing the tree and land shapes this time of year.	• Winter solstice • Hanukkah • Advent and Christmas • Kwanza • Winter and New Year festivals • Groundhog Day
• Look for the first flowers. In the North: spring bulbs of crocus, snowdrop, daffodil. In the South: cactus, amaryllis, poinsettia. • Record the first leaves and tree flowers you see. • Draw sequence of flowers blooming, in high to low elevations.	• Record the rain, mud, snow, and slush. Record signs of warm- and cold-weather changes. • Look for animal tracks in mud. • Days get noticeably longer after March 21 or 22. • Draw a little landscape scene showing early signs of spring in trees and land.	• Vernal equinox • International Earth Day • Easter • Passover • May Day • Spring planting festivals • First day of summer in Celtic calendar
• Record the productivity of backyard gardens, parks, abandoned lots, fields, and meadows. • Plant your own garden and draw and record its growth. • Get out a field guide to plants and learn to identify what's growing where.	• Use your local newspaper, radio station, TV, planetarium, and almanacs to learn about weather. Document the weather daily for a month. • Days are getting shorter after June 21 or 22. • Draw a little summer landscape.	• Summer solstice • Native American sun-dance festivals • August 1 is Lammas, fall in the Celtic calender • International harvest festivals

March 17
St. Patrick's Day
Signs of Spring
in Cambridge —
warmish·sunny
blue· blue skies
While walking Max at
2:30, I spy:

tiny willow leaves
budding out

saucy red
cardinal atop
maple

robins chasing
about in
yards

my enduring snowdrops
blooming since early Feb.
were flattened by cold — now
standing strong + firm
what persistence

crocuses
in full
bloom

daffies up 3"
They say spring is really
early this year. Some things
are early — some are not ···

A Sampling of Seasonal Journal Entries

The following four chapters show examples of journal pages from all four seasons, primarily from Clare's journals. The pages were chosen to inspire, delight, and illustrate exercises you might want to try in your journal.

Clare's Journaling Journey: In Her Own Words

I began my study of nature as an artist, learning bit by bit about the world around me by keeping year-long journals. In June, September, January, or whenever my previous journal ended, I would begin a new one. Now nineteen years later, I use my stack of journals over and over again for reference on events seen, blooming dates, first snowfalls, children's parties, and travels to many different places for teaching. Just recently someone said, "Spring is really late this year." I went back through spring in a number of my journals and found that I had quoted a similar sentiment many times through the years. Yet, year after year, I documented phoebes, grackles, and red-winged black-birds back by mid-March, and

leaves on the Norway maples around May 1. Nature continues to surprise us New Englanders!

The great Canadian wildlife artist Robert Bateman once said to me, "I will sell you my paintings, I will send you photocopies of my journals, but these precious spiral pads are my most important belongings. They contain the soul of my study." I feel the same about my journals.

I keep a year-long journal because it gets me outdoors regularly and keeps me alert, curious, and awake to even the slightest turn of a leaf. It has also become a constant in my life — part of my daily mantra, as it were. As a student of mine said, "Without a journal going, I feel somewhat lost, missing a companion to help me sort out life."

In the following chapters, I cannot represent all of my journals. Nor can I give you anything but an interrupted view of how I cycle through the seasons. But I can show you examples, suggestions, bits and pieces to hopefully get you out there, too.

As you look through the following pages, it will be helpful for you to know several things about the background and experiences I bring to my work. I primarily keep one ongoing, annual journal, 8^1/$_2$ X 11 inches hardbound, that I finish before beginning another. If the book runs beyond a year, or is finished in less than a year, that is fine. When I go on a special trip or to a conference, I often take along a small journal that I keep just for that event. I like experimenting with sizes from tiny to large, and with varieties of paper, from rough to smooth to colored. As you'll discover, various sizes of blank journals abound in art and stationery stores. Experiment!

My journals reflect my life and where I live — we have a small apartment in Cambridge, Massachusetts, and an old farmhouse in rural Vermont. We journey back and forth between the urban and rural settings, and have for over twenty years. I have two children who vary in ages according to which journal is represented. And I have an understanding husband who has always known me drawing and reporting on something. I have no formal studio — just several drawing tables and one large bookshelf. I have learned to draw anywhere, and I do!

As my pages show, the seasons in my native New England change dramatically. A number of pages show the journaling I have done outside of New England, to point out the differences and similarities of habitats.

The pages show variations in style. I'm a professional artist, and my "portfolio" drawings and paintings are much more detailed, complex, and "finished." In my journal, though, I draw basically for myself; so will you. Sometimes I'm sloppy, sometimes I'm crisp. Sometimes I have 30 seconds to journal, sometimes two hours. Sometimes I'm drawing with eight-year-olds, sometimes with college students. I selected material to reflect that variety in the hope that the subjects I chose may apply to your own journaling possibilities.

Some of the selections may seem a bit jumpy and unconnected. Besides keeping a journal for myself, I also use my journal as I teach. A number of these pages were done in workshops or courses. I hope you can get ideas from any of these pages, whether you are journaling alone or with others, in a class or on a trip.

loud rattling + twitching about

Sit down to draw + hear a loud croaking + fluttering about in maples/birches

Wed. Nov. 20
Mount Auburn. Camb.
Sunny but chilly
not a cloud

6:42 am ⎫ 9 hrs
4:18 pm ⎭ 36 min

Begun outside.
Ended in car—
hands shaking
+ body raw.
The winter
regiment."

CHAPTER 5

The Autumn Journal

European beech

Autumn is a good time to begin a nature journal. School is starting again. Summer is over. The heat that makes us drag and feel lazy is leaving the earth. With cooler mornings and less light from the sun, a new season is coming on. Animals and plants are readying for the coming of the colder months. Even if you live in a warm climate year-round, animals and plants go through cycles of change — perhaps between wet and dry seasons, rather than warmer and cooler. Where we live, September, October, and November are the fall months. Of course, if you live in the Southern Hemisphere, these months are different.

Autumn Observations

The subjects you draw and write about in your journal will vary, of course, depending on where you live — in the city, suburbs, or country; by the sea, in the woods, or in the desert. To begin, take a walk around your neighborhood and observe and draw signs of fall. Create a two-page spread, letting images flow one after the other.

Following are some topics covering various subjects you might explore in more detail this time of year. (See Suggested Reading for books to help you with your exploring.)

When Is Fall?

The autumn season is also commonly called fall. In regions with many deciduous trees, *fall* refers specifically to late autumn, when leaves literally fall from the trees. We use the terms *autumn* and *fall* interchangeably.

leaves collected off Mt. Auburn
on a snowy, dark Sunday eve.
The glow of crimson crabs and
basswood leaves caught
my eye. Color in
gray....

Nov. 24
lightening skies after
weekend's darkness
Sunrise: 6:46 am
Sunset: 4:16 pm
9 hrs 30 min light
6/24 = 15 hrs 17 min light
12/24 = 9 hrs 4 min light

Plants

What plants still have flowers; what have seeds? Find different grass, rush, and sedge seed heads, and draw them. Draw five different leaves from plants and contrast their shapes. What plants have leaves turning color? Draw and identify five wildflowers near you. Were they ever used in cooking, for medicine, or to dye wool? Roger Tory Peterson's *A Field Guide to Wildflowers* is a good resource to have (see Suggested Reading).

Trees

What trees turn color? Draw five different leaves with different colors and shapes. Do trees of the same kind all have the same colors? Do different kinds of trees each have their own fall color change? Read about fall foliage changes. Identify and draw seeds, fruits, and nuts of trees and shrubs. Draw the differences between evergreen and deciduous trees. Draw five tree shapes near you and identify the trees. Which trees are native to your areas; which have been imported?

Animals

Read about and draw the eight most common animals you think live near you: rabbits, squirrels, foxes, frogs, fish, butterflies, ants, salamanders, turtles, and so on. Draw from life, if possible; if not, use photographs or a trip to the zoo. Learn animal tracks by drawing them and noting the size of each print, the distance between tracks, the width between front or back tracks. Don't forget small creatures — insects, sow bugs, snails — and how they seem to be preparing for winter.

Birds

What birds live near you? What birds will migrate? What birds will stay nearby all winter? Draw from life, or from photographs, five local birds: such as crow, robin, blue jay, pigeon, magpie, kestrel, chickadee, and nuthatch.

Weather and Season

Which phases of the moon do you see and when? Draw cloud patterns and note sky color. Learn the cloud types and what kind of weather each indicates. Keep a daily weather and temperature chart so you can begin to predict weather in your area. What does fall mean to you? What are the festivals of fall? How does our American Thanksgiving in late November relate to the fall harvest festivals of other cultures?

Yourself

How does autumn weather make you feel? What is your response to the changing fall colors? Draw events that symbolize the season for you.

All birds fly in to face towards low morning SE light

Wed. Nov. 27
Mt. Auburn Cem.
9–11 am
sunny + bright
Snow remains on oak leaves

12 robins gobbling scarlet crabapples
flock of 30+ starlings swoops in to feed — in winter color
a flicker flash — flicker!
several juncos

flicker in crab!

Several juncos

Young + mature

All facing SE. bellies to Sun!

to assembly I must go

white

shaking tail at birds?

Squirrel also!!

in maple

Too hesitant to jump to crab. goes to ground to wait birds' departure!

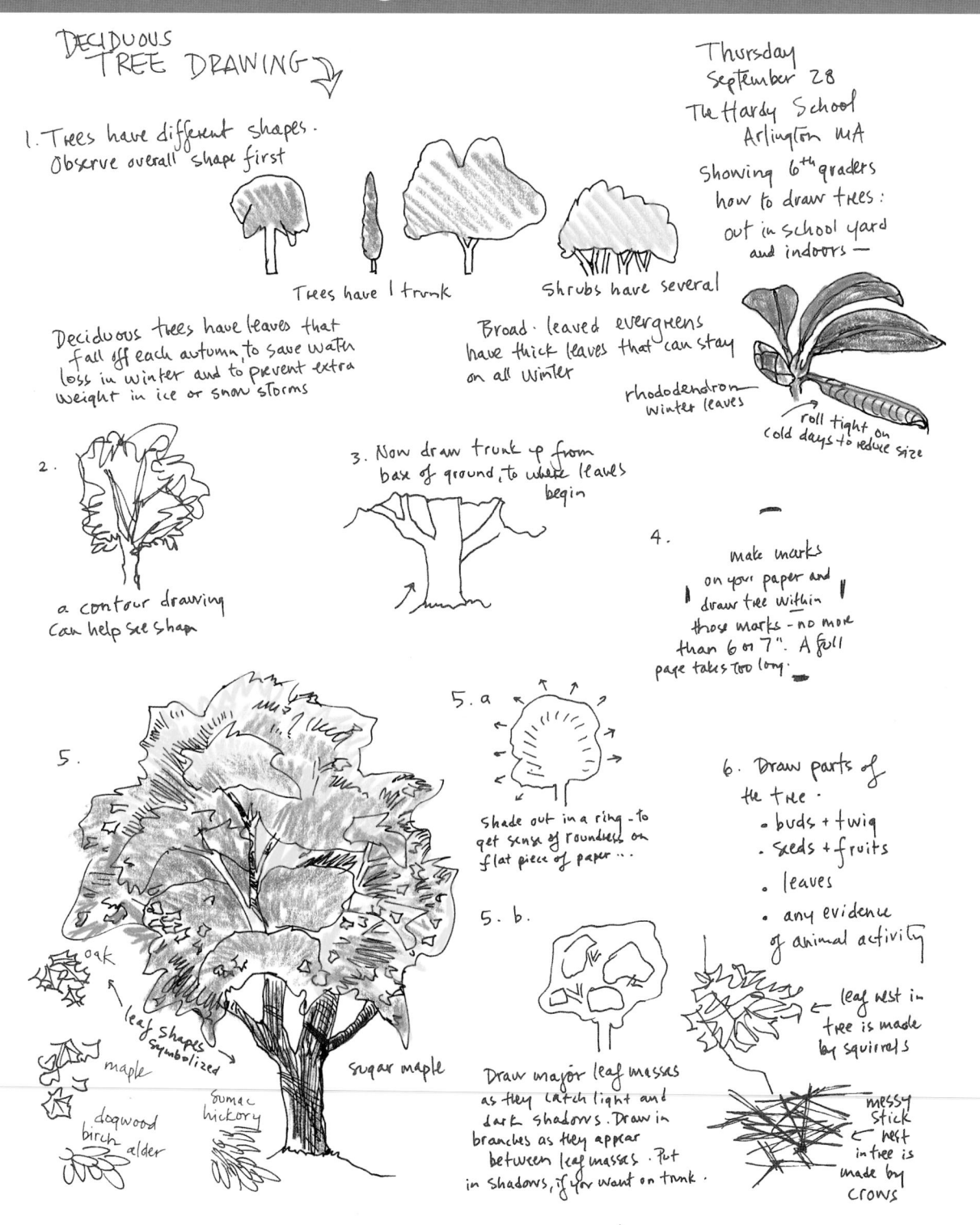

DECIDUOUS TREE DRAWING →

1. Trees have different shapes. Observe overall shape first

Trees have 1 trunk

Shrubs have several

Thursday September 28
The Hardy School Arlington MA

Showing 6th graders how to draw trees:
out in school yard and indoors —

Deciduous trees have leaves that fall off each autumn, to save water loss in winter and to prevent extra weight in ice or snow storms

Broad-leaved evergreens have thick leaves that can stay on all winter

rhododendron winter leaves

roll tight on cold days to reduce size

2.
a contour drawing can help see shape

3. Now draw trunk up from base of ground, to where leaves begin

4. make marks on your paper and draw tree within those marks - no more than 6 or 7". A full page takes too long.

5.
oak
leaf shapes symbolized
maple
sugar maple
dogwood birch alder
sumac hickory

5. a
Shade out in a ring - to get sense of roundness on flat piece of paper ...

5. b.
Draw major leaf masses as they catch light and dark shadows. Draw in branches as they appear between leaf masses. Put in shadows, if you want on trunk.

6. Draw parts of the tree.
• buds + twig
• seeds + fruits
• leaves
• any evidence of animal activity

leaf nest in tree is made by squirrels

messy stick nest in tree is made by crows

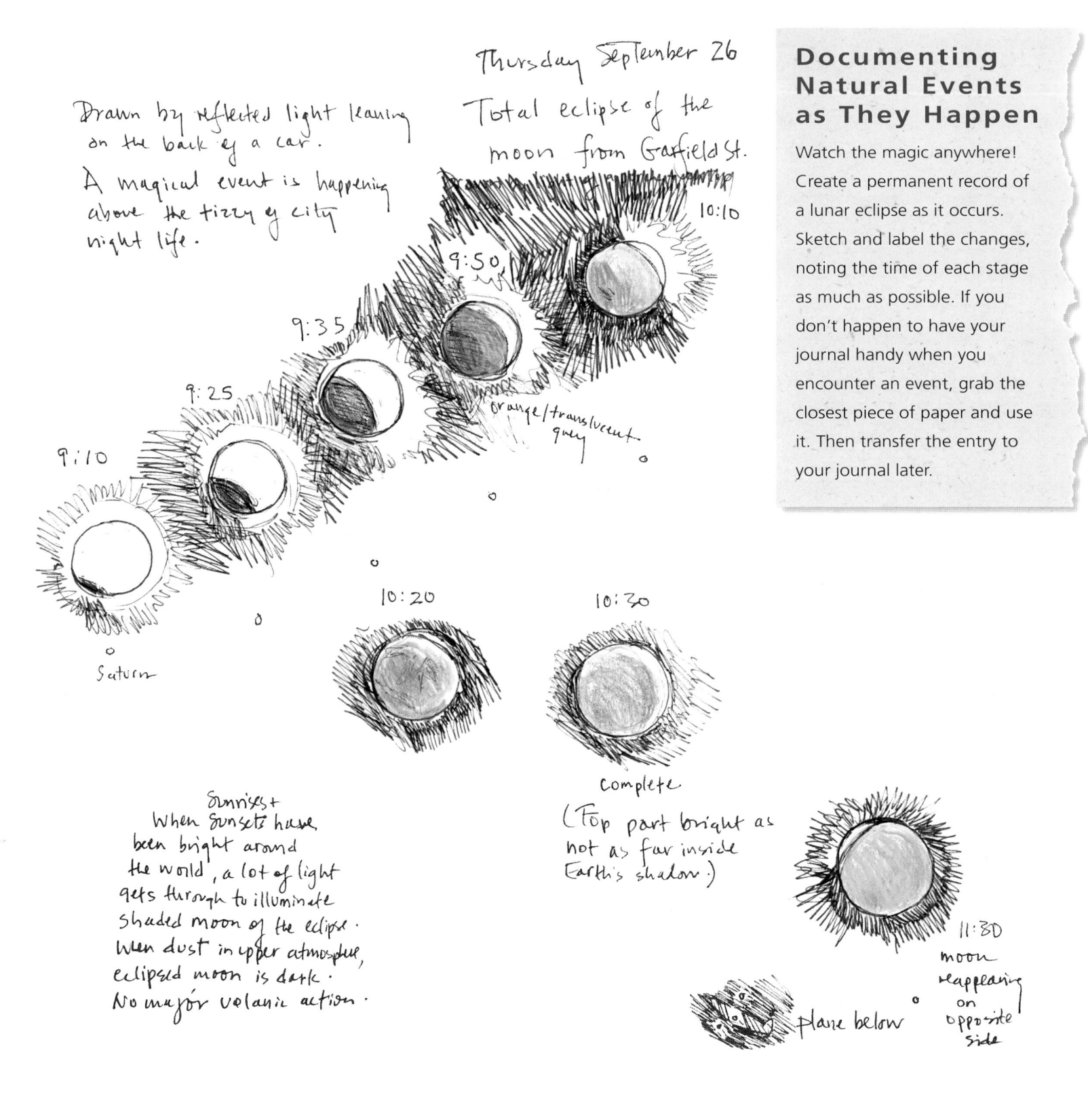

Drawn by reflected light leaning on the back of a car.
A magical event is happening above the tizzy of city night life.

Thursday September 26
Total eclipse of the moon from Garfield St.

10:10

9:50

9:35

orange/translucent grey

9:25

9:10

Saturn

10:20

10:30

Sunrises +
When sunsets have been bright around the world, a lot of light gets through to illuminate shaded moon of the eclipse.
When dust in upper atmosphere, eclipsed moon is dark.
No major volcanic action.

complete
(Top part bright as not as far inside Earth's shadow.)

11:30
moon reappearing on opposite side

plane below

Watch the magic anywhere! Create a permanent record of a lunar eclipse as it occurs. Sketch and label the changes, noting the time of each stage as much as possible. If you don't happen to have your journal handy when you encounter an event, grab the closest piece of paper and use it. Then transfer the entry to your journal later.

Observe Shapes and Color

Shapes of plants can be quite distinctive. Note the details of each plant you record. These are very useful when you're trying to identify the plant later in a guidebook.

If you're looking for a theme for a particular day, try focusing on colors. Look about you and note the various colors you see, then record all the objects that display each of these colors.

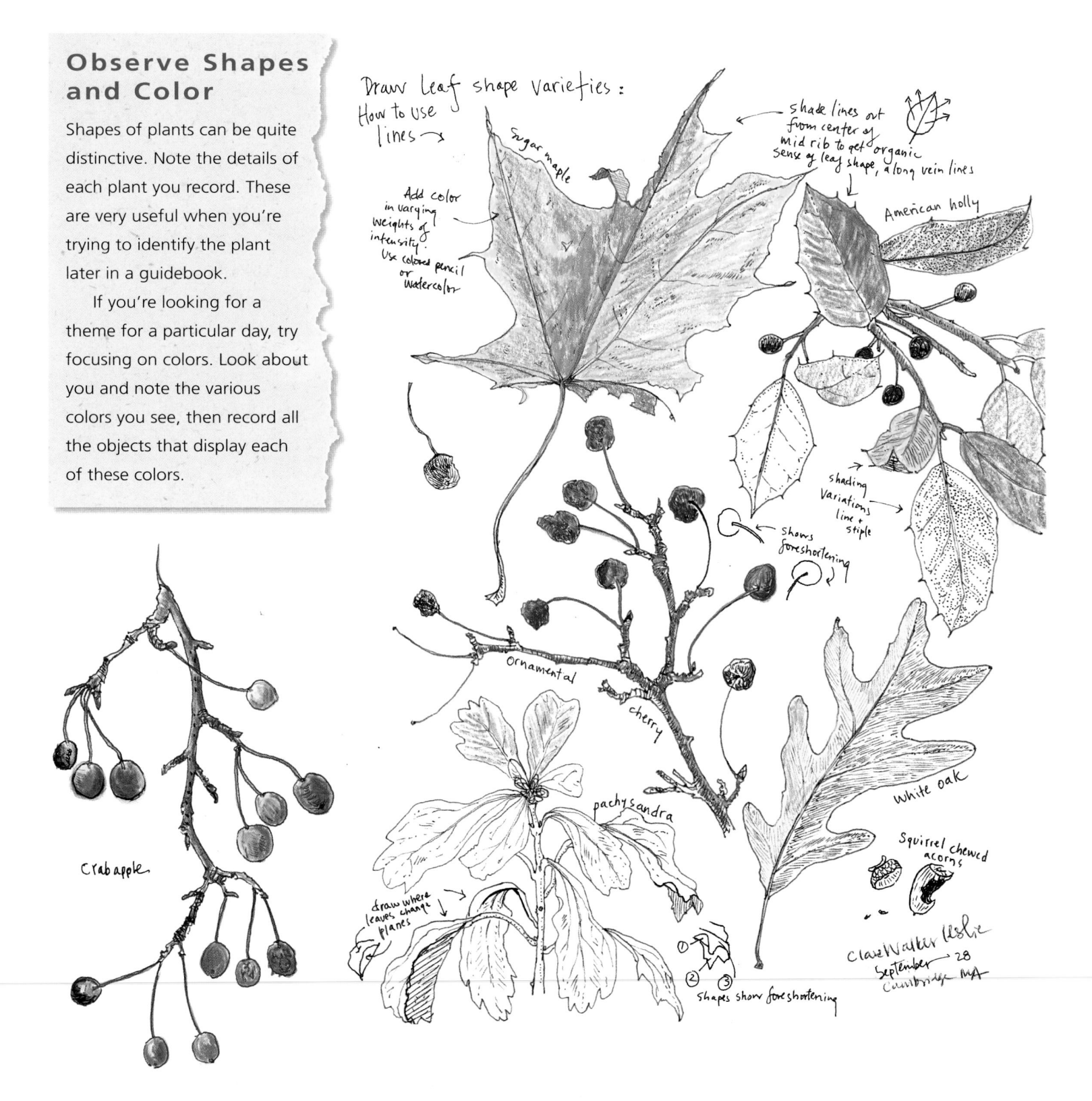

Draw leaf shape varieties:
How to use lines →

sugar maple

Add color in varying weights of intensity.
Use colored pencil or watercolor

shade lines out from center of mid rib to get organic sense of leaf shape, along vein lines

American holly

shading variations line + stiple

shows foreshortening

Ornamental cherry

pachysandra

draw where leaves change planes

① ② ③
shapes show foreshortening

white oak

squirrel chewed acorns

Clare Walker Leslie
September 28
Cambridge MA

Crabapple

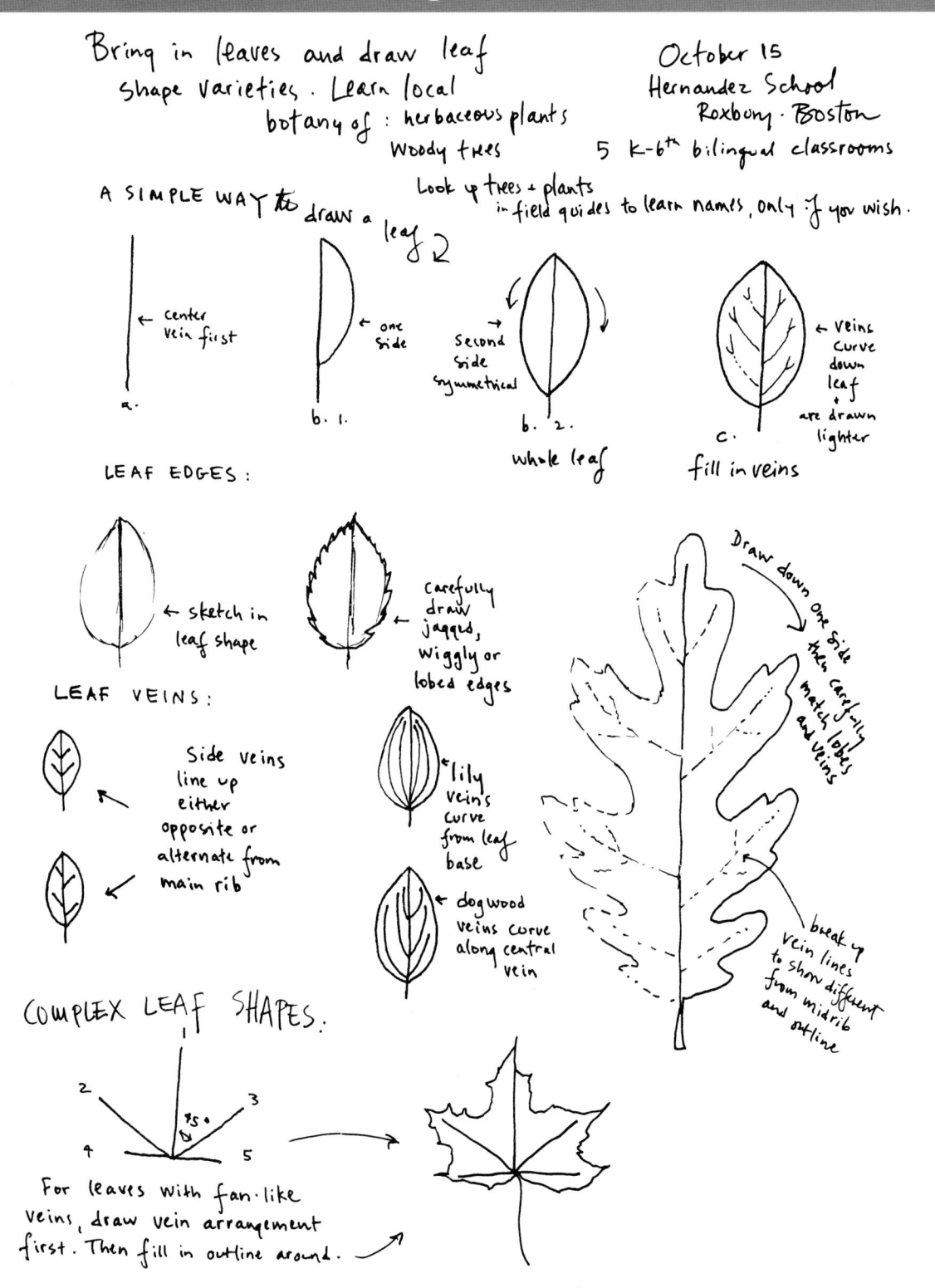

Bring in leaves and draw leaf shape varieties. Learn local botany of: herbaceous plants Woody trees

October 15
Hernandez School
Roxbury · Boston
5 K-6th bilingual classrooms

Look up trees + plants in field guides to learn names, only if you wish.

A SIMPLE WAY to draw a leaf

← center vein first
a.

← one side
b. 1.

Second side symmetrical
whole leaf
b. 2.

← veins curve down leaf + are drawn lighter
c.
fill in veins

LEAF EDGES:

← sketch in leaf shape

Carefully draw jagged, wiggly or lobed edges

LEAF VEINS:

Side veins line up either opposite or alternate from main rib

← lily veins curve from leaf base

← dogwood veins curve along central vein

Draw down one side then carefully match lobes and veins

break up vein lines to show different from midrib and outline

COMPLEX LEAF SHAPES:

2
3
45°
4
5

For leaves with fan·like veins, draw vein arrangement first. Then fill in outline around.

Record Seasonal Celebrations

Many of our observances have ancient roots in the cycles of nature and the earth. Halloween marks the end of the harvest and the beginning of winter in the old Celtic calendar. It is a time of great mystery, death, imagination, and, for many people, spiritual connection with the earth. Record how different people observe the holiday, and what elements from nature play a symbolic role in the celebration. Go to the library and research more about Halloween and other earth festivals, then record your new knowledge in your journal.

HAPPY HALLOWEEN!

Many elaborate pumpkin faces perched on porch railings or in windows.

Lancaster St.   10·31
5 min. sketch
standing with journal

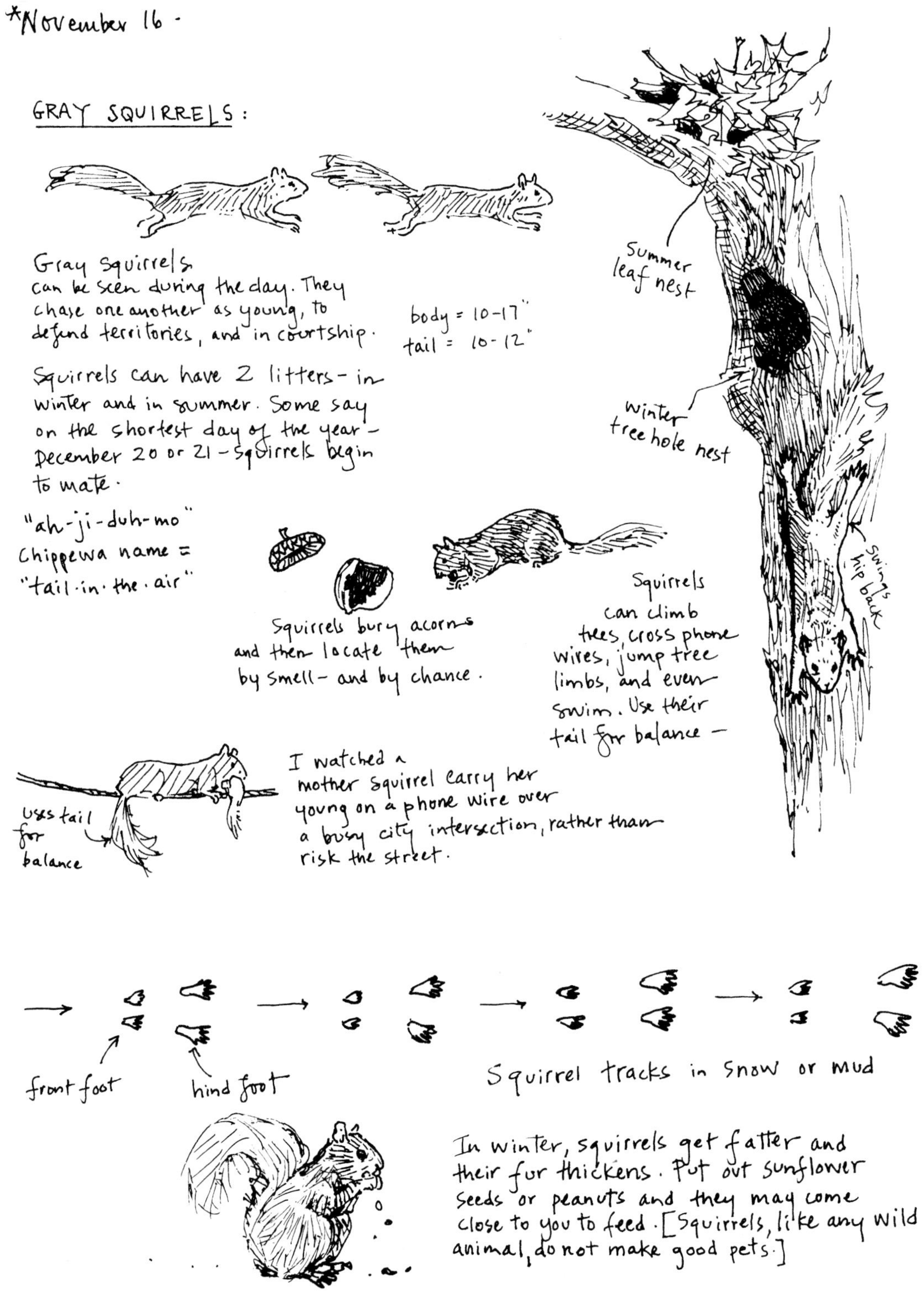

*November 16 -

GRAY SQUIRRELS:

Gray squirrels
can be seen during the day. They
chase one another as young, to
defend territories, and in courtship.

body = 10-17"
tail = 10-12"

Squirrels can have 2 litters - in
winter and in summer. Some say
on the shortest day of the year -
December 20 or 21 - squirrels begin
to mate.

"ah-ji-duh-mo"
Chippewa name =
"tail·in·the·air"

Summer
leaf nest

winter
tree hole nest

Squirrels bury acorns
and then locate them
by smell - and by chance.

Swim's
hip back

Squirrels
can climb
trees, cross phone
wires, jump tree
limbs, and even
swim. Use their
tail for balance -

uses tail
for
balance

I watched a
mother squirrel carry her
young on a phone wire over
a busy city intersection, rather than
risk the street.

Set Up a Research Project

When a particular plant, animal, or event captures your imagination, stay with it — launch an intensive study to find out more about it. Make as many field observations of the object as possible in your journal. Then go to the library and research its nature, origins, and unique characteristics and habits. Incorporate some of these written findings into your field sketch. Your research may direct your observations in new directions as well, and you'll add more field sketches to your study. See how much you can learn and observe by staying with this focus for an extended period of time.

front foot   hind foot   Squirrel tracks in snow or mud

In winter, squirrels get fatter and
their fur thickens. Put out sunflower
seeds or peanuts and they may come
close to you to feed. [Squirrels, like any wild
animal, do not make good pets.]

Explore A New Place

Plan a weekend trip, or join a naturalists' group trip, where you can devote a longer, more intensive time to record in your journal in a new place, uninterrupted for hours. On a weekend teaching for the Appalachian Mountain Club's Pinkham Notch Camp in Gorham, New Hampshire, Clare had two full days to teach drawing and to explore unfamiliar habitats with a class of adult students. The first day, they began by drawing small objects. The next day, they expanded their vision to sketch larger elements of the landscape.

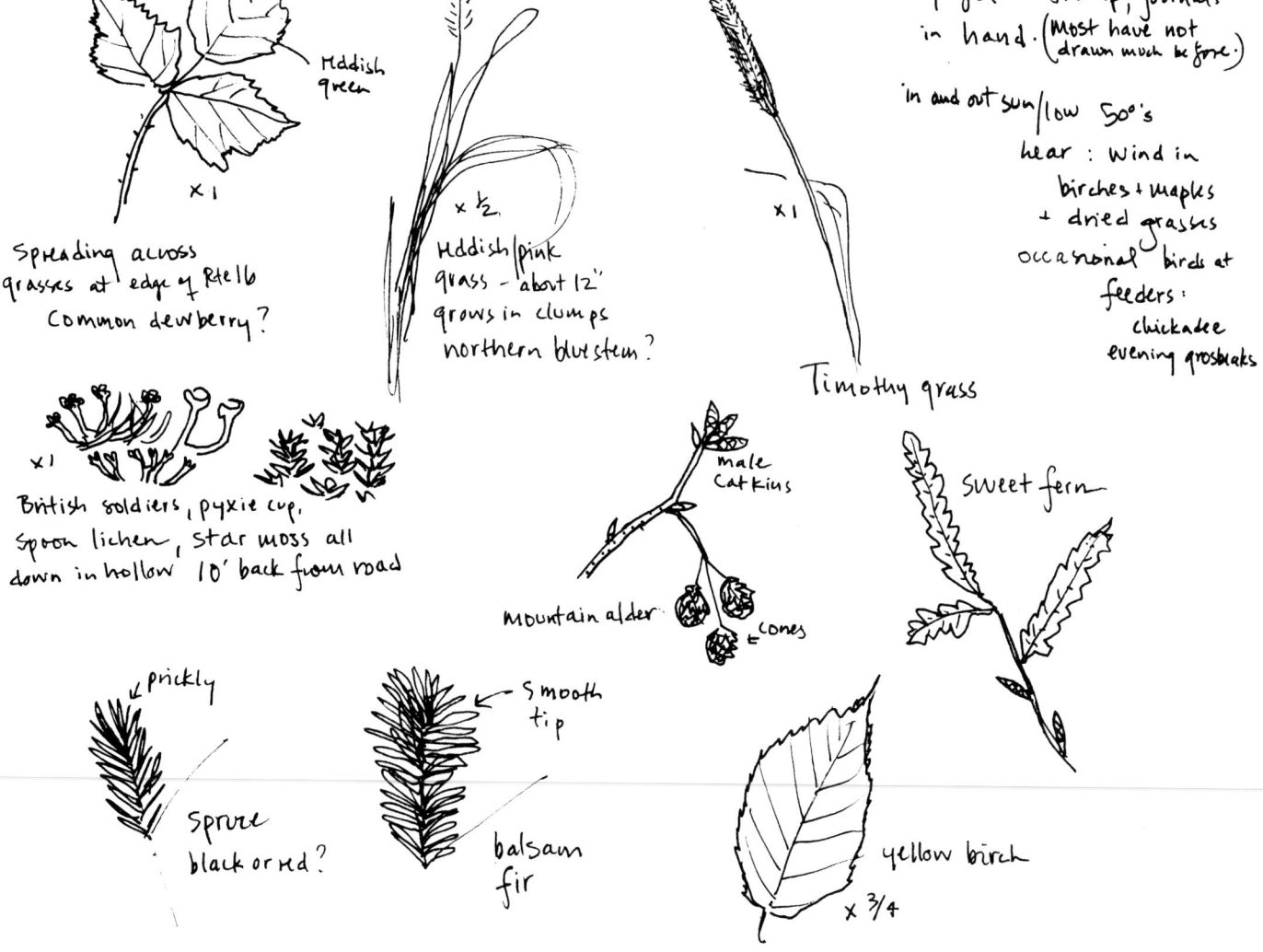

reddish green

x 1

Spreading across grasses at edge of Rte 16
Common dewberry?

x ½
reddish/pink grass - about 12"
grows in clumps
northern bluestem?

x 1

Timothy grass

x 1
British soldiers, pyxie cup,
spoon lichen, star moss all
down in hollow 10' back from road

male catkins

sweet fern

Mountain alder
cones

prickly

smooth tip

Spruce
black or red?

balsam fir

yellow birch
x ¾

November 18
Appalachian Mountain Club
Pinkham Notch Camp
Gorham NH
9:30 am

12 adults come to draw nature in the mountains - in late fall. Although it's raw outdoors, we dress warmly and go for a tramp, journals in hand. (most have not drawn much before.)

in and out sun/low 50°'s
hear : wind in birches + maples + dried grasses
occasional birds at feeders:
chickadee
evening grosbeaks

Students drawing
in 40°'s grey fog
at Cascade falls
2 pm
Cold + raw
people too focused
to notice! 11·18 Pinkham Notch AMC
New Hampshire

Record the Human Element

If you are drawing or observing with others, enter quick studies of your friends or fellow students as *they* draw or observe. Even if you are sitting alone drawing, there may be others around you who are appreciating the natural scenery. Capture a quick sketch of the other humans who are interacting with the environment along with you, for you are all part of the natural scene.

Getting Down to Details

A great way to hone your observational skills is to gather five or six objects when you're out on a walk. Put them on your desk and then set aside one to two hours to draw each object carefully, in detail. These studies can seldom be done as well outdoors; indoors, however, you can take the time to work on developing your drawing technique. This particular drawing was done with a .35 technical drawing pen.

findings along the trail behind Pinkham Lodge Gorham NH.

yellow birch catkins

beech

various mosses

sugar maple

lichen on yellow birch bark

red spruce

balsam fir

I go for a fast walk around the neighborhood with a friend, before heading in to Harvard Square to teach.

Shadows are reaching across lawns and buildings are darkening as the sun drops behind barren tree silhouettes.

It is a walk of silhouettes and warm talk. Squirrels dart in and out of our path; a dog sniffs along on a leash; two cardinals flash by!

We peek into people's warmly lit kitchens and see plants perched on window ledges.

I do quick sketches.

Cambridge · MA
November 23
4 pm
mid 300's
sunny but brisk
sun setting now at
4:15 pm

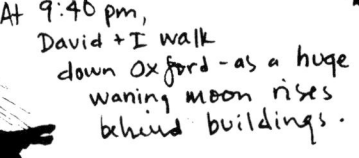

← Squirrel heading up tree with summer leaf nest

deepening lapis lazuli sunset sky

At 9:40 pm, David + I walk down Oxford - as a huge waning moon rises behind buildings.

Everywhere - there rises the moon.

← tabby heading home for the night - or out mousing?

Tell Stories In Your Journal

The journal is a wonderful place to recount the day's events, both great and small, that you observed in nature. You don't need to have your journal with you; try recording from memory, just as if you were telling one of your friends about the day's activities. Use a mixture of writing and images spread out on one or more pages. Try creating an interesting layout of these relatively unconnected experiences. Use a variety of markers, colors, or even collage to enrich the story.

Reflecting on a Piece of Time

We all benefit from periodically taking a moment to step back and reflect on a particular period of our lives, whether it be a changing season, the conclusion of a trip, a study, or a series of personal journeys. The journal pages offer a place to sum up our feelings and experiences. In this entry, Clare reflects on the fall hunting where she lives in Vermont.

leaden grey skies

a smearing of snow on the mountains

brilliant oranges + reds of October give way to lavenders and rusts of November

← hunters in wool black + red plaid or bright orange

bow hunters wear camouflage

deer hide + come out after dusk

our dog wears orange tape + a sign saying "DOG"

November 28 - Granville · Vermont

In some places it's still balmy and sunny. Here, the ending of one season and the beginning of another is on us.

Tuesday the wind chill made it -20° and it was wild.

Wednesday the kids were out in T shirts.

Thanksgiving day was driving wind and rain.

Just wait a moment and you'll have the weather you want, here in New England...

Thanksgiving weekend in Vermont ends deer and bear hunting season. For those of us who do not hunt, the woods and fields and not safe. For those who do hunt, this is the grand, yearly time to stalk, hunt, kill and continue a ritual both ancient and terrifying.

Our neighbors have 5 lordly buck hanging by ropes lashed to an old maple in their front yard.

We go outdoors decked out in bright orange.

The world I love is not mine the month of November

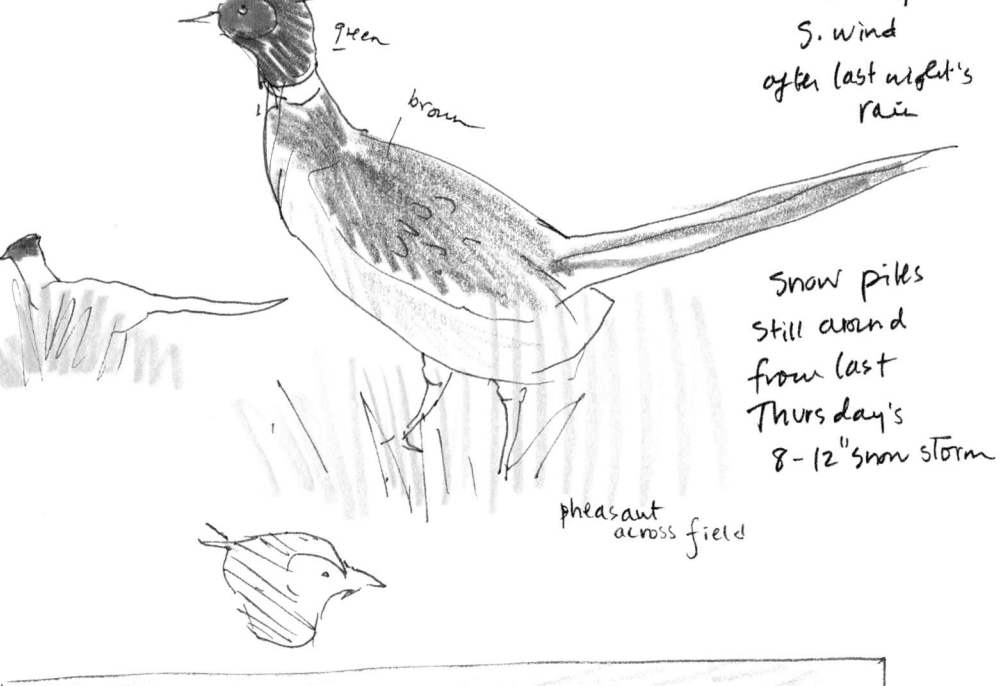

Duxbury —
November 18
12:40 pm
60's — warm
sunny
S. wind
after last night's
rain

red

green

brown

pheasant
across field

snow piles
still around
from last
Thursday's
8-12" snow storm

CWL

Alone here for 3 days working on MKH
N.P.R. - listening to Senate final book.
hearings on Iran Contra invest.

Make Your Journal Your Sidekick

Keep your journal by your side as much as possible, no matter where you are or what else you are doing. You never know when an opportunity will arise for observation and recording. It might just be a fleeting moment when you happen to look up at the sky, or stop to take a deep breath and stretch your legs. With her journal resting ready on the windowsill, Clare was able to quickly record the marching pheasant in the field and the view across the saltwater, while on a three-day writing retreat near Cape Cod.

Norway maple

December 1   Sunday of Thanksgiving weekend
Hunting still on → red plaid clad men with long
rifles, nimble deer tracks in the snow around
our pond. I call to one hunter —
    "Hope you know your aim."
    Some don't....

The Winter Journal

indentation in snow = 8"

2"

3 part dimple in pad is characteristic

8"

Bob cat

2"

eating bud

deer foraging under the snow

Winter is a good time to learn about the basics of nature. There are fewer things going on than in other seasons. The world outdoors initially seems barren — until you focus in. Then you begin to see the skeletal shapes of trees, the patterns of animal tracks in snow and mud, the dried remains of last summer's plants, and the cocoons of silk moths. Winter is an important time in the year's cycle as the earth rests before reproducing and growing anew. In the northern hemisphere, December, January, and February are the heart of this season.

Winter Observations

No matter where you live, whether there is a dramatic change in temperature or more subtle changes from the other seasons, winter is the time of basic regeneration in nature. A good book to read this time of year is *A Guide to Nature in Winter* by Donald Stokes (see Suggested Reading). An amateur naturalist, Don began his study of nature by writing this book. Today he is widely known for his nature books, particularly on birds. Here are some journaling studies you might want to undertake this season.

Images while walking:

red ozier dogwood

found in a wet lowland area

? in bloom now?

apartment building for 3 wasps or midges in a goldenrod

Plants

Identify the plants that remain as dried stalks. Find five different dried plants; cutting carefully, bring them inside to study. Do any of them have unusual growths on them, such as the galls on goldenrod stems? Can you identify milkweed, Queen-Anne's-lace (wild carrot), or evening primrose in their winter state? (*Weeds in Winter* by Lauren Brown is a useful aid in this process; see Suggested Reading.) Can you find some plants that stay green all winter, such as Christmas fern or pachysandra?

Trees

Practice drawing the silhouettes of various types of evergreen and deciduous trees to get to know their distinctive shapes. Explore the differences between trees and shrubs, broad-leaved evergreens and evergreens with needles. Examine and draw the twigs, buds, and any fruits and nuts you find. Look at bark patterns of trees; can you learn to recognize a number of trees from their bark alone?

Animals

Read about and draw the five most common animals you think live near your home. Do each of these stay active all winter? Which ones sleep some of the time? Which ones hibernate? Can you find the places where they sleep or hibernate? Which ones can you observe directly, or indirectly by the signs they leave? Go to your local library and look for books on what animals do in winter. There are a number of good ones, especially in the children's section. Become a careful investigator of the area you live in and record all signs of animal activity, including tracks, chewed seeds, and dens. Draw what you see and label it by name, where you found it, and what it tells you. In New England, woodchucks, brown bats, and jumping mice are the only deep hibernators. Bears arouse easily in winter, although they sleep deeply for extended periods.

Eastern Coyote

fox

coyote in snow

Birds

What birds live near you? Study five birds that do not leave your area in winter. Where do they find shelter? What do they eat? Do they travel in single-species flocks or in mixed-species flocks? How do they communicate in winter? Notice that on bright, sunny days more birds are out singing and flying about. By February, birds such as pigeons, house finches, and sparrows are actively courting. (And in the wild, great horned owls and mourning doves are, as well.)

Winter is pair-forming time for many ducks. Watch them in patches of open water and record their courtship behavior.

Weather and Seasons

Much has been written about the rigors of winter. Survival through this season has been very difficult for many human cultures and many kinds of animals. What does winter mean to you? Record what you like and don't like about the season. Keep a monthlong record of weather, moon phases, and precipitation. Carefully chart sunrises and sunsets from mid-December to mid-January so you can determine the actual length of each day (in daylight), and track the changes before and after the winter solstice — the longest night (and shortest day) of the year.

If you live in a snowy region, record the snow-crystal patterns, the depth of snowfalls, and the type of snow received in each fall. If you live in a southern region, record periods of rainfall or drought. Participate in and record the activities of winter festivals of various cultures.

Yourself

How does winter weather make you feel? What is your response to the cold, snow, and ice? Draw events that symbolize the season for you.

full moon
1·27

icicles   everywhere

Seeing Signs of Winter

Focusing in on the signs of winter is a good beginning project. This exercise is particularly useful if your habitat is limited, time is limited, or, as was the case with this drawing, you are working with students for whom English is a second language. Drawing is a universal language.

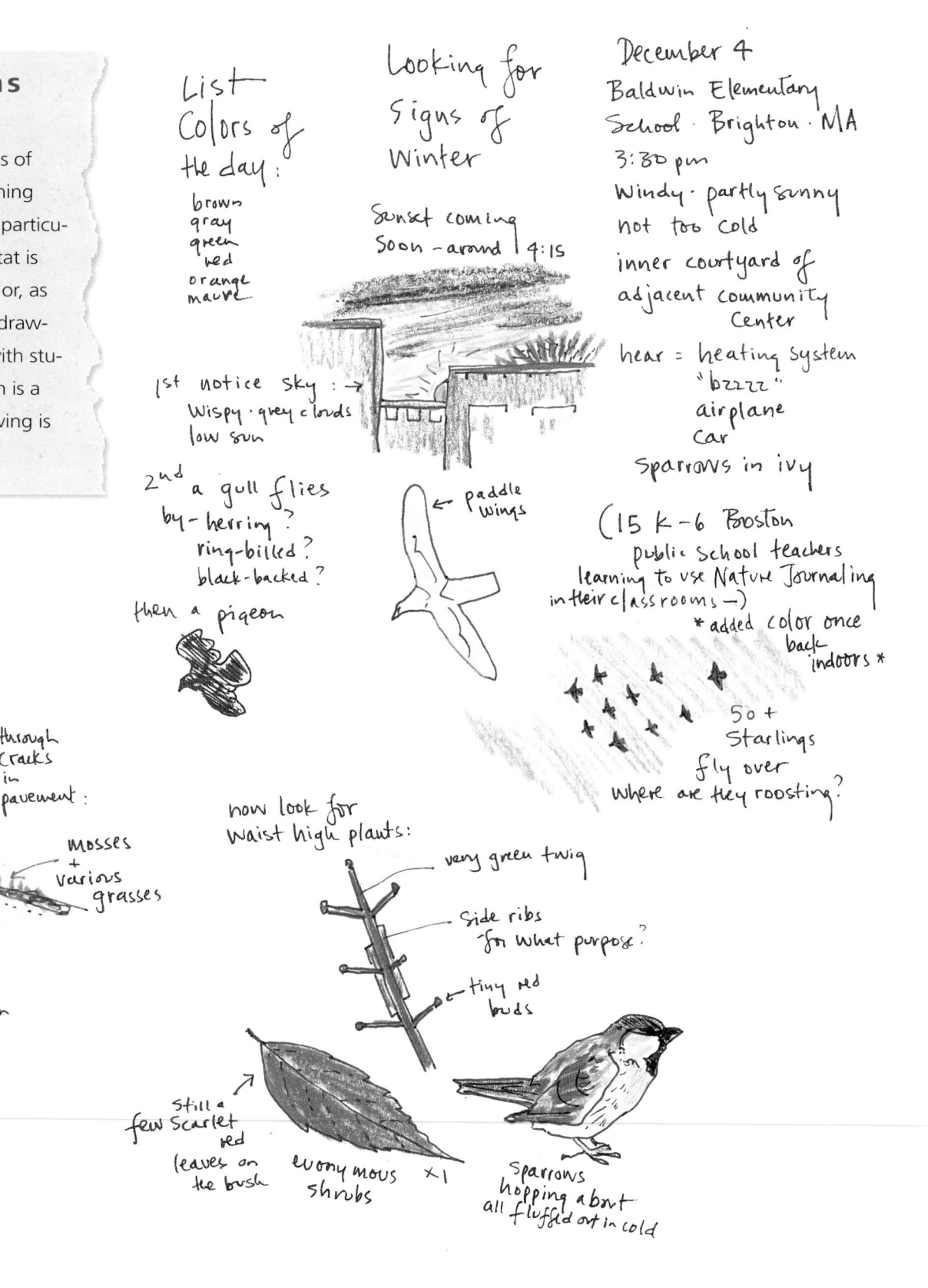

List Colors of the day:
brown
gray
green
red
orange
mauve

Looking for Signs of Winter

Sunset coming soon - around 4:15

1st notice sky : → Wispy·grey clouds low sun

2nd a gull flies by - herring? ring-billed? black-backed?

then a pigeon

← paddle wings

Now draw 3 ground plants:

dandelion

through cracks in pavement:

mosses + various grasses

plantain

December 4
Baldwin Elementary School · Brighton · MA
3:30 pm
Windy · partly sunny
not too cold
inner courtyard of adjacent community Center
hear = heating system "bzzzz"
airplane
car
Sparrows in ivy

(15 K - 6 Boston public school teachers learning to use Nature Journaling in their classrooms —)
* added color once back indoors *

50 + Starlings fly over
where are they roosting?

now look for waist high plants:

very green twig

Side ribs for what purpose?

tiny red buds

Still a few scarlet red leaves on the bush

euonymous shrubs x1

Sparrows hopping about all fluffed out in cold

January 13

10° → 20° F

up + down Temperatures

snow · sleet · snow

at 9am

, gorgeous sun

making everything brilliant

+ glistening —

ice
diamonds
as sun hits
snow
on forsythia

WILLIAMS
STUDENT

purple +
yellow pants

Journaling for Focus

Nature journals are used in English, geology, and environmental studies classes at various colleges around the country. Journaling gives students an opportunity to get out of the classroom and learn directly from the environment in which they live. Here the assignment for students at Williams College in Williamstown, Massachusetts was to draw the day. By finding the time to focus specifically on local habitat, you can develop the ability to look and analyze at close range, a skill you can use in more conceptual work as well.

Honoring the Seasons

For several years, Clare and her friend Sharon Bauer have been meeting for walks in a nearby sanctuary, Mount Auburn Cemetery, in Cambridge, Massachusetts to honor each solstice and equinox. It has become a wonderful ritual that briefly takes them out of their busy daily lives to focus on a cycle happening all around, every year.

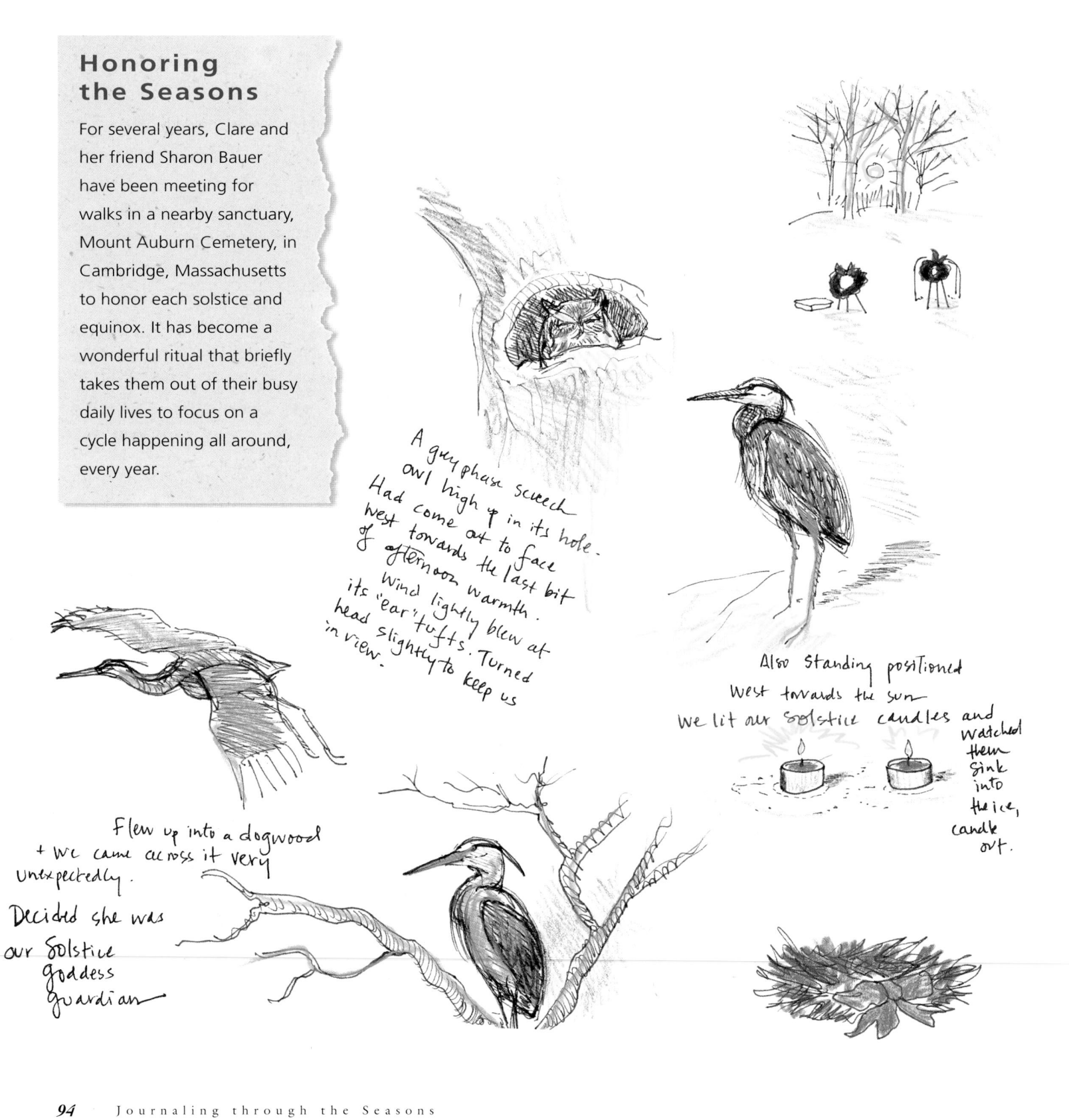

A grey phase screech owl high up in its hole. Had come out to face West towards the last bit of afternoon warmth. Wind lightly blew at its "ear" tufts. Turned head slightly to keep us in view.

Flew up into a dogwood + we came across it very unexpectedly.

Decided she was our Solstice goddess guardian.

Also standing positioned West towards the sun We lit our solstice candles and watched them sink into the ice, candle out.

← S

Winter Sunset = far south with sun low in sky by mid afternoon

4 pm WINTER

N →

Summer Sunset = far north with sun high in sky in mid afternoon

4 pm SUMMER

Dec. 1 = Sunset = 4:13 pm   9 hrs 19 min daylight
Sunrise = 6:54 am

June 1 = Sunset = 8:15 pm
Sunrise = 4:10 am

Dec. 14 = Sunset = 4:12 pm   9 hrs 6 min
Sunrise = 7:06 am

6 hrs difference

15 hrs 5 min of daylight!

Dec. 20 = Sunset = 4:14 pm   9 hrs 4 min
Sunrise = 7:09 am

Dec. 21 = Sunset = 4:14   9 hrs 4 min ← WINTER SOLSTICE Sun "stands still" for several days
Sunrise = 7:10

Dec. 25 = Sunset = 4:17   9 hrs 5 min   days begin to lengthen
Sunrise = 7:12

Jan. 14 = Sunset = 4:36   9 hrs 25 min   difference of light first in sunsets lengthening
Sunrise = 7:11

☀ Charting the Winter Sun's path ☀

activity outside on our balcony

♀ house finch

Max + Cleo romp all over the house, unable to go outdoors —

We make paper snowflakes, paper chains for the tree, and bake cookies

We put out lights, candles, sprays of holly, and poinsettias to help us live in these dark days.

flowering narcissus and

If you record regularly and return to reflect on your earlier observations, your journal record becomes a rich resource for detecting nature's subtle changes that, over time, result in dramatic effects. At left, Clare created a chart of sorts, tracing the flow of daylight and darkness. By December in the Northern Hemisphere, the early sunsets, long nights, changing daily moon phases, and weather and temperature fluctuations can be fun to reflect on. Come early January, the days may be the year's coldest, but the nights are also getting shorter as you move inevitably toward spring.

Whether you live in the North, South, East, or West, or even below the equator, seasonal changes influence how you spend your time. Humans, too, are part of the cycle of nature. In the North we spend more time indoors, lighting candles, making gifts, and baking things to give as presents. Create a drawing or prose journal page of what the winter season means to you.

A watchful eye, a little extra attention to detail, and a sharpened sensitivity to seasonal changes can uncover a veritable Serengeti Park just beyond the bedroom window. All you have to do is learn to see.

There is a popular belief abroad in this country that holds that the most interesting things in the natural world can only be found in faraway places or specifically designated areas.

JOHN MITCHELL,
A FIELD GUIDE TO YOUR OWN BACK YARD

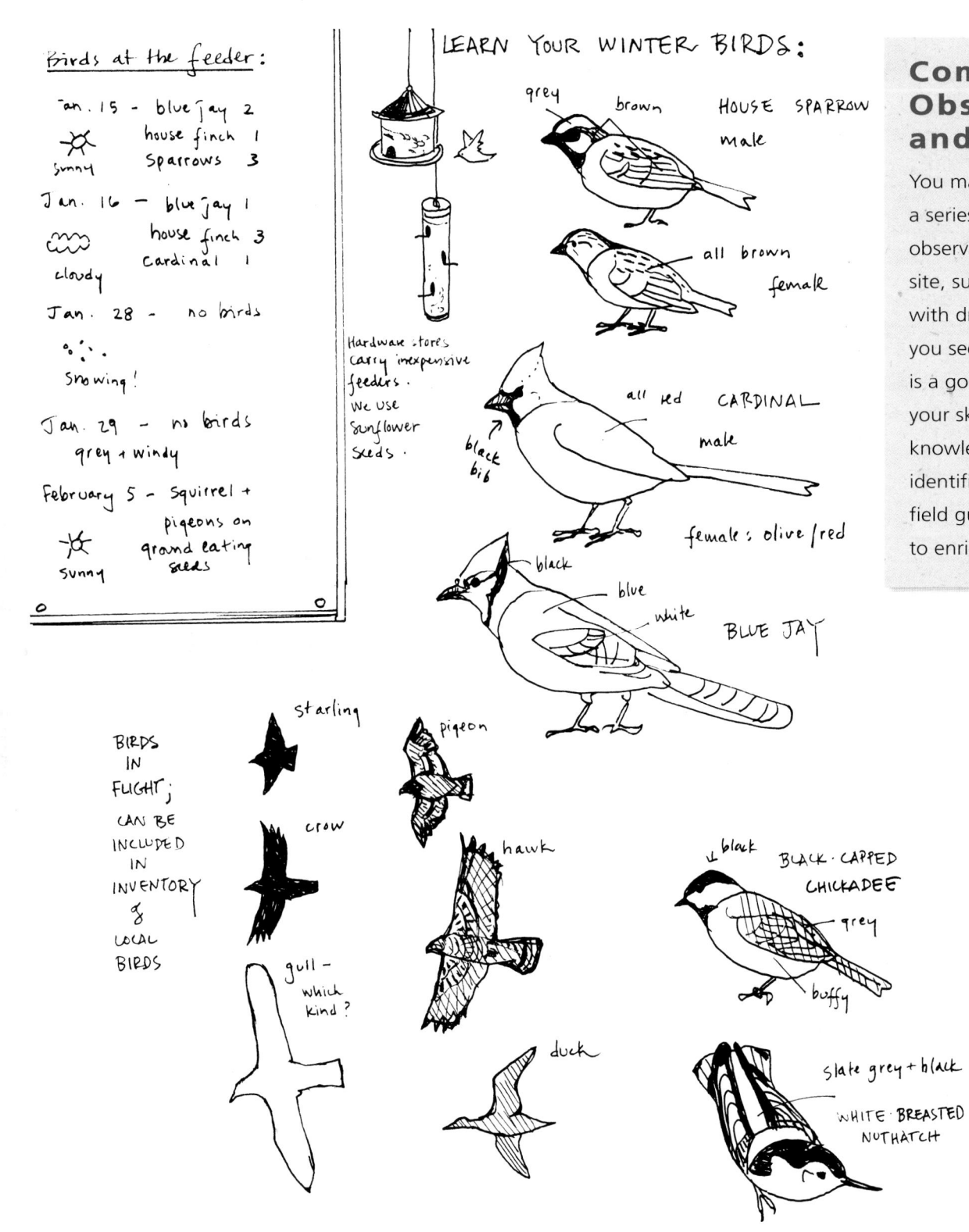

Birds at the feeder:

Jan. 15 — blue jay 2
☀ house finch 1
Sunny   Sparrows 3

Jan. 16 — blue jay 1
〰 house finch 3
Cloudy   cardinal 1

Jan. 28 — no birds
·°·°·
Snowing!

Jan. 29 — no birds
grey + windy

February 5 — Squirrel +
☀ pigeons on
Sunny ground eating
seeds

LEARN YOUR WINTER BIRDS:

grey   brown   HOUSE SPARROW
male

all brown
female

Hardware stores carry inexpensive feeders. We use sunflower seeds.

all red   CARDINAL
black   male
bib
female: olive/red

black
blue
white
BLUE JAY

BIRDS IN FLIGHT;
CAN BE INCLUDED IN INVENTORY & LOCAL BIRDS

starling
pigeon
crow
hawk
gull — which kind?
duck

↙ black   BLACK-CAPPED CHICKADEE
grey
buffy

slate grey + black
WHITE-BREASTED NUTHATCH

Combining Observation and Research

You may want to combine a series of daily written observations about a given site, such as a bird feeder, with drawings of the birds you see there. Drawing birds is a good way to develop your skills, as well as your knowledge of bird species for identification purposes. Use field guides or other sources to enrich your drawings.

Recording Change — Create A Story

Narcissi, amaryllises, crocuses, irises, and tulips are all spring flowers, but you can get a jump on spring and enliven winter by growing them indoors. Start your bulbs indoors on a windowsill, then record the daily changes as the plant sprouts from the bulb or corm, capturing the flowering activity little by little until the plant reaches full bloom.

To bring more people to appreciate the beauty of their world and fellow beings is the one supremely worthy purpose of the arts.

ROCKWELL KENT, *SPIRIT AND NATURE: VISIONS OF INTERDEPENDENCE*

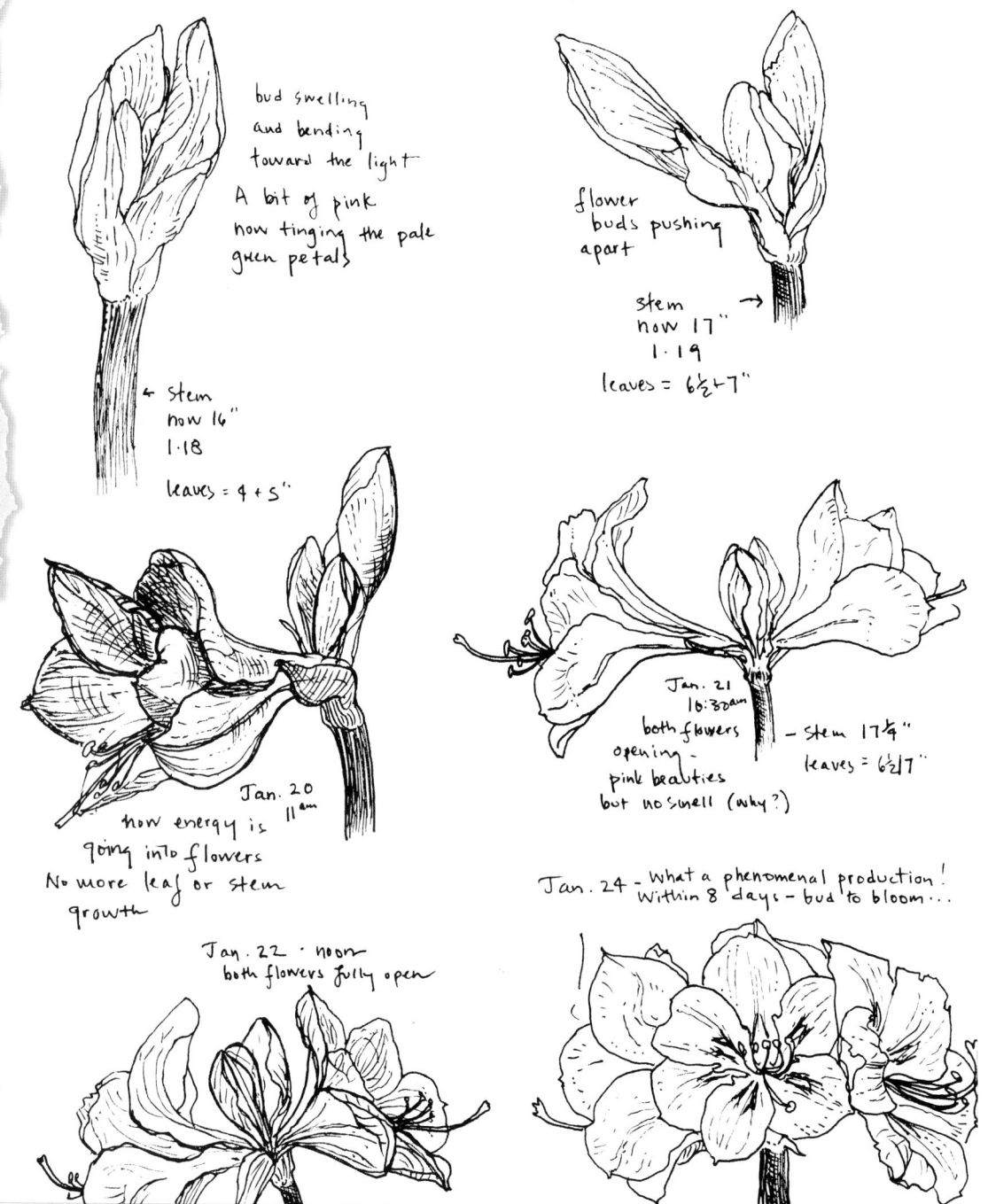

bud swelling and bending toward the light
A bit of pink now tinging the pale green petals

← stem now 16"
1·18
leaves = 4 + 5"

flower buds pushing apart

stem now 17" →
1·19
leaves = 6½ + 7"

Jan. 20 11am
now energy is going into flowers
No more leaf or stem growth

Jan. 21 10:30am
both flowers opening -
pink beauties but no smell (why?)
— stem 17¼"
leaves = 6½|7"

Jan. 22 · noon
both flowers fully open

Jan. 24 - What a phenomenal production!
Within 8 days - bud to bloom...

Evergreen Tree Drawing

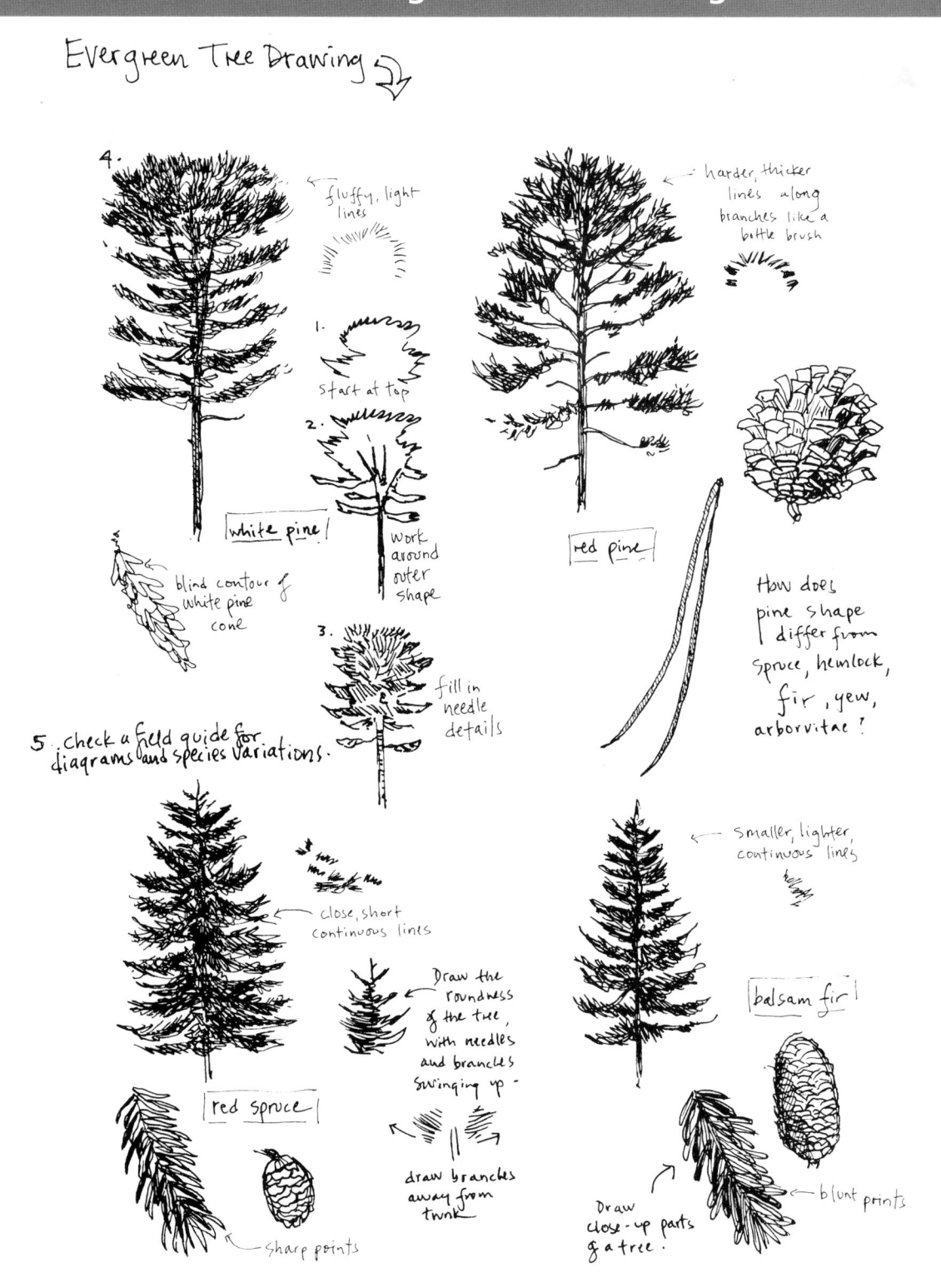

4.

fluffy, light lines

1. start at top

2. Work around outer shape

white pine

blind contour of white pine cone

3. fill in needle details

5. check a field guide for diagrams and species variations.

harder, thicker lines along branches like a bottle brush

red pine

How does pine shape differ from spruce, hemlock, fir, yew, arborvitae?

close, short continuous lines

Draw the roundness of the tree, with needles and branches swinging up -

draw branches away from trunk

red spruce

sharp points

smaller, lighter, continuous lines

balsam fir

Draw close-up parts of a tree.

blunt points

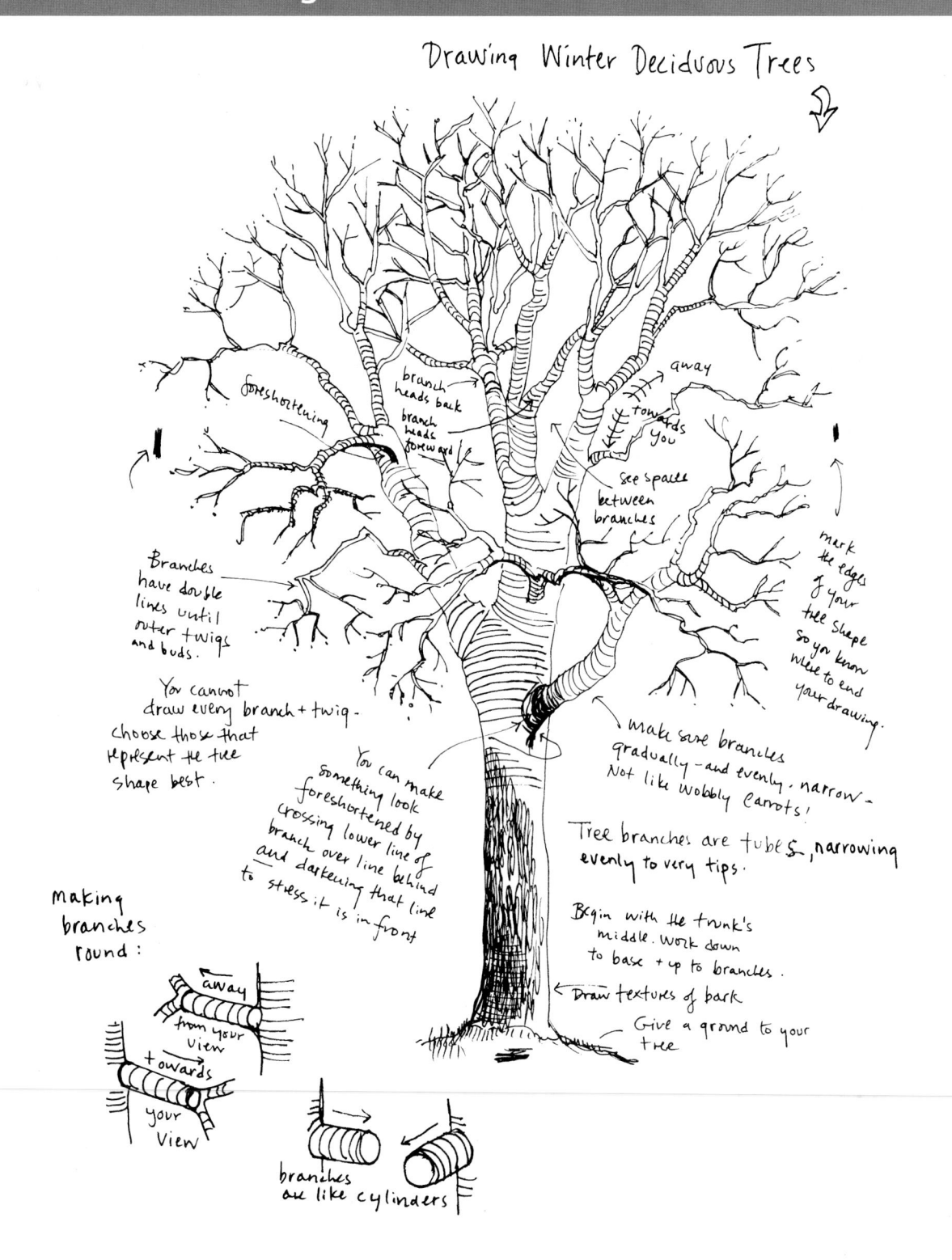

Drawing Winter Deciduous Trees

foreshortening

branch heads back

branch heads forward

away

towards you

See spaces between branches

Branches have double lines until outer twigs and buds.

You cannot draw every branch + twig. Choose those that represent the tree shape best.

mark the edges of your tree shape so you know where to end your drawing.

You can make something look foreshortened by crossing lower line of branch over line behind and darkening that line to stress it is in front

make sure branches gradually – and evenly – narrow – Not like wobbly carrots!

Tree branches are tubes, narrowing evenly to very tips.

Begin with the trunk's middle. Work down to base + up to branches.

Draw textures of bark

Give a ground to your tree

making branches round:

away from your view

towards your view

branches are like cylinders

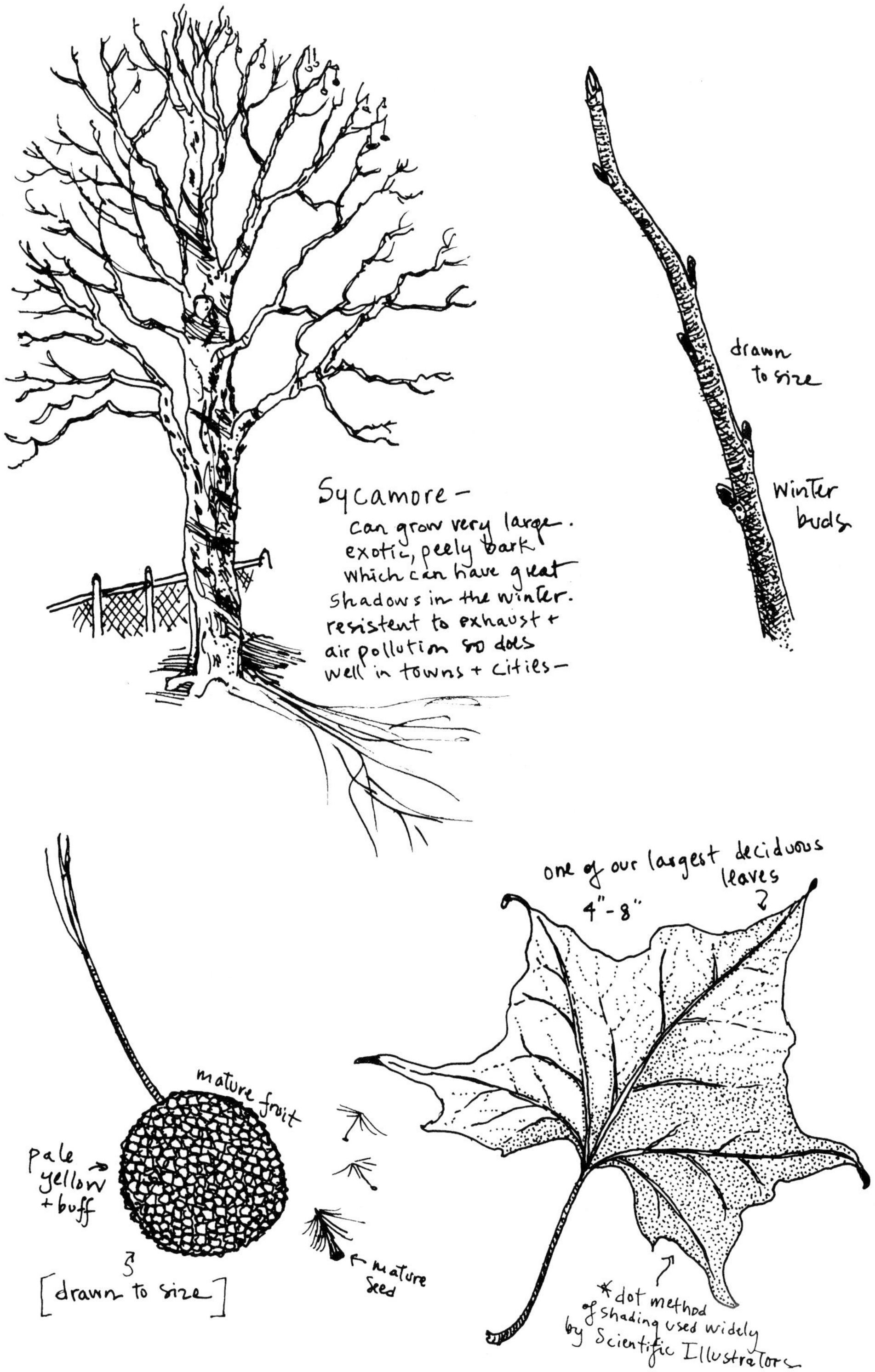

Winter Tree Project

Make an inventory of the trees that grow in your area. Write descriptions of each; measure the leaves, fruit, and buds; draw a map indicating where each type of tree is located; draw full-tree silhouettes, and details of the twigs, buds, seeds, and dried leaves as best you can.

Observe the activity in one of your trees. What creatures are spending the winter in your special tree? What roosts in your tree and why? Which trees in the area are healthy; which are being adversely affected by human activities? What activities have various effects?

Sycamore —
can grow very large.
exotic, peely bark
which can have great
shadows in the winter.
resistent to exhaust +
air pollution so does
well in towns + cities —

drawn
to size

Winter
buds

one of our largest deciduous leaves
4"-8"

mature fruit

pale
yellow
+ buff

[drawn to size]

← mature
seed

* dot method
of shading used widely
by Scientific Illustrators

Snow Script

Walkers in snow leave tracks. Each track is like a letter of the track alphabet. Clusters of tracks — two for birds, four for mammals — create simple animal words. Some represent simply standing still; others show patterns of movement, such as hopping and running. A string of tracks begins to spell out the story of what the creature was doing. Follow some tracks, see where they go, and record what the tracks indicate about what the animal was doing.

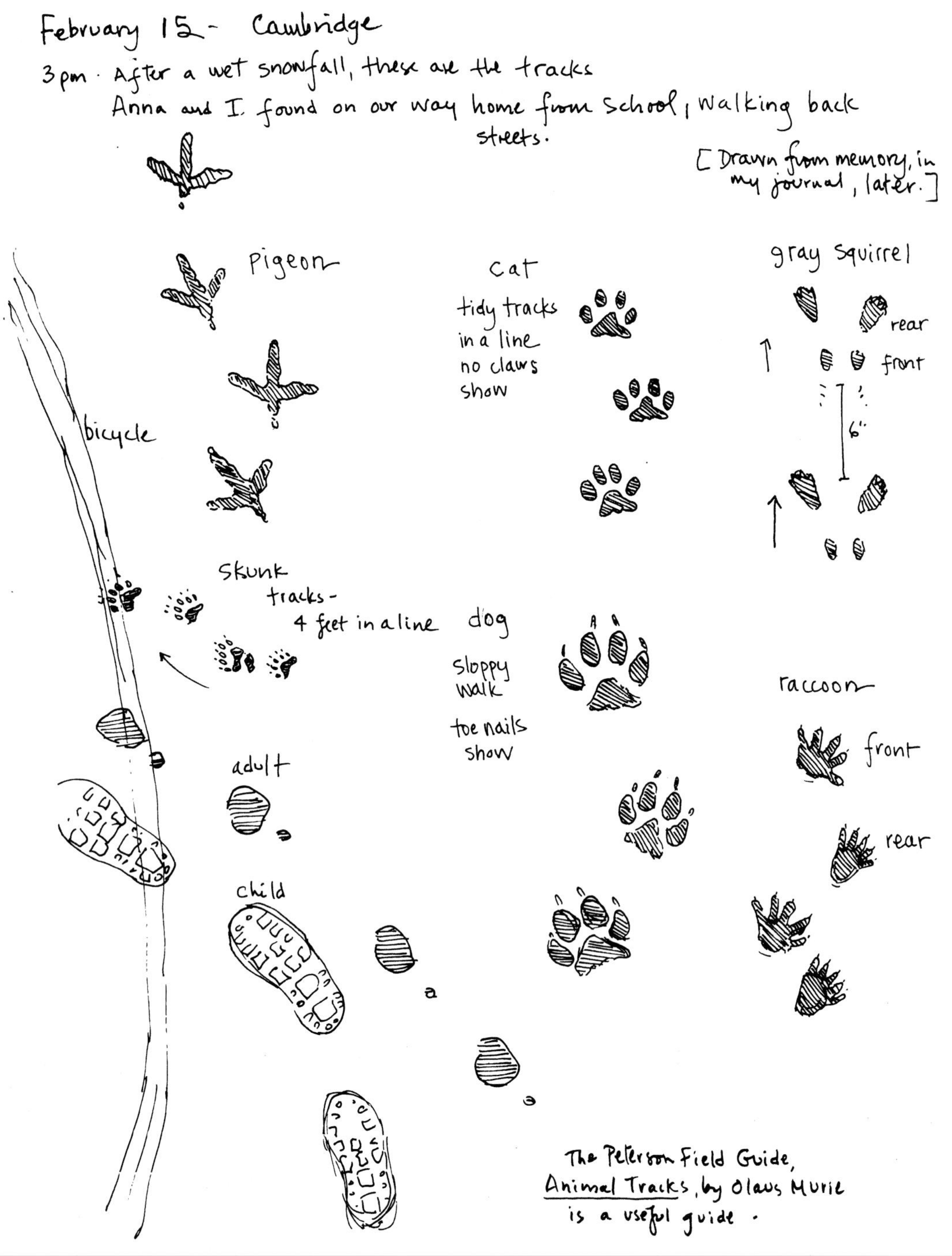

February 15 - Cambridge

3 pm · After a wet snowfall, these are the tracks Anna and I found on our way home from school, walking back streets.

[Drawn from memory, in my journal, later.]

Pigeon

bicycle

Skunk tracks - 4 feet in a line

adult

child

cat
tidy tracks in a line no claws show

dog
sloppy walk
toe nails show

gray squirrel
rear
front
6"

raccoon
front
rear

The Peterson Field Guide, Animal Tracks, by Olaus Murie is a useful guide.

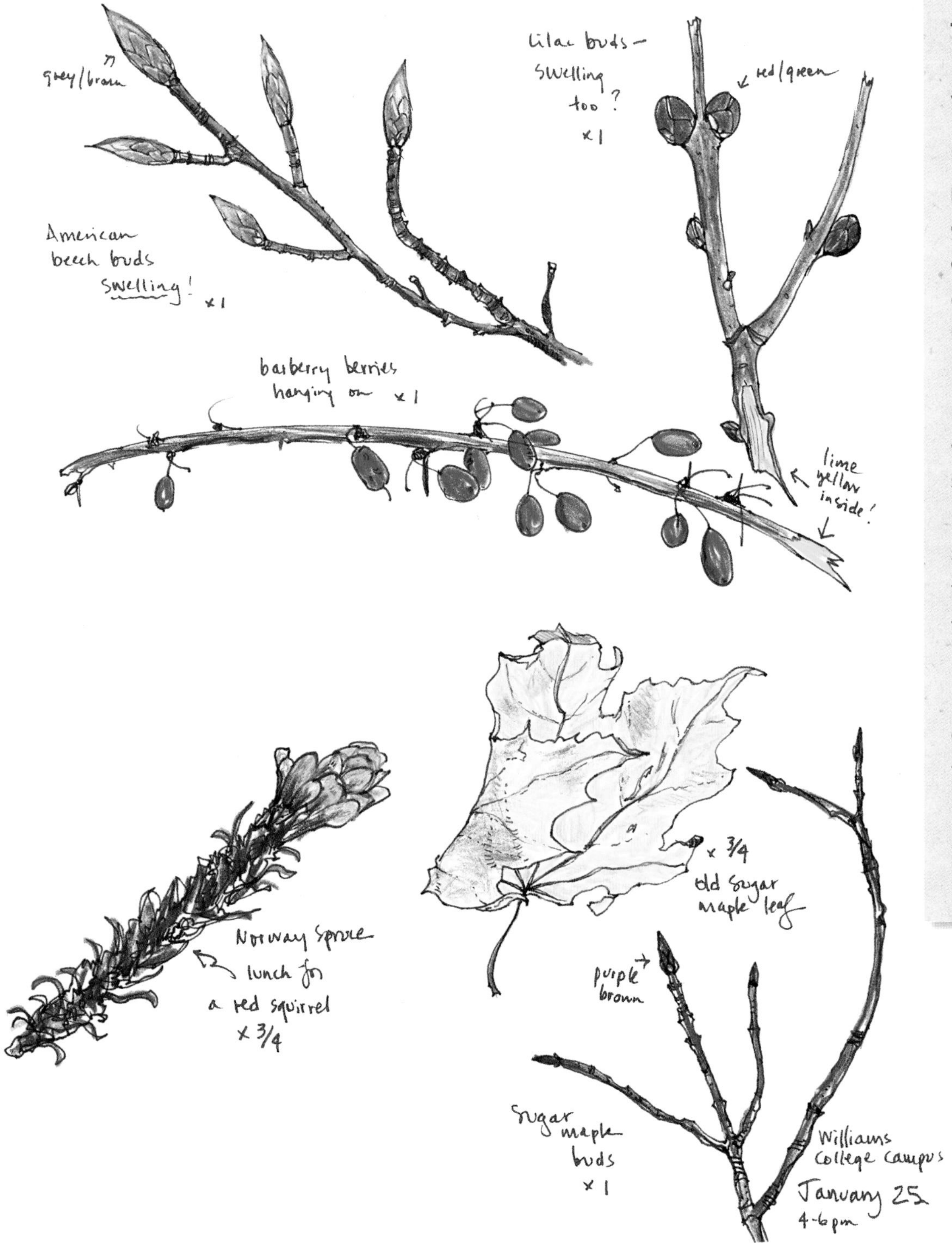

grey/brown

American
beech buds
swelling! ×1

Lilac buds—
swelling
too?
×1

← red/green

barberry berries
hanging on ×1

lime
yellow
inside!

Norway spruce
lunch for
a red squirrel
× 3/4

× 3/4
old sugar
maple leaf

purple
brown

sugar
maple
buds
×1

Williams
College campus
January 25
4–6 pm

Taking a Microscopic View

If it is too cold or rainy for prolonged observation outdoors, take a walk and collect objects such as winter twigs, dried weeds, galls, and the like. (Take only small specimens, and respect private property.) Then bring the objects indoors for close-up study using your eyes and a magnifying glass. Observe shapes, patterns, and textures. Record your observation in sketches and words.

Here, Clare collected 8- to 10-inch twig samples, then carefully drew and labeled them. She used a felt-tipped pen and colored pencil; students working with her used pen, pencil, and color.

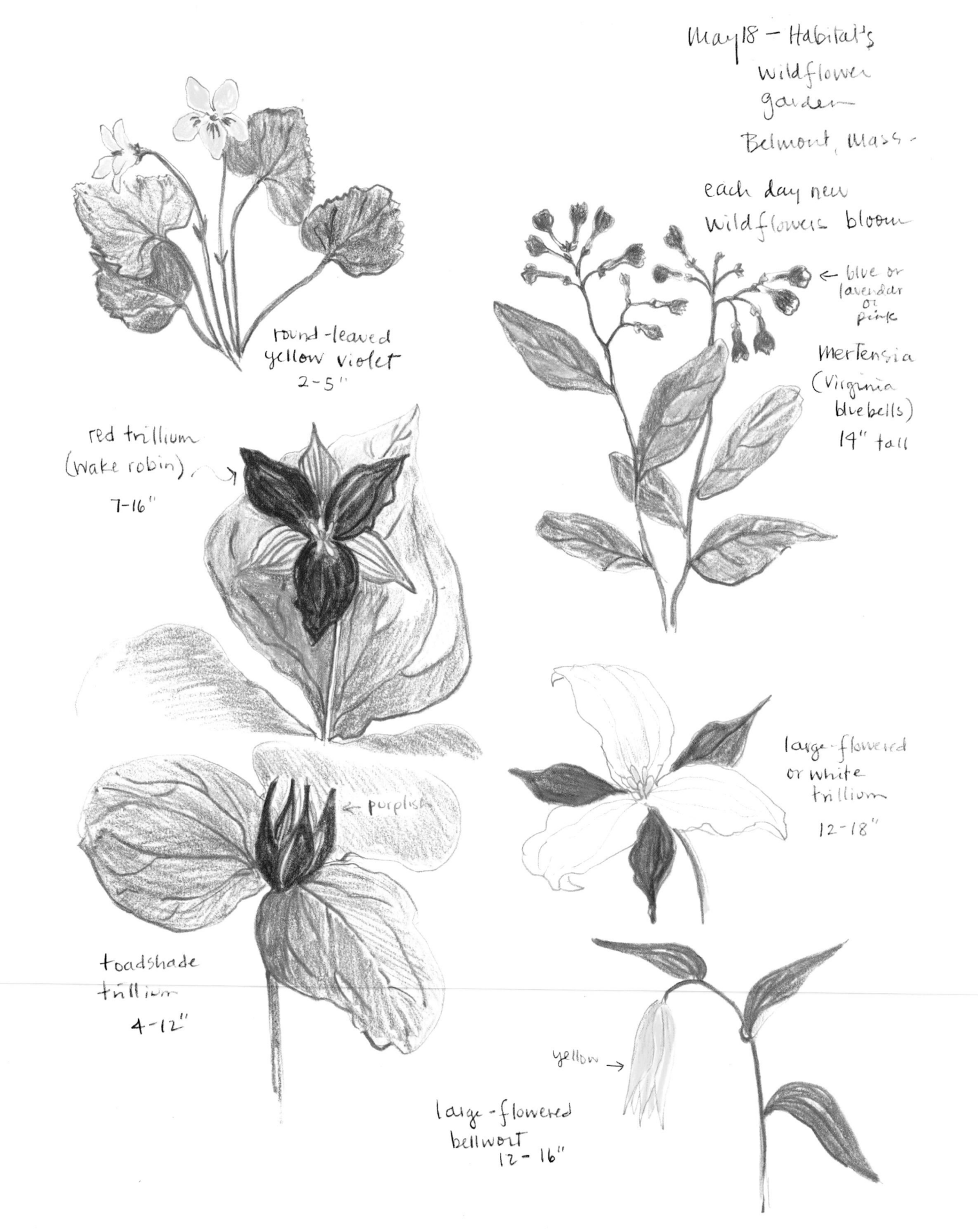

round-leaved
yellow violet
2-5"

May 18 — Habitat's
Wildflower
garden
Belmont, Mass.

each day new
wildflowers bloom

← blue or
lavender
or pink

Mertensia
(Virginia
bluebells)
14" tall

red trillium
(wake robin)
7-16"

large-flowered
or white
trillium
12-18"

← purplish

toadshade
trillium
4-12"

yellow →

large-flowered
bellwort
12-16"

The Spring Journal

Spring is when many of us would rather be outdoors than in! The months vary depending upon where you live. Here in New England, spring begins creeping in on sunny days in March, warm days in April, or finally with the retreat of mountain snows in May.

Spring Observations

What are some spring subjects to observe and record in your journal, based on where you live? Finally, the earth is warming up once more and the increased light activates daily, no longer weekly, changes indoors. We find if we blink on a spring day, we miss out on something happening. Ten minutes a day in your journal can help you keep track of how fast spring comes on.

Plants

What early green shoots appear near you — planted bulbs of snowdrops, crocuses and daffodils, or grasses and woodland flowers? Take a walk and draw the green things growing on the ground. Be sure to record the date, because growth changes almost daily now.

Trees

Draw the buds as they expand and come into bloom. Date your daily observations. What do new

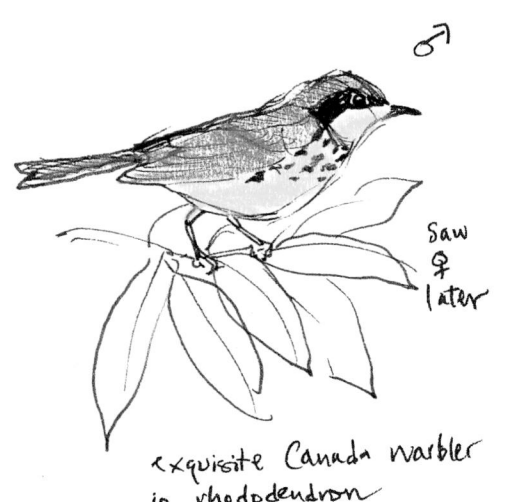

new honeysuckle leaves

Saw ♀ later

exquisite Canada warbler in rhododendron

poplars in bloom!

leaf shapes and colors look like? What fruits do you still see on trees, shrubs, and evergreens? Where do trees leaf out earlier — in sunny warm places, or colder darker places? Cut branches of forsythia, apple, pussy willow, dogwood. Bring them in and put them in water, then watch the leaves and flowers open and expand, recording the activity as it happens.

Animals

What are local animals doing around you? Do you see them during the day or at night?

Skunks mate in February and are out more at night, as are raccoons. Grey squirrels around us have courted in late December through January, and are raising young in April. Do you have deer, foxes, elk, mice, rats? Listen for the beginning of the annual chorus of mating frogs. Which kinds do you hear earliest in the year? When do other species join the chorus? What evidence of animals can you find: holes, burrows, chewed branches? Record as much as you can of the lives of the animals that live near you.

chipmunks have emerged looking fresh + clean

A red fox appears from a dune + crosses onto tarmac. Pauses, watches us, goes across to marsh. stops to look again

Surprisingly Red fur

Birds

What birds have been with you all winter? What new birds appear first as part of the spring migration? What are the dates of the first bird of each species that you see returning in spring? Look for the brightly colored males in breeding plumage; they may be very different looking than when they passed southward in fall. Locate a local birdwatcher to go afield with you, and have him help you learn to recognize new kinds of birds.

Weather and Season

Much has been written about spring. The season comes early in some places and much later in others; it depends in large part on the latitude of your home, or its altitude. Do you have snow in May, floods in April, hail in February? Keep at least a monthlong record of weather, moon phases, precipitation, sunrises, and sunsets. This is the time when, in the Northern Hemisphere, the earth is pointing more toward the sun. Meanwhile, in the Southern Hemisphere, the reverse is true, and residents are experiencing not spring but fall. What are the spring celebrations in your area — Easter, Passover, Earth Day, May Day?

Yourself

How does spring weather make you feel? What are your responses to the pastel colors of spring, the showers, the warm moist air, the new plant growth, the returning migrant birds? Draw events that symbolize the season for you.

marsh hawk

SIGNS of SPRING
watch today =

① In Vermont, warm mushy ski at Sugarbush vs 4. Rime ice crystals at top on trees, like candy.
② Raked flower beds. Little bulbs there. In A+E's garden — crocuses! A+E play in "town" until past dark making "cookies" + building a fire. (Eric awakes today really sick. I am still → a weird one: everything out of focus)

Robins in Vermont
Harold sugaring —
always mystical

As I get into the car, a mourning cloak butterfly floats along the street. What a sign of hope!

Hermit Thrush in honeysuckle underbrush

Neighbor's purple crocuses in bloom. Crocuses in bloom everywhere in Cambridge.

Home Pages

Devote a journal page every now and then to reflecting on what is happening in and around your home. You might record your thoughts of the season, images of change you see in your yard and nearby surroundings, or what has been happening to you and your family over the past month, week, or day. These pages are fun to refer back to and reflect on over the year, just like an old page of family photos.

Granville · Vermont

(Mud season here –
Swallows cars, kids, kittens…)

What's happening outdoors on this balmy Sunday
Should I:
* write a poem
* paint a picture
* go for a walk – or a ski
* watch the sunset while cooking dinner
* notice the earth beginning to move
(I did all of the above –)

March 21
The first day of Spring!
Sunrise = 5:44 am
Sunset = 5:55 pm
        almost
        equal Day + Night

Snow fleas are hopping about across our snow
called "Collembola" or "Springtails" also

Sitting huddled in a gully of snow + mud – a Woodcock!

flies up with a whir + a "bleep"

Stanley now sugaring
40 gal of Sap
make 1 gal of Syrup!
8 cords of wood burned
in wood-fired furnace
below boiling pans –
an intoxicating
steam room is the sugar house
in March

first of the returning red-winged blackbirds   grackles   cowbirds   starlings also

December 21
4:12 pm

Sept 21 + March 21
5:49 pm   5:55 pm

June 21
8:40 pm
sunset

View West from our house

Winter   Spring   Summer
                          fall
Sun's western setting path year upon year

Winter without
Spring eternal
within
3.23.97

Bright Spots for Gloomy Days

For those rainy spring days, brighten up your spirits by buying a bouquet of spring flowers. Draw them and write about them. What do the colors, the shapes, the smells make you think about? You might write just a sentence or two, a few phrases, or even a poem. Try wrapping the words around the flowers as if they were part of the bouquet.

Drawing for Observation Clues

Sometimes it helps you get acquainted with local birds if you first draw them from good photos or the drawings in bird identification guidebooks. By drawing particular birds, you fix their most prominent field marks in your memory, and you'll find that you're better able to accurately identify them when you see them in the field. The journal then becomes a great tool for sharpening your observation of birds' movements and activities. In this study, Clare was learning to distinguish the breeding plumages of several male warblers.

black-and-white Warbler

♂ breeding

blackpoll warbler

♂ breeding

magnolia Warbler

♂ breeding

Cape May warbler
♂ breeding

Blackburnian Warbler

♂ breeding male

learning ♂
Warbler spring breeding
plumages · Cambridge MA
May 8
...technical pen +
colored pencil...

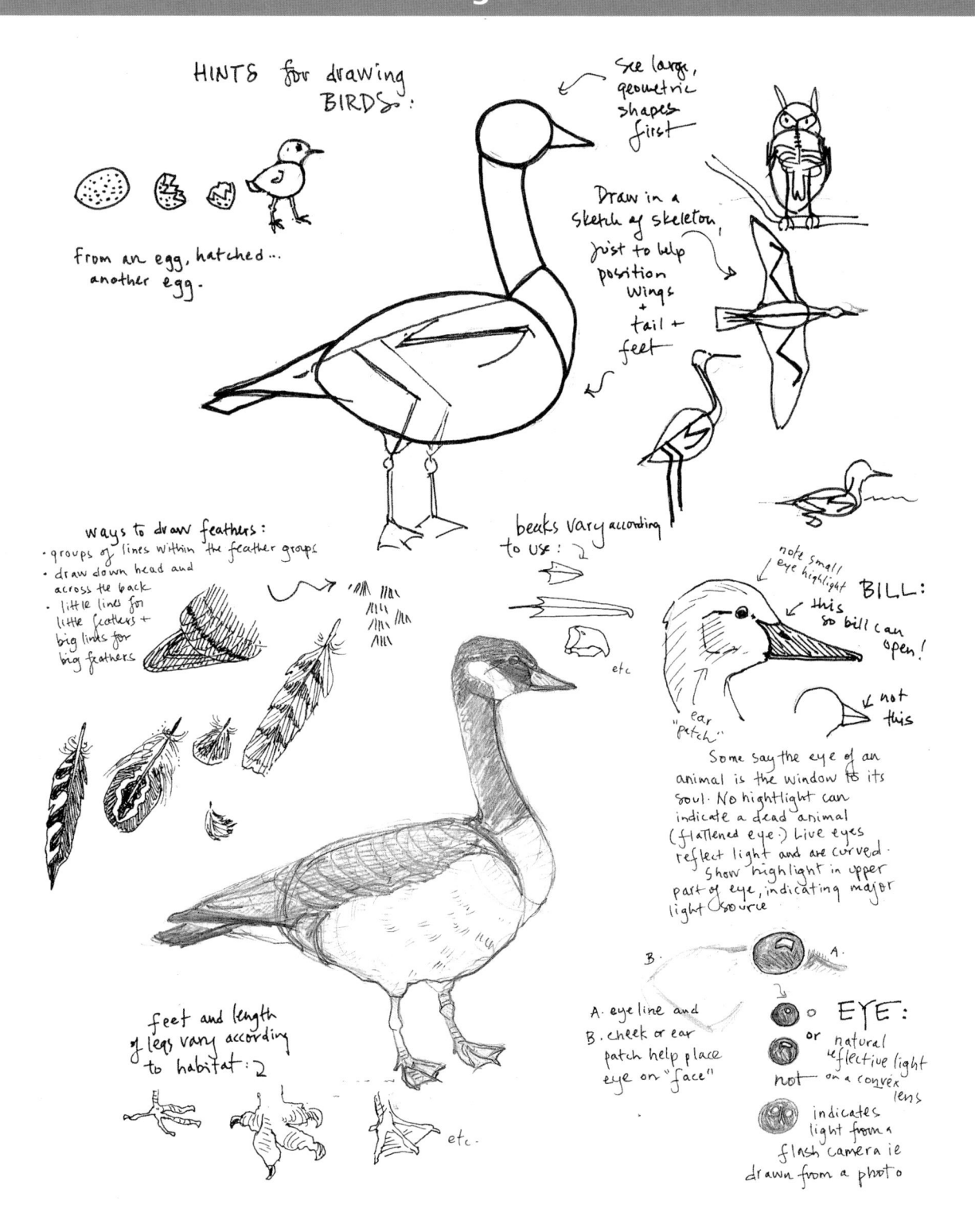

HINTS for drawing BIRDS:

From an egg, hatched...
another egg.

See large, geometric shapes first

Draw in a sketch of skeleton, just to help position Wings + tail + feet

beaks vary according to use :

etc

note small eye highlight

BILL: this so bill can open!

"ear patch"

not this

Some say the eye of an animal is the window to its soul. No highlight can indicate a dead animal (flattened eye.) Live eyes reflect light and are curved. Show highlight in upper part of eye, indicating major light source.

ways to draw feathers:
· groups of lines within the feather groups
· draw down head and across the back
· little lines for little feathers + big lines for big feathers

feet and length of legs vary according to habitat :

etc.

B.

A.

A. eye line and
B. cheek or ear patch help place eye on "face"

EYE:
or natural reflective light on a convex lens
not

indicates light from a flash camera ie drawn from a photo

Drawing for Information

By combining indoor study with outdoor nature observation, you learn about nature as naturalists have done throughout history. Reading books, asking questions, and learning why and how animals do what they do helps improve both your knowledge and your ability to accurately depict the animals' activities in your field drawings.

A PIGEON REPORT=

Pigeons were first brought to this country to raise for their meat and to carry messages. Their relatives, the rock doves, nest on cliffs and have abilities to fly through narrow spaces and land on almost anything. (Because of their adaptability, pigeons have easily adapted to most of our cities.)

* BIRD REPORTS are good subjects for your NATURE JOURNAL

choose local birds

STAR

couples make messy stick, string, paper nests in various enclosed places. They generally begin courting + nest building in late January but interactive couple behaviors can be observed all year long.

Pigeons can clap their wings in take-off as a kind of courtship message.

PIGEON POSTURES IN A NEARBYE PARK=

① ♂ lowers head, puffs out feathers to show power to mate or group

② ♂ male struts about, feathers puffed + tail down. Showing off to group or possible mate.

③ ♂ chases ♀ around within or away from a group of pigeons. Rather like ♂ showing off his ♀ to the group.

④ Female puts bill inside male's mouth. Together their heads bob up + down. Part of a courtship pattern.

⑤ ♀ and ♂ preen head feathers as a courtship pattern.

(see A Guide to the Behavior of Common Birds)

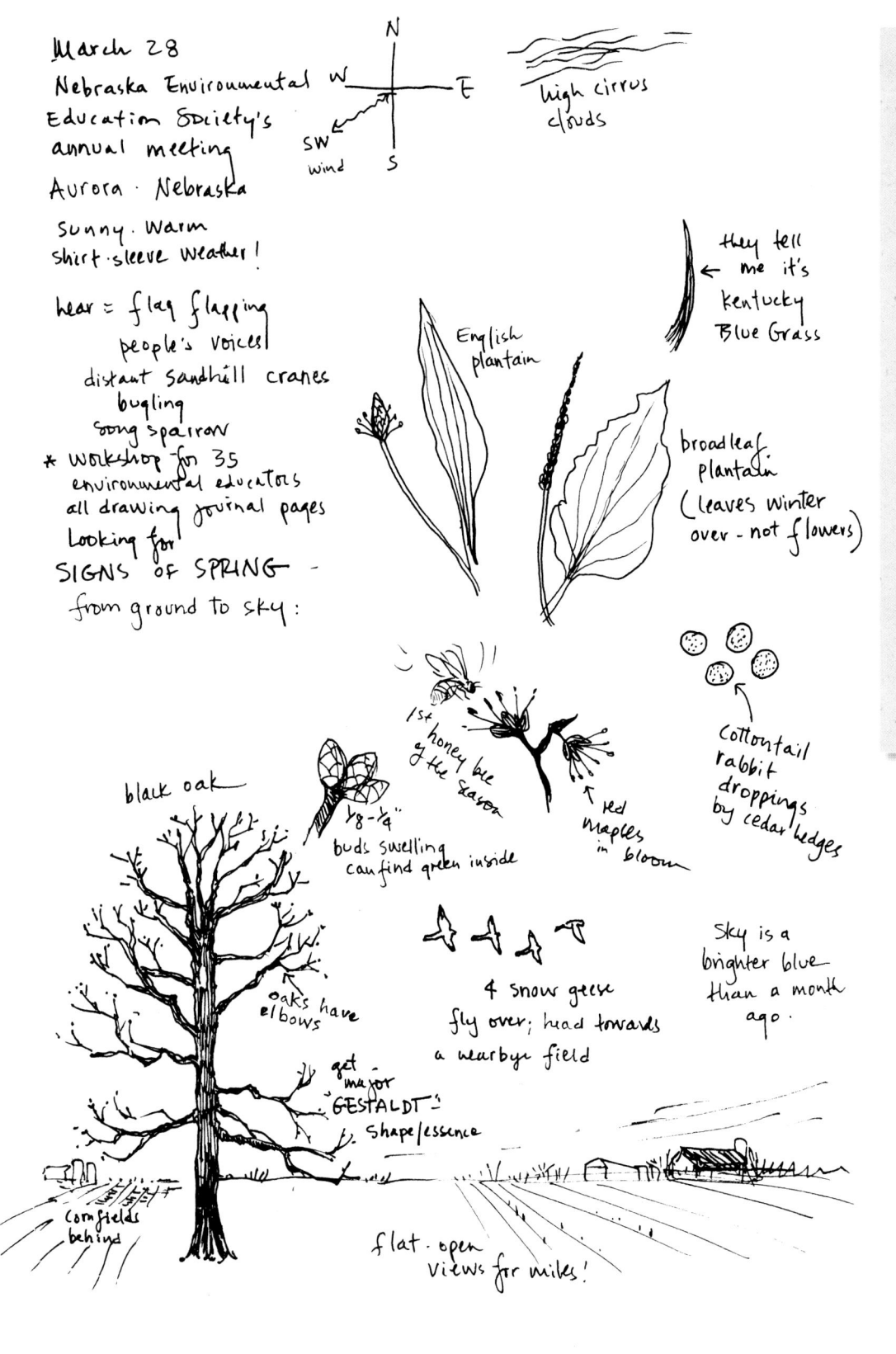

March 28
Nebraska Environmental
Education Society's
annual meeting
Aurora · Nebraska

sunny · warm
shirt · sleeve weather!

hear = flag flapping
        people's voices
    distant sandhill cranes
        bugling
    song sparrow
* workshop for 35
    environmental educators
    all drawing journal pages
    Looking for
SIGNS OF SPRING –

    from ground to sky:

N
W   E
SW
wind
S

high cirrus
clouds

they tell
← me it's
   kentucky
   Blue Grass

English
plantain

broadleaf
plantain
(leaves winter
over - not flowers)

black oak

1st
honey bee
of the season

⅛-¼"
buds swelling
can find green inside

red
maples
in bloom

cottontail
rabbit
droppings
by cedar hedges

oaks have
elbows

get
major
"GESTALDT"
shape/essence

4 snow geese
fly over; head towards
a nearby field

Sky is a
brighter blue
than a month
ago.

cornfields
behind

flat · open
views for miles!

Noting Contrasts in Place

As you travel, be sure to take your journal along. This is a great opportunity to observe and record the things that set these new habitats apart from the ones with which you are most familiar. Note the differences and the similarities between this new place and the spot you live. Clare recorded these observations on a visit to Nebraska; note how different the flat, open landscapes are from the hilly country of New England.

Look for Nature Everywhere

Even in urban spaces, you can note signs of the season: sky condition, position of the sun, type of vegetation and stage of growth, animal evidence and survival. Clare made this drawing during a forty-five-minute session with a group of elementary schoolchildren in Cambridge, Massachusetts. All were amazed at how much nature could be found right around the school yard. Journaling is a great way to confront unfounded fears about nature, as well. Once the children spent time drawing and learning about earthworms, they were no longer afraid of them.

April 5
Peabody Elementary School
Cambridge
1:30 pm

One of our 1st warm, sunny days!
50°
* 35 2nd graders, plus
2 aides, 1 teacher, and
me in the school's courtyard. We all draw together as best we can — from ground to sky:

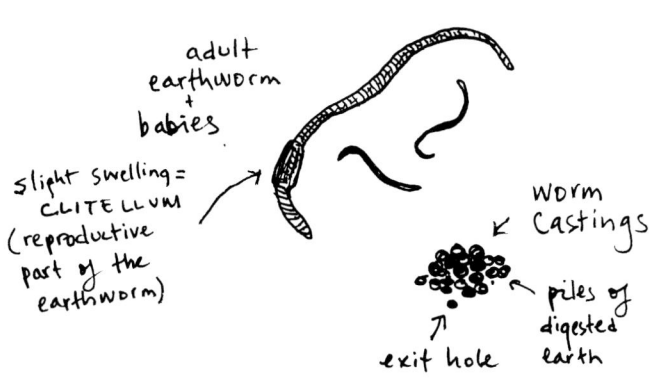

½" Sow bug dark brown/black

adult earthworm + babies

slight swelling = CLITELLUM (reproductive part of the earthworm)

WORM Castings

piles of digested earth

exit hole

tree flowers

Silver maple

buds getting bigger

Norway maple

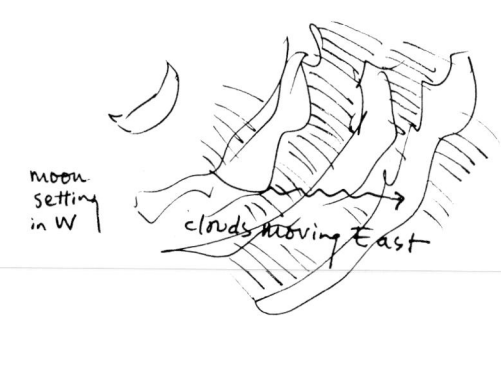

moon setting in W

clouds moving East

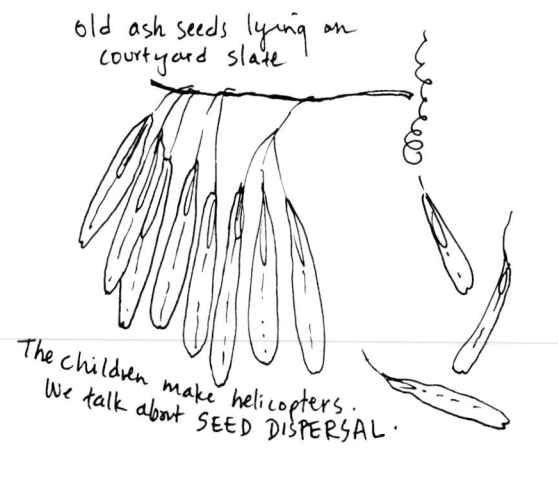

old ash seeds lying on courtyard slate

The children make helicopters. We talk about SEED DISPERSAL.

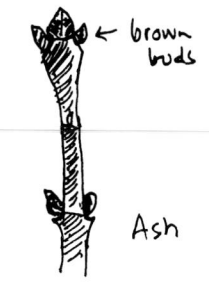

← brown buds

Ash

May 1
7:30 am walk around my neighborhood
       to honor MAY DAY
60° already!
I leave the house with NO
coat on for the first time this year —

sounds = cars · people going to work ·
  trash being dragged to street · a
  lawnmower!
calling = starling · crow · mockingbird · cardinal
  mourning dove · house finch · house sparrow

in leaf = lilac · barberry · weeping willow
  privet ; red maple + elm in flower +
       Norway maple

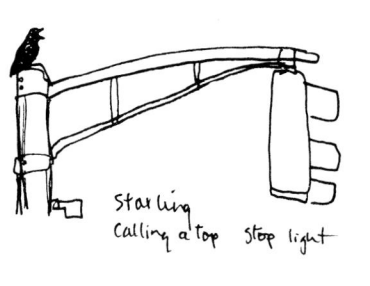

Starling
calling a top   stop light

barberry in leaf

What's Moving in Your Neighborhood?

May is a time of movement and renewal. Look for signs of action in your area. Observe flowers opening in trees and from the ground. Watch for the return of migrating birds. Insects are emerging from pupae and cocoons to repopulate the spring landscape. Take a walk once a week and keep a record of changes over a month, several months, the year.

house finch
eating red maple
florets

crimson red
♂ flower parts

star magnolia in full flower

first mourning cloak
butterfly of the season
floats across the street

Linnaean St.

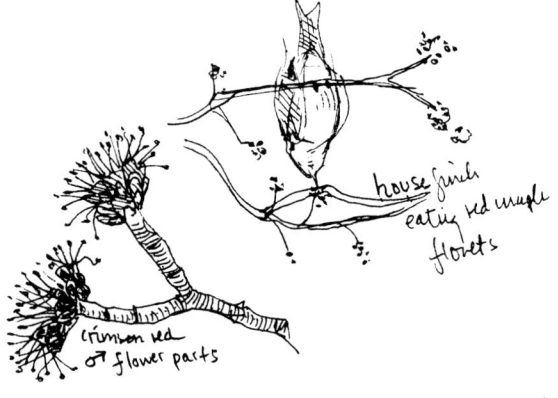

Windows open + cat watches passersby ····

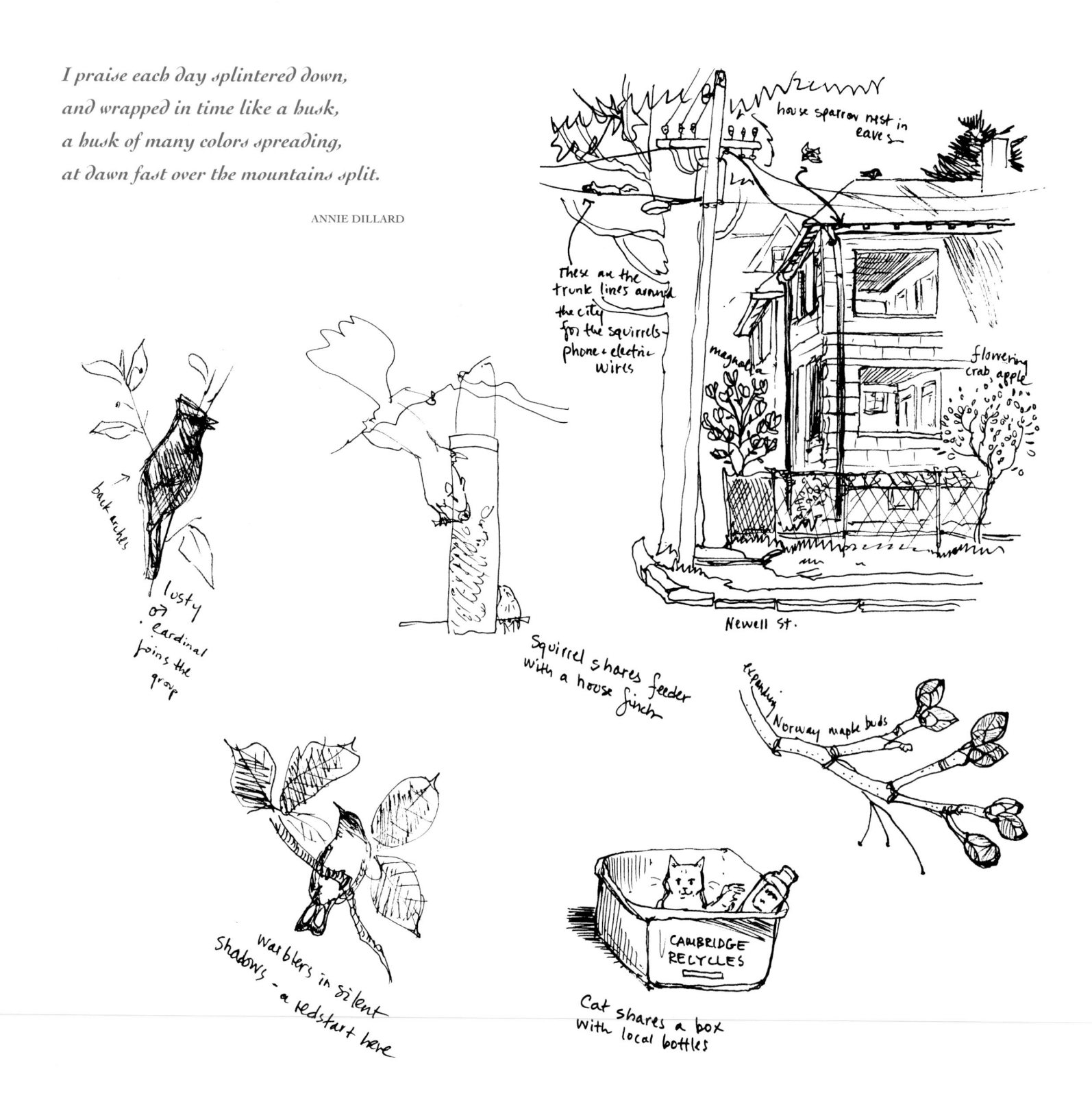

I praise each day splintered down,
and wrapped in time like a husk,
a husk of many colors spreading,
at dawn fast over the mountains split.

ANNIE DILLARD

house sparrow nest in eaves

These are the trunk lines around the city for the squirrels— phone & electric wires

magnolia

flowering crab apple

Newell St.

back arches

lusty ♂ cardinal joins the group

Squirrel shares feeder with a house finch

expanding Norway maple buds

Warblers in silent shadows - a redstart here

CAMBRIDGE RECYCLES

Cat shares a box with local bottles

May 27 · Tuesday
Mount Auburn Cemetery · Cambridge MA
   5 pm
Sunny. blue/blue skies
   bit chilly + slightly windy
      low 60's

☾ moon

Sunrise = 5:13 am
Sunset = 8:10 pm

length of day = 14 hrs 57 min

hear = oriole   great crested flycatcher
      cardinal   robin
      goldfinches   titmouse
      Wind   catbird
      crows

on Cambridge
Streets today — black throated green
               magnolia or parula?
               yellow
                  ?? warblers

to hear Wind in leaves!
to walk just to look
   at exceptional images
evening is lost to us
   who cook and end
   the day with home
   duties

dogwood white on
      green

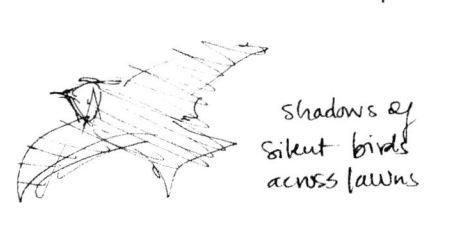

shadows of
silent birds
across lawns

memory

Catch the black beady eye of
a catbird before it shadows into
a low shrub. Then begins "meowing"
at me minutes later —

Sandstone
markers
bleaching
out
names
+
age

IIIIIII

live

heard
preening in
azalea
flew off when I
dropped my bag

2"
of
lime green
new growth
on darker green
yew branches

16-20"
long

✳ I brown
½" ant

1-2,000
Some appear dead
large over small dead
#'s

large aggregate of tiny
brown ants obviously
agitated by something . ?

Nature Drawing Exercise: Color

Colored pencils are a great way to begin adding color. You can use them much the way you do crayons — just color in green for leaves, red for flowers, yellow for bumblebees, and so on. The colors are already mixed in the pencils. If you want to mix and vary your colors, just layer one over the other in various weights (color densities). Be sure to get the thick lead pencils, because these are richer in color than the thin leads, and the waxy texture of the lead allows the colors to blend nicely. The white or cream colors are good for softening or highlighting. You can mostly erase colored pencils if you make a mistake. You can also mix them with other media, such as watercolor, watercolor pencils, crayons, and pen and ink. Colored pencil is better added to a pen and ink drawing than a pencil drawing, since the pencil edges can smudge, and make the colors muddy. *The Colored Pencil* by Bet Borgeson (see Suggested Reading) is also a very useful book. Some people develop color-coding systems to categorize their observations: one color for all weather-related entries, another color for plant observations, another for animal observations, and yet another for reflective comments.

Working in Watercolor

Watercolor is too big a subject to cover adequately here; we will only mention how we use it. There are many good books available on how to use watercolor for landscapes, plants, and wildlife. You might also look for courses in your area — but we suggest you first find out how the teacher uses watercolor, and if this matches your interest.

Here are several methods we use:

• Apply watercolor pencils the same way as colored pencils; then add a brush of plain water to blend in the wash. Use a permanent ink or pencil, so the line will stay. The trick is not to have too much water on your brush, or the colors will puddle.

• Learn how to mix colors, and what colors result. For example, mix red, blue, and yellow together. What do you get?

• Do a pencil drawing, laying in major shapes. Then develop tones and color washes using both wet and dry layers. Brush size, type of paper, and the amount of water in your brush all make a big difference in your results. Experiment. Record your experiments and the results in your journal for future reference.

Colored pencils do not mix colors like watercolor. They blend them.

erasing

cream

white

shade   tint

Shade out from the midrib, as you did shading with pencil.
Layer colors Light to Dark.

Add a little red to the green and green to the red to help connect colors. See paintings of Van Gogh, Cezanne, Monet for help on use of color!

Shade petals out from center. Make center of flower round, using ≡ and \\\ lines.

Try using a wash of water on a brush, over a pen and ink drawing.

primary (unmixed)   secondary (mixed)
Colors

A colored pencil drawing can take from 5 10 minutes to 10 hours.

blue gray   black
                black
buffy

black

? nuthatch about 5" on sugar maple Williamstown 1·10

Colored pencils are used a great deal in the field for quick color notations, as done here.

Let pencil lines show if you want

mop out extra color with paper towel

try pen and watercolor

wet on wet

dry on wet

let colors puddle

technical pen

felt·tipped pen

pencil

June 24   6:30pm

On my way to pick up
D's bike, I went looking
for roses to draw.

Even in the city,
there can be connections
to nature :

While drawing, the soft
sounds of evening ensuing
around me -
      children being fed
      cars returning home
      Sparrows chattering
       Swifts
      nighthawks
      robin
      mockingbird playing cardinal (!)

CHAPTER 8

The Summer Journal

Summer is a terrific time for nature journaling. Many people who don't have time to journal during the rest of the year (or think they don't!) find time to unwind and relax in the summer. You might find yourself craving a way to get closer to nature and experience its beauty more fully while on vacation. Keep fifteen- to twenty-page journals so you feel the satisfaction of completing your journal. Title it appropriately as a one-event journal, such as: My Summer Vacation, My Trip to Spain, Our Hike In Wyoming, My Garden Journal, Birding in Nova Scotia. In the northern hemisphere, the summer months are June, July, August.

Summer is a wonderful time to explore the nature sanctuaries, public parks, reservations, state forests, and wildlife refuge areas around your home. Each place offers its own distinct pathway to nature, with trails through woods, meadows, or mountains, or along riverbeds. See what quiet wonders lie within an hour's drive of your home. Then you can say to friends, as one college student did, "I saw events I go by daily and never had seen before, until stopping to draw, and so to notice. There is much more out there than I had realized, going on daily despite my not noticing. It makes me more conscious of protecting these wild places that I now know well."

surf clam
quahog

green crab

Summer Observations

The world is rich and full of life in summer. It's all around you. You may have the chance to experience some new places and observe different kinds of living things than those at home. Begin by simply recording the date, place (including state), time, and weather, then go on to record all you can hear, see, feel, smell. Record what is special about wherever you are.

Plants

Observe and draw five plants that grow in the sun and five that grow in the shade. What things does each need to grow? Can you observe a blooming succession among these plants? Which bloom in June? Which bloom in August? What insects are attracted to which plants? Label the size, the color, and any distinctive characteristics of each plant, along with where you found it growing. Would these plants grow near your home or school?

Watercolor drawings

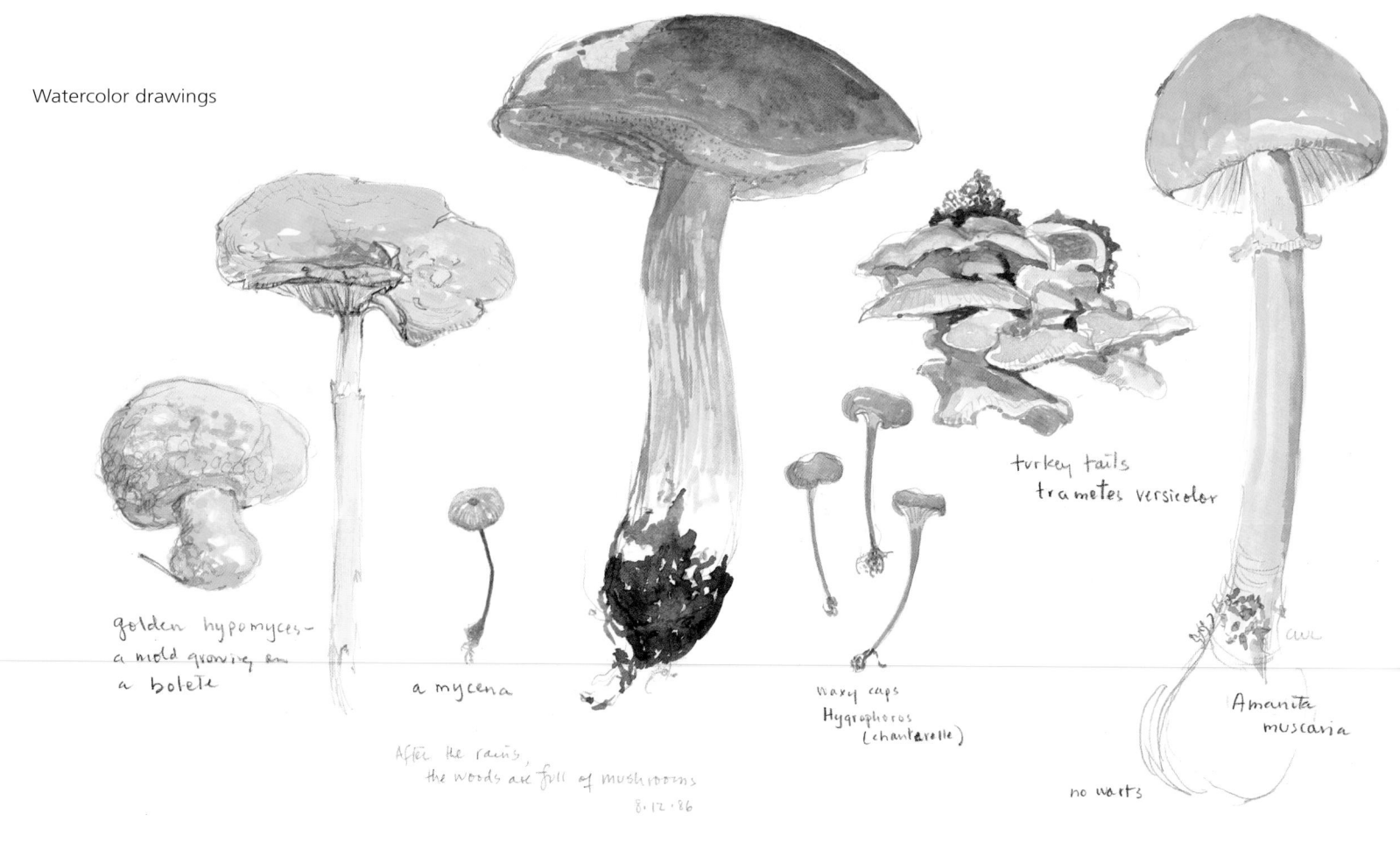

golden hypomyces—
a mold growing on
a bolete

a mycena

After the rains,
the woods are full of mushrooms
8.12.'86

waxy caps
Hygrophoros
(chanterelle)

turkey tails
trametes versicolor

no warts

Amanita
muscaria

Trees

If you are visiting a new place, get to know the trees there by drawing five different tree shapes you see. Keep the drawings small. Compare the shapes of the trees with leaves to the drawings you did of tree skeletons in winter. Do you have similar kinds of trees at home? What animals need each of these trees for food or protection?

Animals

Draw five animals, including insects, reptiles, and amphibians, living in the habitat where you are journaling. What do these creatures do in the summer? Go to a library and read about five that interest you. Search your habitat for clues that these animals are living there, and make notes about them in your journal drawings. You may discern their presence by tracks, chewings, holes, or scat, even if you don't spot the animals themselves.

Birds

What five birds are in your habitat? Are they year-round residents or do they arrive in spring and leave in fall? Are these shorebirds, water-birds, pelagic or seabirds, hawks, owls, woodpeckers, or songbirds? Take the time to learn to use a field guide and binoculars for observa-

tion. Perhaps you can find a nesting bird and, without disturbing the parents, observe and record the growth of the youngsters. Find a friend, join a group, and go birding with companions.

Weather and Season

Ah, summer! This is a great time to get out at night and learn the major star constellations. It is also a good time to study cloud patterns and figure how they affect weather formations. Of particular interest is observing and recording the formation of thunderheads from simple cumulus clouds to towering cumulonimbus forms with developed anvils on top. Swimming and fishing might be among your summer activities; try studying aquatic life, including everything from frogs to nesting fish. Summer includes the longest day of the year in the Northern Hemisphere — the summer solstice.

Yourself

How does summer weather make you feel? What is your response to the parade of flowers, the nesting birds, fireflies and dragonflies, summer storms, the life of ponds and streams and tide pools? Draw events that symbolize the season for you.

Compare to Old Horizons

Take time to compare the new places you visit with those close to home. Revisit your favorite places, scenes, and natural neighbors often and record what they're up to this season. These drawings were sketched in pen while walking, and filled in with watercolor at home.

July 15 Rochester. Vermont

3:50 pm

. the North Hollow walk - with Eric 1½ hrs

Sunny but clouds have been in + out w/ showers

brisk !

about 65°

hear - king bird · crows · red squirrel
cows munching hay · red wings

whiff of manure everywhere ...

ox-eye daisy at dirt road edge

one huge bullock !

♀ now eating

One mean. ugly bullock !

Good view of a pileated woodpecker
(1st we heard a raucous woodpecker call)

An all black kitty
joins us "mha·mha".
Is it wild? Many are.

Lots of little bird activity.
in + out of Trees — fall beginning
to activate
them?

24"

huge
holes
in
maple
tree by
road

Kestral chasing
flicker over the
trees

The cloud
shapes this
summer have been tremendous
(good for painting)

Spotted 10 bluebirds
bouncing along the
Phone wires by Harvey's Mtn. View

Drawing Animals - in action or not...

When animals are moving, look hard at overall form. Do several combination contour and gesture sketches, getting major geometries. When animal moves go to another drawing. You can have 2/3/4 sketches going at once, moving from one to the other as the animal takes those positions again. When you are familiar enough with the form, you can draw the details in from memory.

sleeping

See geometries in sketch

washing itself

trying to sleep

Had

neck

shoulders

belly

hips

mouse eyes are huge - add highlight to show eye is convex

deer mouse found in our trash basket kids put it in our old terrarium "for a pet"... July 20

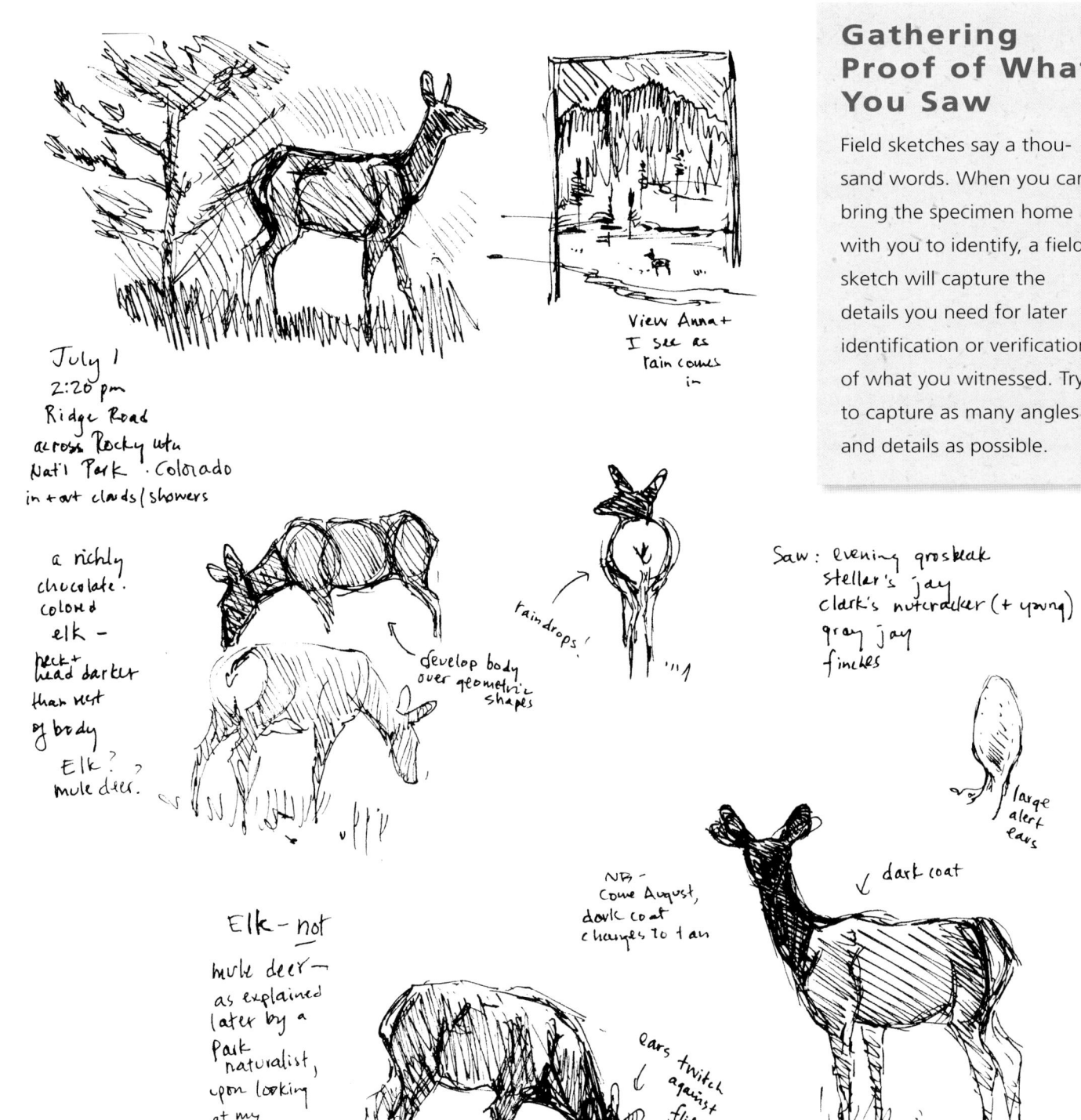

Gathering Proof of What You Saw

Field sketches say a thousand words. When you can't bring the specimen home with you to identify, a field sketch will capture the details you need for later identification or verification of what you witnessed. Try to capture as many angles and details as possible.

July 1
2:20 pm
Ridge Road
across Rocky Mtn
Nat'l Park . Colorado
in + out clouds/showers

View Anna +
I see as
rain comes
in

a richly
chocolate-
colored
elk –
neck +
head darker
than rest
of body
Elk ? ?
mule deer.

develop body
over geometric
shapes

raindrops!

Saw: evening grosbeak
Steller's jay
clark's nutcracker (+ young)
gray jay
finches

large
alert
ears

NB –
Come August,
dark coat
changes to tan

dark coat

Elk – not
mule deer –
as explained
later by a
Park
naturalist,
upon looking
at my
drawings....

ears twitch
against
flies

Listen to the Insect Orchestra

On slow summer days, go for a ramble or just sit outdoors and listen to the insect orchestra. Try to observe the individual players so you can match the sound to the player. You can use field guides to identify the players; there are recordings that can help you identify sounds and players when you can't find the insects themselves. If you get a chance, watch the insects make their sound. Look for edges of wings being rapidly vibrated back and forth, or legs rubbing on wings.

true katydid

♂ sings by rubbing rasps + ridges of outer wings rapidly back + forth. A tree dweller looking like part of a leaf. Very long antennae. A number of different species.

true katydid
1¼" pale green

"Katy·did·she·didn't·she·did"

red·legged grasshopper

Land dwellers, moving by short vertical flights. makes a "tzzip" crackling sound with its wings as it flies up. Short antennae. Makes rasping sound rubbing femur of hind leg across hardened veins on fore wings.

red·legged grasshopper
¾"-1¼"
green/brown

"tzzip·zipp" crackly sound

field cricket

Largely nocturnal, makes chirping sounds by rubbing slightly raised wings back + forth across one another. Likes warm places — even buildings

field cricket
5/8"
black
♀ ovipositor pierces earth to lay eggs
"treat·treat·treat"

snowy tree cricket or "temperature cricket"

Males make a soft, slurred call from trees and bushes. The number of "chirps" in 15 seconds, plus 40, gives approximate local Farenheit temperature. The colder the temperature, the slower the call.

snowy tree cricket
¾"
soft green

"churr·churr·purrrrr·churr" soft lisping

annual or "dog day" cicada

On hot days, a long + rising crescendo of buzzing emerges from somewhere in a tree. Males make the sound with "voices" boxed at the base of their abdomen, not by wings.

Cicada
dark brown
1¼"

"bzzzzzz" very loud

orthoptera — "straight wing"

hemiptera — "half wing" true bugs

homoptera — "same wing" shape

coleoptera — "sheath winged" beetles

hymenoptera — "membrane wings"

lepidoptera — "scale wings"

diptera — "two wings"

odonata — "tooth jaws"

✱ Insects are not bugs. Only hemiptera are bugs! Ladybugs are really ladybird beetles

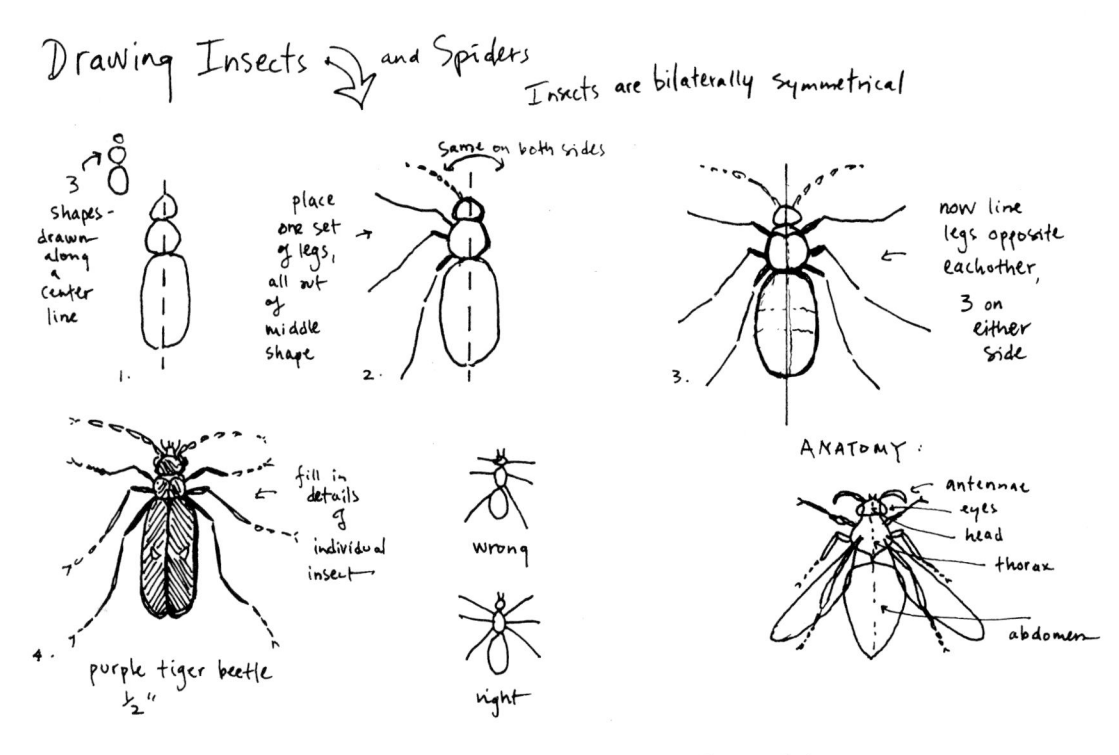

Drawing Insects and Spiders

Insects are bilaterally symmetrical

3 shapes - drawn along a center line

1.

Same on both sides

place one set of legs, all out of middle shape

2.

now line legs opposite eachother, 3 on either side

3.

fill in details of individual insect

4. purple tiger beetle ½"

wrong

right

ANATOMY:
antennae
eyes
head
thorax
abdomen

SPIDERS are related to insects, but they are NOT insects. They each have distinctive numbers of body sections and legs.

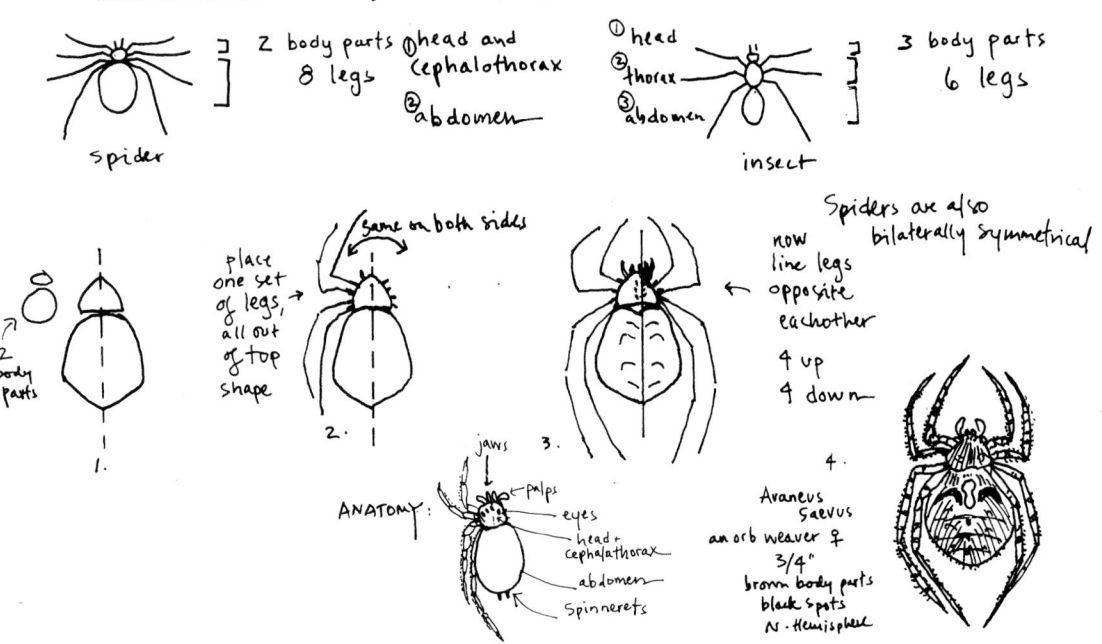

2 body parts
8 legs
① head and cephalothorax
② abdomen

spider

① head
② thorax
③ abdomen

3 body parts
6 legs

insect

2 body parts

1.

Same on both sides

place one set of legs, all out of top shape

2.

now line legs opposite eachother
4 up
4 down

Spiders are also bilaterally symmetrical

3.

ANATOMY:
jaws
palps
eyes
head + cephalothorax
abdomen
spinnerets

4.

Araneus Saevus
an orb weaver ♀
3/4"
brown body parts
black spots
N. Hemisphere

Drawing to Identify Species

The drawing at right is one Clare did while conducting an adult nature-journaling workshop. Sponsored by the National Wildlife Federation, this weeklong summit took place at Estes Park next to Rocky Mountain National Park in Colorado. We were joined by Roger Tory Peterson who spoke with Clare on the values of this kind of field identification sketching.

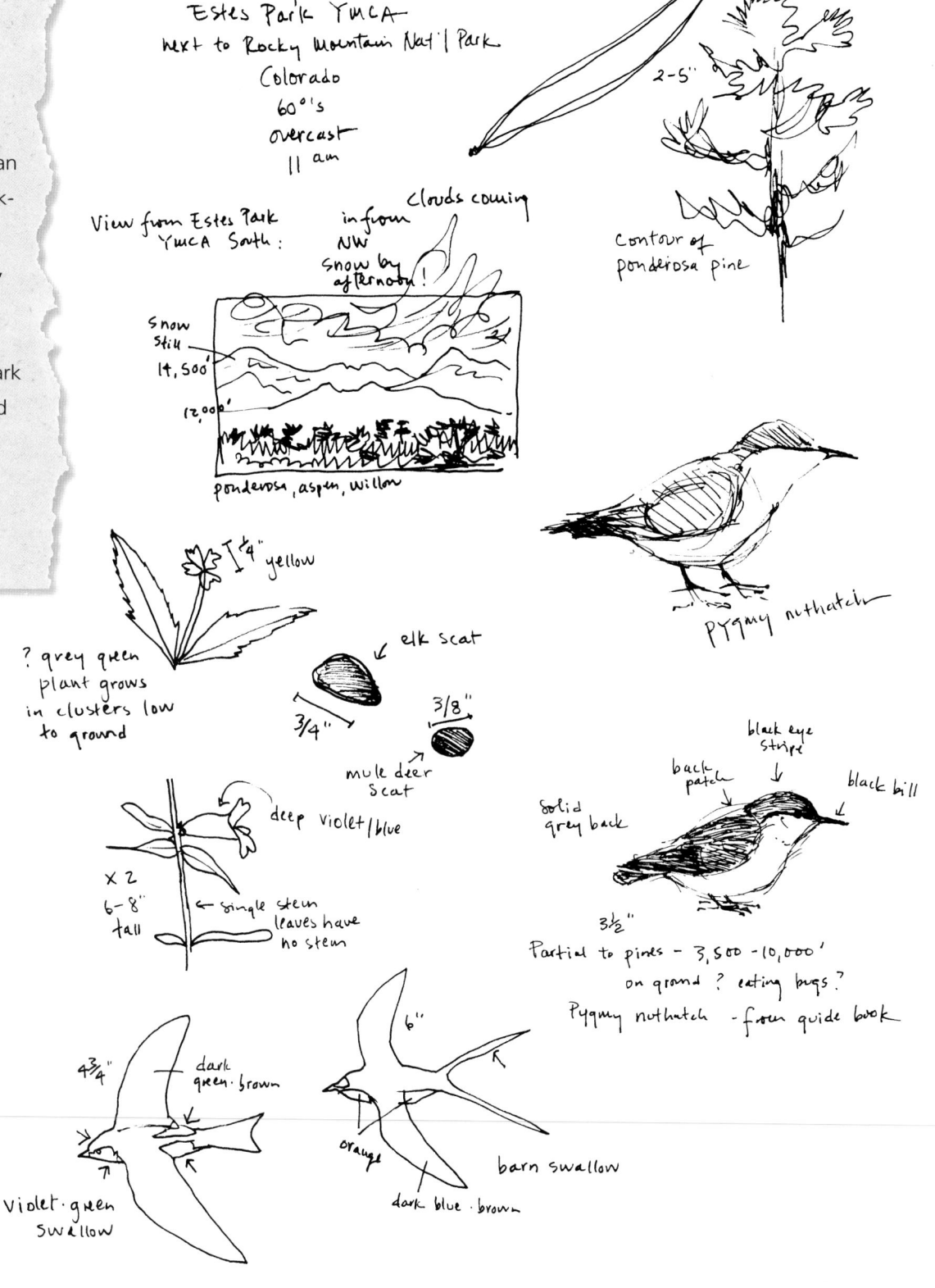

July 1
Estes Park YMCA
next to Rocky Mountain Nat'l Park
Colorado
60°'s
overcast
11 am

View from Estes Park YMCA South:

Clouds coming in from NW
snow by afternoon!

snow still 14,500'

12,000'

ponderosa, aspen, willow

2-5"

Contour of ponderosa pine

? grey green plant grows in clusters low to ground

I ¼" yellow

elk scat

3/4"

3/8"

mule deer scat

deep violet/blue

X 2
6-8" tall

single stem
leaves have no stem

Pygmy nuthatch

black eye stripe

back patch

black bill

solid grey back

3½"

Partial to pines — 3,500 –10,000'
on ground ? eating bugs?
Pygmy nuthatch — from guide book

4¾"

dark green-brown

violet-green swallow

6"

orange

dark blue-brown

barn swallow

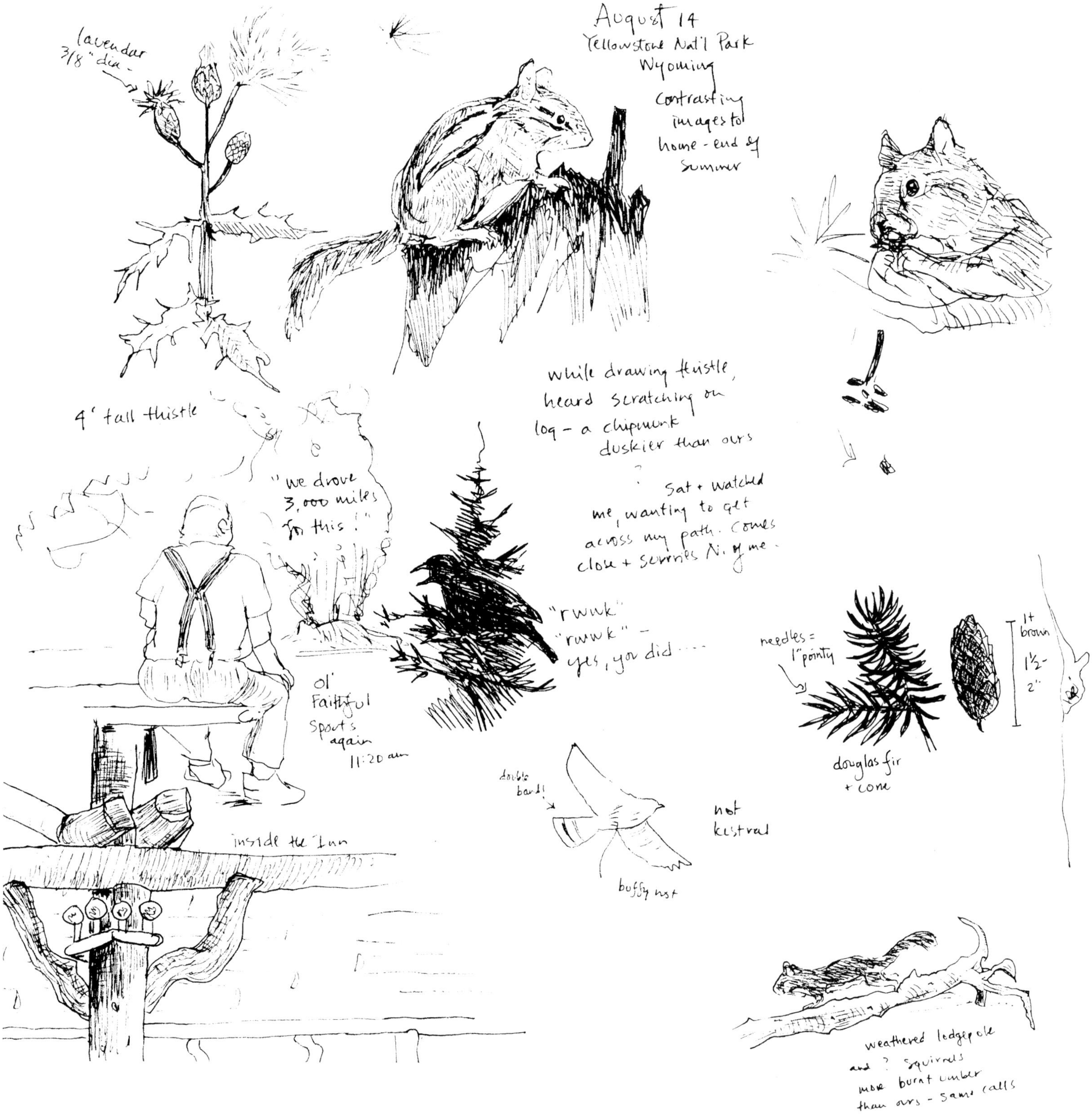

lavender 3/8" dia

August 14
Yellowstone Nat'l Park
Wyoming
Contrasting
images to
home - end of
Summer

4' tall thistle

while drawing thistle,
heard scratching on
log - a chipmunk
duskier than ours
?
Sat + watched
me, wanting to get
across my path. Comes
close + scurries N. of me.

"we drove
3,000 miles
for this!"

"rwwk"
"rwwk" -
yes, you did ....

Ol'
Faithful
Spouts
again
11:20 am

inside the Inn

needles =
1" pointy

douglas fir
+ cone

It
brown
1½ -
2"

double
band!

not
kestral

buffy rest

weathered lodgepole
and 2 squirrels
more burnt umber
than ours - same calls

Drawing household pets - When it's rainy out, evening, or you want an indoor project

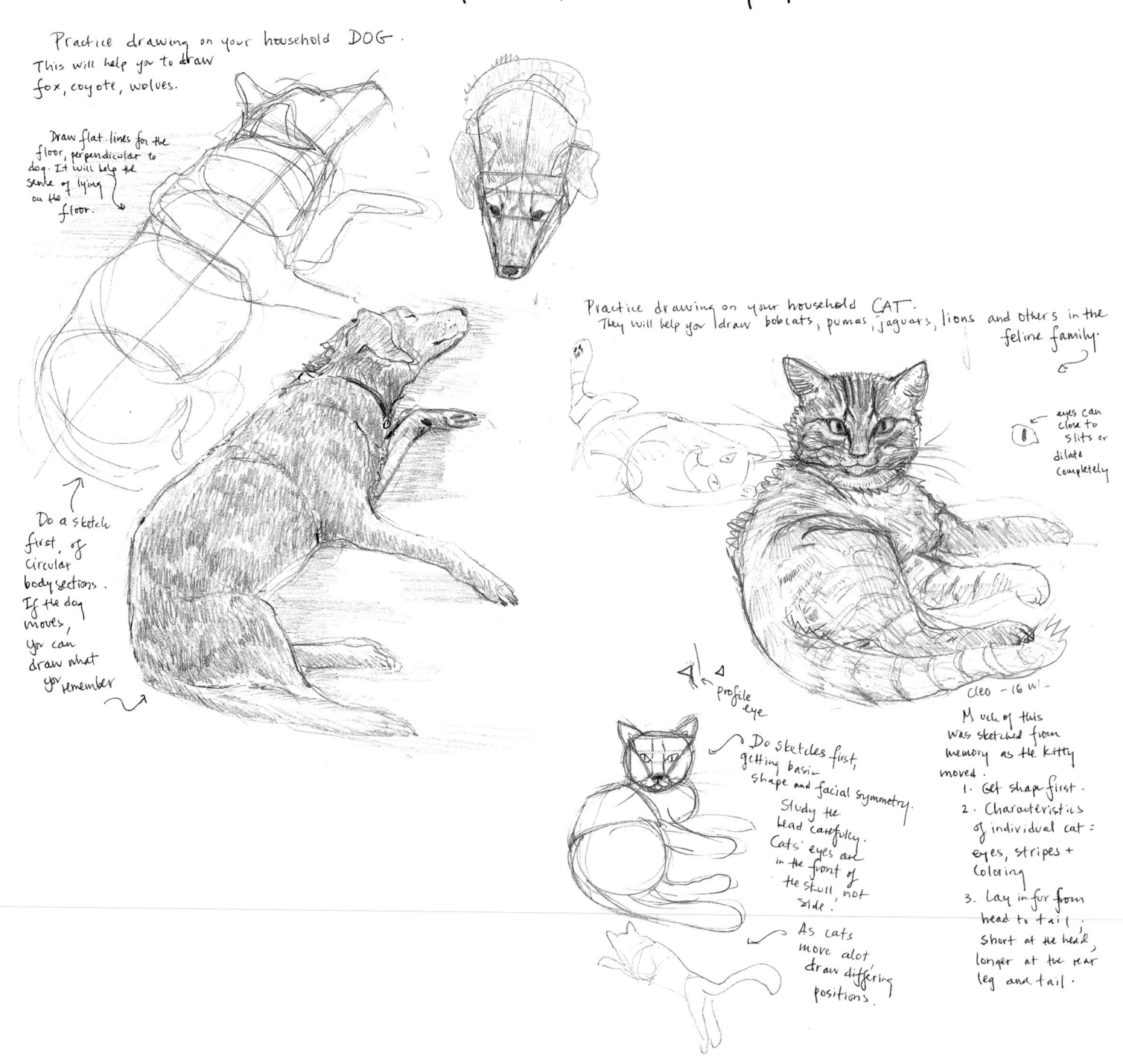

Practice drawing on your household DOG. This will help you to draw fox, coyote, wolves.

Draw flat lines for the floor, perpendicular to dog. It will help the sense of lying on the floor.

Do a sketch first, of circular body sections. If the dog moves, you can draw what you remember

Practice drawing on your household CAT. They will help you draw bobcats, pumas, jaguars, lions and others in the feline family.

eyes can close to slits or dilate completely

Cleo - 16 w -

Much of this was sketched from memory as the kitty moved.
1. Get shape first.
2. Characteristics of individual cat = eyes, stripes + coloring
3. Lay in fur from head to tail. Short at the head, longer at the rear leg and tail.

profile eye

Do sketches first, getting basic shape and facial symmetry.
Study the head carefully. Cats' eyes are in the front of the skull, not side.

As cats move alot draw differing positions.

facing N

wood pile

Compost

Summer
garden
journal

August 3

Granville
Vermont

sugar snap   PEAS   edible podded snow
onions

chard   beets

peppers   3x's lettuces

basil

broccoli

Corn

green
bean

red
potatoes   yellow
              squash   zucchini   gourds

cucumbers

Supper 8.5 = zucchini, a few old beans, tomatoes,
pepper, beets, lettuce

Garden Delights

Summer is the time to garden for many of us, and the garden is a wonderful place to observe at random the miracles of nature — seeds sprouting, growing, flowering, fruiting; insects pollinating and eating your plants; the effects of water and lack of it on plants; the ecosystem of a compost pile — all of which are grist for the nature journal. Try keeping a summer garden journal that allows you to compare the entries from week to week, biweekly, monthly, and year to year. This will help you learn what grows well in your conditions and what doesn't; it will also help you track how you rotate crops in various locations of your garden. Add notes on the dates you planted and harvested, germination success, and the times when various plant pests appeared.

Learning Species in Unfamiliar Places

Making simple drawings of plants, animals, people, and landscapes when in a new place can greatly help you learn about that particular habitat and what makes it different or similar to others you know. These sketches were done while Clare was conducting a week-long field journaling workshop for adults at the Sitka Center for Art and Ecology, in Oregon.

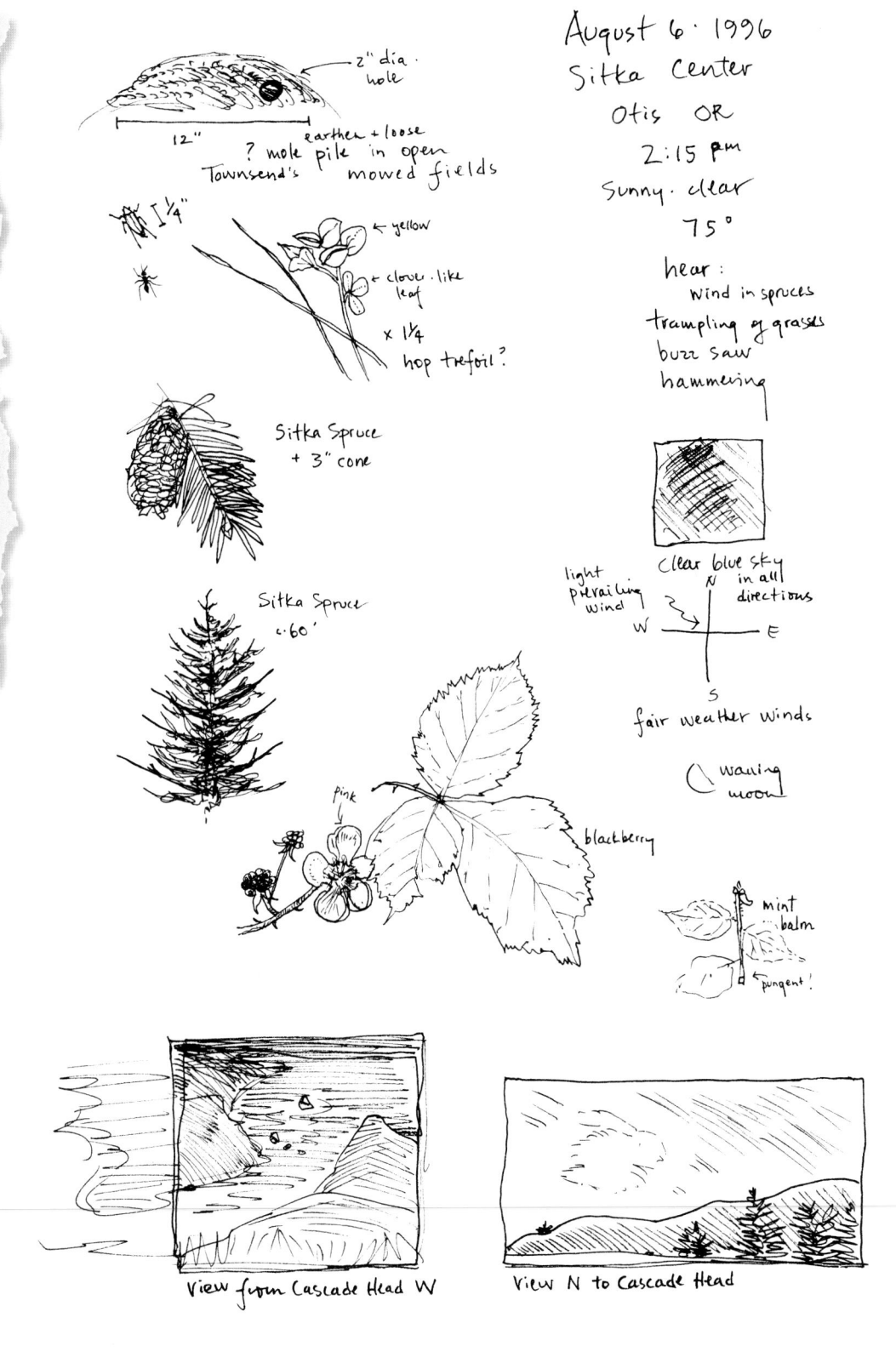

2" dia. hole

12"

? mole pile in open
earthen + loose
Townsend's mowed fields

I¼"

← yellow

← clover-like leaf

× 1¼

hop trefoil?

Sitka Spruce
+ 3" cone

Sitka Spruce
c. 60'

pink

blackberry

August 6· 1996
Sitka Center
Otis OR
2:15 pm
Sunny. clear
75°

hear:
wind in spruces
trampling of grasses
buzz saw
hammering

Clear blue sky
in all directions

light prevailing wind

N
W ——— E
S

fair weather winds

waning moon

mint balm

pungent!

Spruce

red alder

field

View West to
Pacific Ocean from
Sitka

View from Cascade Head W

View N to Cascade Head

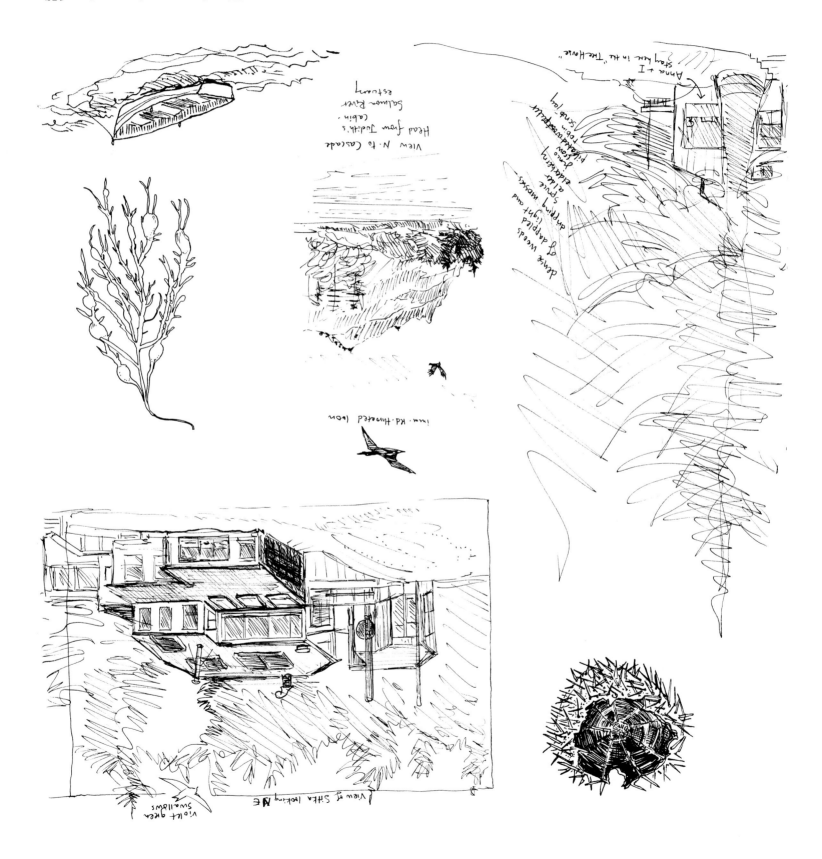

Pocket Pals

While roaming on the beach, through the woods, or even along the side of a country road, see what natural objects you can collect in your pockets. Then, in a quiet moment once back home, at your campsite, hotel, or friend's house, empty the stash and record the items in your journal. This is a good chance to take some time to work on developing your drawing skills (see chapter 9 for more guidance on drawing techniques).

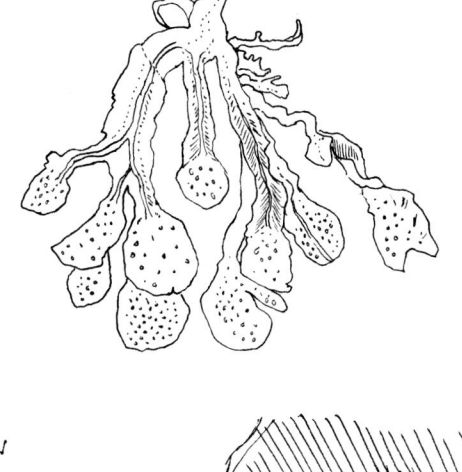

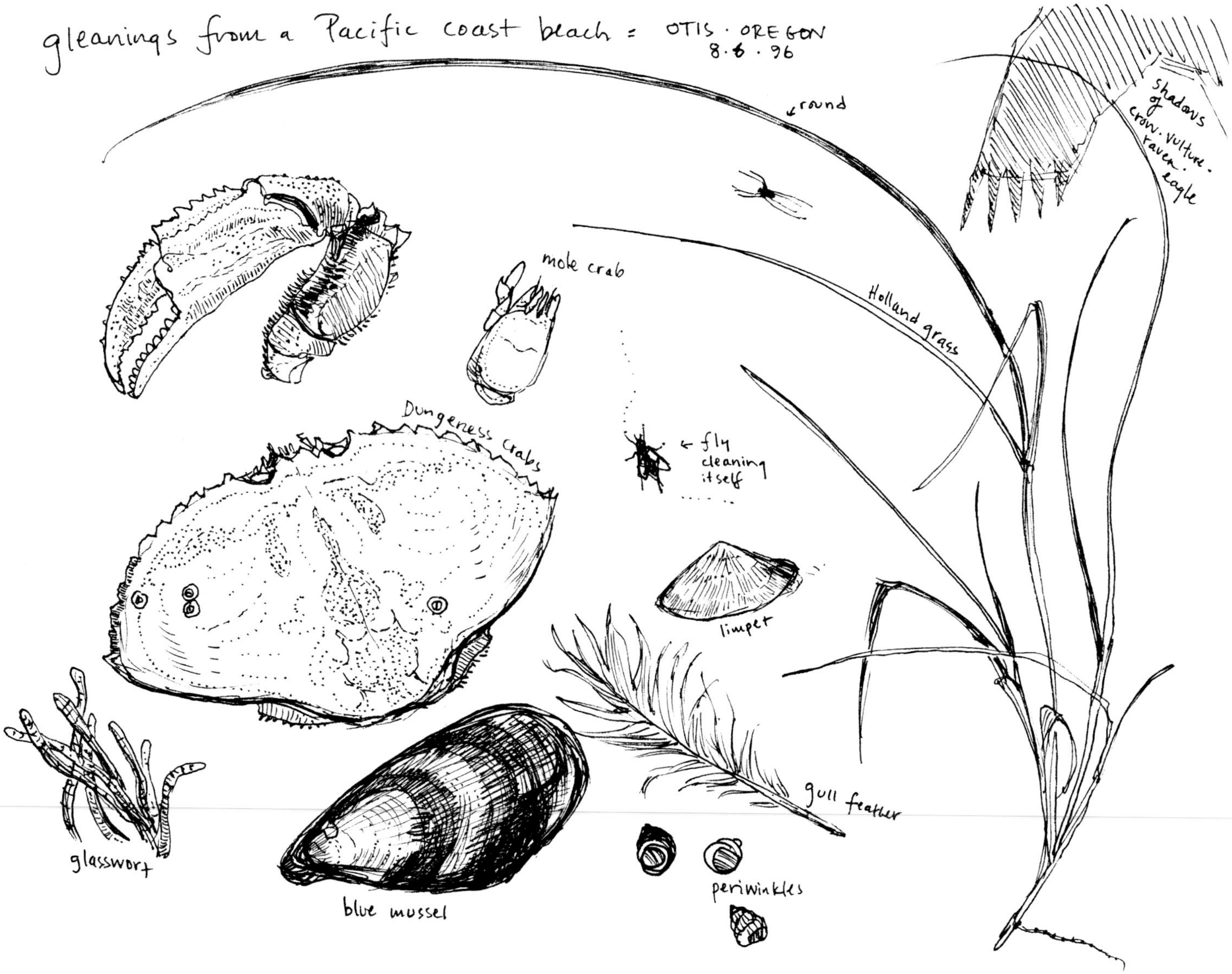

gleanings from a Pacific coast beach = OTIS · OREGON 8.6.96

← round

mole crab

Holland grass

shadows of crow · vulture · raven · eagle

Dungeness crabs

← fly cleaning itself

limpet

glasswort

blue mussel

gull feather

periwinkles

PART 3

Learning & Teaching
Nature Journaling

field study
Acadia NP-ME
6.24.95
cwr

It's amazing how many people have commented on our nature journals. We wish we'd started many years ago. English and art combined in journal writing should be a required course. What a joy to learn early and have nature journaling to enjoy for the rest of your life.

STEVE AND LYNDA CHANDLER, IN A PERSONAL LETTER TO CLARE, FEBRUARY 1998

4/30/97

Jake an oak tree

Getting Started with Drawing

As with any skill, it takes time and discipline and some concentration to learn and sharpen your drawing ability. Interspersed throughout the book up to this point are Nature Drawing Exercises and tips (see pages 76, 79, 99, 100, 111, 118, 126, 129, and 132). In this chapter, you will find some general suggestions for getting started and techniques for expanding your drawing skills. When you are ready to explore nature drawing in more depth, see the Suggested Reading for more in-depth treatments of the topic.

The dynamics of nature journaling may not always be conducive to drawing with a steady hand. You may be standing up drawing a roaming bumblebee or trying to capture the curve of crashing waves. You could be in the dark trying to record the eclipsing moon. Your cat might jump up on you just as you start to draw, or snow might fall on your paper while you're out cross-country skiing and stop a moment to record what you see. All of these are situations any devoted journalist faces and learns to work with; they're just the ins and outs of drawing from nature.

← heavy pressure

← medium

← light

cross hatch for shading

good for grasses whiskers fur

start heavy and flick up releasing pencil

PEN

The first day of Spring...

smudge for tones

erase for highlights

PENCIL

139

Drawing with Children Under 7 Years Old

Children under seven should only be exposed to limited drawing techniques; they are still exploring how they think they see things. An adult intervention could cause them to lose that freedom and possibly cause a long-term inhibition about any kind of drawing. When young kids are ready to learn technique, they will show interest. Give them individual techniques slowly, helping them keep their own self-confidence going.

pigeon

James Howard
age 9

Beginning Drawing Exercises

There are a number of tips and tricks that will help you gain confidence with basic drawing skills. The following eye-hand beginning warm-up exercises are a great way to get loosened up and tuned in to really looking at the form of an object before you begin actually journaling. These exercises do not take more than five or so minutes. They're actually similar to those traditionally used in art school figure-drawing classes. They are also akin to warm-ups before a sport or the warm-ups a musician does before beginning a lengthy practice or performance. In any skill training, warm-up exercises are highly encouraged. (For an excellent explanation of the warm-up exercises used in art schools, refer to the classic *The Natural Way to Draw* by Kimon Nicolaides; see Suggested Reading.)

Whether you're indoors or out, and whether you've done journaling before or not, we suggest a sequence of five warm-up exercises: blind contour, modified contour, quick gesture sketches, diagrammatic drawing, and finished drawing. Try them in sequence, then modify and rearrange them to fit your interests and journaling style.

These general categories of drawing techniques have obvious overlaps. You will soon find which type suits you, and for what purpose. They are best done in sequence, beginning with the blind contour. If you choose not to do them all each time you begin a drawing practice session, at least do one blind or modified contour exercise. Journalists invariably find the contour drawing immensely helpful in beginning to see how to draw any natural form, from shells to horses, clouds to trees. We suggest warming up before any drawing session by doing several sets of these exercises using various small objects that you may have around — leaves, seeds or seedpods, fruits or vegetables, feathers, twigs, or bones. Once you've mastered these, or if you are ready for more advanced techniques, you'll find more suggestions for quick ways to draw various natural objects on pages 147 to 153.

Exercise 1: blind contour.

This exercise is very good to try when you first see an object, and to get your hand onto the paper. It's a good warm-up for loosening and getting focused.

Without looking at your paper at all, keeping your eyes only on your object, "trace" in a continuous line across your paper everything you see. *Don't look, lift your pencil, or stop* until you have drawn all lines, outlines, markings, bristles, veins, eyes, feathers, and so on. You can go around the form from left to right, or right to left; just complete the form. Go slowly and look very carefully at your form. Don't peek at your paper! Think of yourself as a spider threading out a line. Complete in one to two minutes.

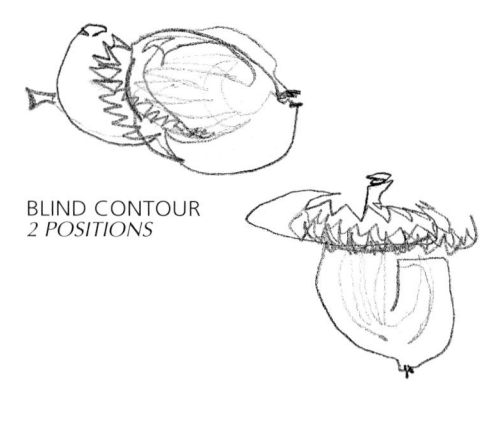

BLIND CONTOUR
2 POSITIONS

Exercise 2: modified contour.

Draw the same form that you made the blind contour of, allowing yourself to look at the paper, but be sure you do not lift your pencil off the paper. Draw with one continuous unwinding line, as before. Go slowly and stop only when you feel you have fully read your object. Complete in one to two minutes.

Compare the blind and modified contour drawings. Do you prefer one to the other? You may find a confident and strong line and a form surprisingly like what you are observing.

MODIFIED CONTOUR

Exercise 3: quick gesture sketches.

This technique is very useful for field artists because much of what we draw moves quickly!

Looking at your paper and the object at the same time, lifting your pencil as needed, now scribble down the whole form as fast as you can for five seconds; then try doing it in ten seconds; finally, take fifteen seconds to get your sketch down. Try to get the major sense of the form by looking hard and drawing the large, identifiable shapes. In art schools, this exercise is done by having the model move in timed sequences. With each move, the students try to capture the "gestalt" or essence of what they see.

If you want, try first a five-second, then a ten-second, then a fifteen-second sequence all on one drawing. We use this method, for exmaple, if a bird comes to a feeder and keeps returning to the same posture.

QUICK GESTURE SKETCHES

5 SECONDS

15 SECONDS

10 SECONDS

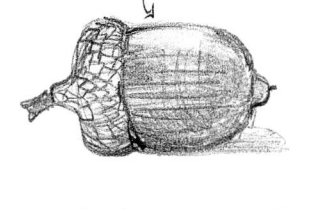

woody stem →

shallow, scaled cap

← large acorn about ¾"

smooth · brown

slight lines

DIAGRAMMATIC DRAWING

FINISHED DRAWING
10–15 MINUTES

Exercise 4: diagrammatic drawing. This technique is useful when you spot something you want to identify, but you don't have a field guide with you, can't take a specimen home, or are with a group that's hiking too fast for you to linger. We call these "proof-in-court" drawings, because they can prove invaluable evidence of things seen but not collected. This is the most common technique used by beginning nature journalists.

Make a simple line drawing, as if for a field guide identification. Add written notes of the object's size, color, shape, and name if you know it. Record enough to help you identify it later. Complete in three to five minutes.

Exercise 5: finished drawing. Use this technique to produce a more complete drawing. Now add volume, shading, and the various surface details of the shell, leaf, banana, rabbit, or whatever it is you are drawing. Often these lengthier drawings are done indoors from photographs, or from animals that do not move very much — owls, zoo animals, or museum mounts. You may use one of the sketches from your journal as a basic reference for a finished drawing. What begins as a quick sketch may end up as a finished drawing if, for example, the cow lies down, or the hen stalks closer. But, more often, the desired finished drawing ends as a

contour

half-sketch, when the hawk flaps off or the cat leaps away!

Set a time for yourself — fifteen minutes, one hour, two hours, or however long you wish. Draw a natural object or an assemblage of objects. Try one drawing in pencil and one in pen. Try one in colored pencil, and another in watercolor. Experiment!

Capturing Basic Shapes

Before you begin drawing, look at your object to see what geometric shapes you can find within the form. Having these shapes within in one or two blind or modified contour drawings first (see page 29) can help you get a handle on the real form. Draw over your contour to identify the major triangle, circle, or square shapes you see in the object. Draw an axis line if it helps. This will also help you with perspective issues. Connect the lines around the geometrics to get the overall shape of the object.

Next, try doing a gesture sketch using the knowledge you have of the geometric forms in your object. Thinking of forms as cylinders will help

you understand the third dimension or roundness of an object, such as the shell. This will also help you decide which direction you should use for shading lines.

Finally, do a finished drawing. Whenever applying pencil or pen, use lines or dots to show how your form curves and what is in shadow and what is not.

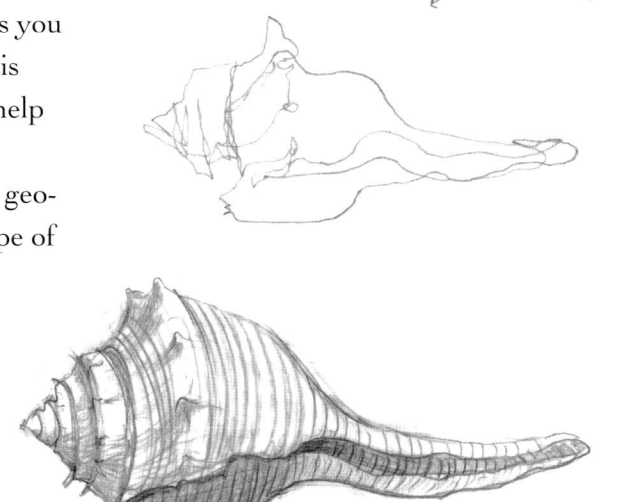

A good artist, scientist, or observer of any kind eventually becomes skilled at recounting from memory. We have found that many of the best wildlife artists paint or draw a great deal from memory. If, for example, that butterfly drifts off, keep drawing as much as you remember, and finish the details later from a guidebook.

Make a careful observation of something you see outdoors, such as a hawk flying through the sky. Memorize key features — tail shape and markings, shape of wings, color of belly, and approximate size. Draw a sketch from memory when you reach home. The best way to practice this skill is to stare at the object, memorizing five key features; when it hops away, draw what you remember.

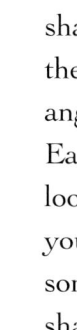

Try the Opposite Hand

If you want, try doing a blind or modified contour with your opposite hand. Also with the opposite hand, stand up, with your paper at arm's reach on a table. Now draw, and notice how loose and strong your drawings are getting. Have fun!

Opposite hand drawing

Foreshortening of Natural Objects

Objects will not always be in full profile. Try drawing them at an angle, or foreshortened, to see how their shape appears to change. Squint to flatten your depth of field, or use a contour drawing to see those "new" shapes.

Getting the Right Perspective

One of the trickier things to accomplish in a drawing is the proper perspective. When you view some-thing from the side or directly from the front you can re-create the basic shape fairly easily. When you view the same object from different angles, however, the shapes change. Earlier you were encouraged to look for geometric shapes within your object. Now you need to gain some experience drawing the basic shapes — circles, cubes, and cylinders — from different angles. Once you understand these forms, use them in sketching natural objects from the same angles by again including the modified geometrics in your contour or gesture sketches.

To get a sense of perspective in a drawing, you also have to determine in your mind where the horizon line would be. The horizon line is a basic reference point in almost everything we see; we perceive other objects in relation to that real or imaginary line. In drawing objects of the same size one behind another, the farther-away objects will appear smaller than those in the foreground. Parallel lines, such as road edges, railroad tracks, and the like, will appear to converge and get smaller toward the horizon line.

Some Basic Rules of Perspective

• Surfaces that are parallel to the picture plane appear in their "true" shape.

• Objects appear smaller in relative proportion to their distance from your eye.

• Receding parallel lines seem to converge away from the eye at a common vanishing point.

• Surfaces are foreshortened in relative proportion to their angle away from the picture plane.

• A circle that is parallel to the picture plane appears as a circle.

• A circle observed at an angle to the picture plane is foreshortened and appears as an ellipse.

• An object appears less distinct in proportion to its distance from your viewer's eye.

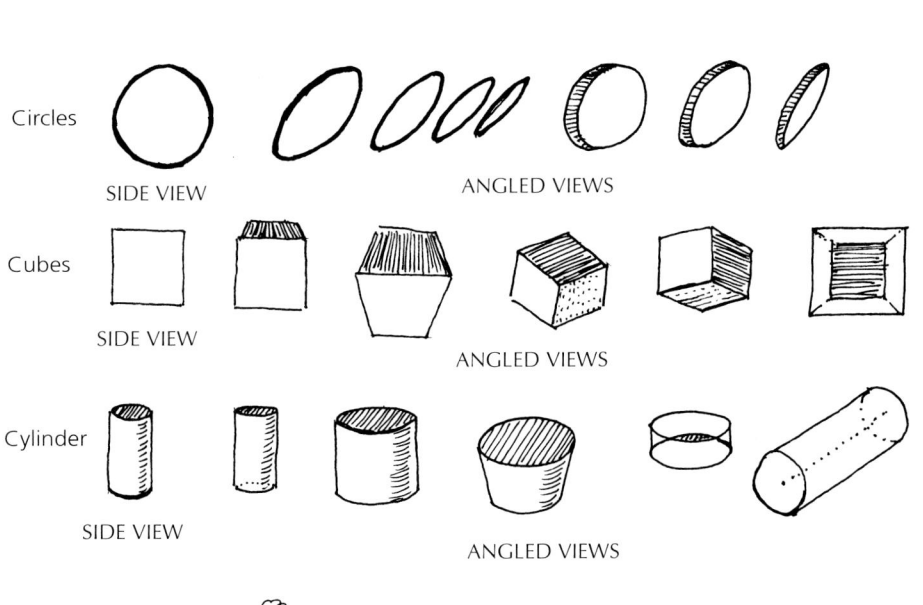

Circles — SIDE VIEW — ANGLED VIEWS

Cubes — SIDE VIEW — ANGLED VIEWS

Cylinder — SIDE VIEW — ANGLED VIEWS

Parallel lines and horizon line

Shading and Foreshortening

Shading can be done in pen with lines — parallel or cross hatches — or by using dots placed close together for dark shading and farther apart for light shading. Pencil shading can be done the same way, but more often it is done by solid rubbing, with greater pressure applied to dark areas than to light.

When shading, be sure to choose a direction from which light is coming, or from which you are going to assume light is coming. Be consistent about this light source throughout the drawing. For more exercises on drawing leaves, see page 79.

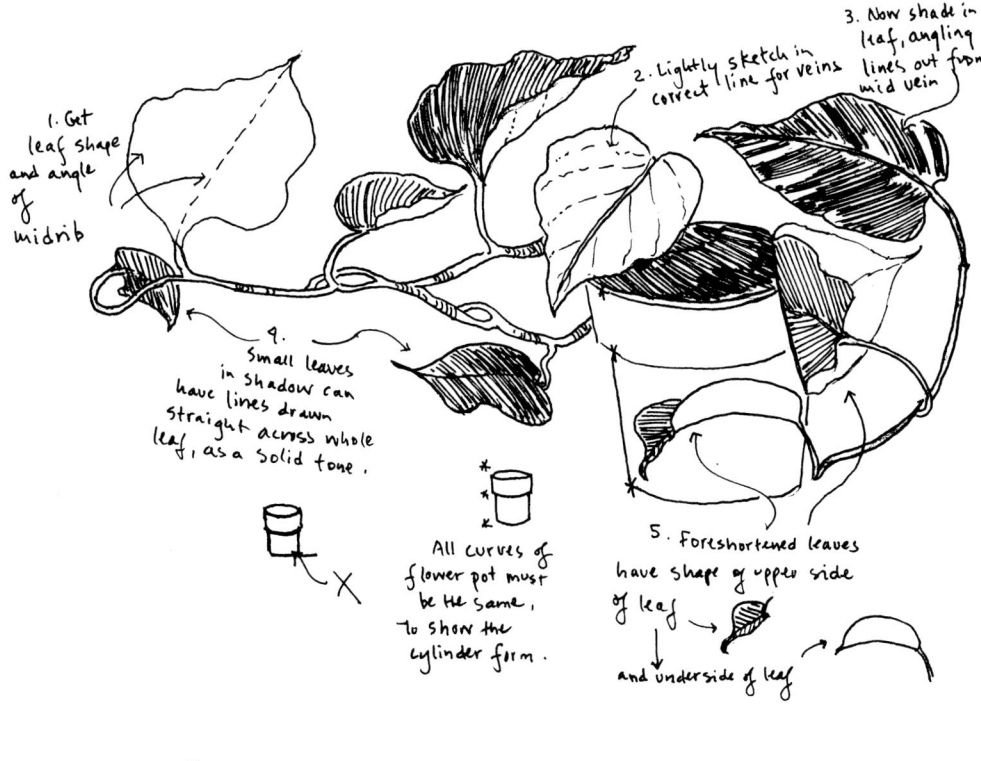

1. Get leaf shape and angle of midrib

2. Lightly sketch in correct line for veins

3. Now shade in leaf, angling lines out from mid vein

4. Small leaves in shadow can have lines drawn straight across whole leaf, as a solid tone.

All curves of flower pot must be the same, to show the cylinder form.

5. Foreshortened leaves have shape of upper side of leaf

and underside of leaf

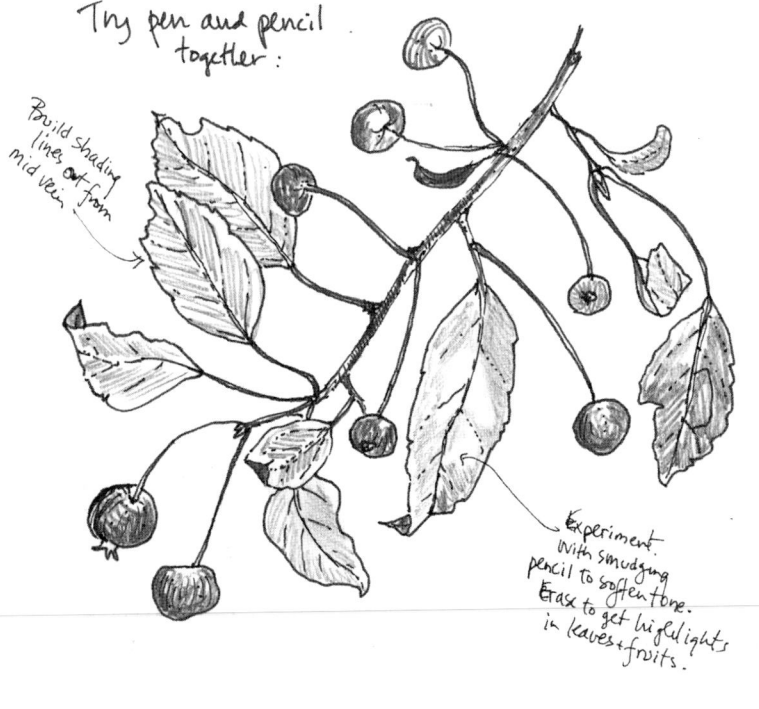

Try pen and pencil together:

Build shading lines out from mid vein.

Experiment with smudging pencil to soften tone. Erase to get highlights in leaves + fruits.

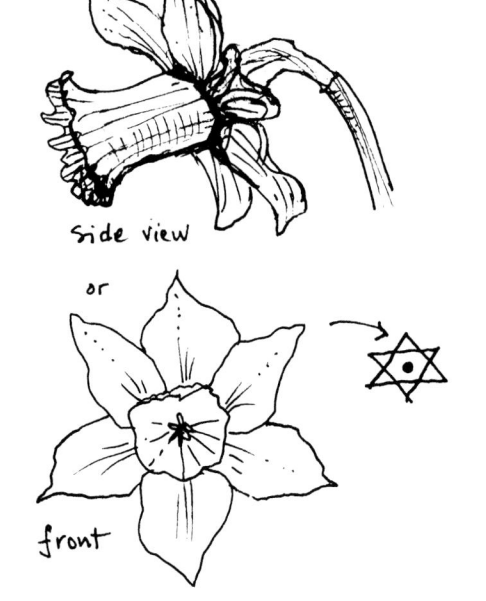

Profile   or

top view

Drawing Flowers

When you draw a plant with flowers, try following this sequence of steps and questions:

1. Observe the basic shape first.

2. See how the flower is put together. Where do the various flower parts attach to one another — petals, stamens, pistil, leaves, stem? Note which parts overlap one another.

3. Keep the drawing simple. If you're doing a complex flower head, like goldenrod, ragweed, or aster, do only part of the whole. Refer to illustrations in plant guides or gardening magazines for ways to draw plants and flowers.

4. Record where this flower grows; whether it is a tree, herbaceous plant, or grass flower; whether it is wild or cultivated.

Record the habitat in which you found it.

5. Trees, shrubs, grasses, and wild and cultivated herbaceous plants all have flowers, although the various parts of the flowers may be placed quite differently in the different kinds of plants. Where is the flower placed?

6. Keep a record of when various flowers bloom over the course of a year. You can learn a lot about weather, habitat, and soil type by tracking where and when particular flowers bloom.

For techniques on drawing deciduous trees, see page 76; for leaves, see page 79; for evergreens, see page 99; for winter deciduous, see page 100.

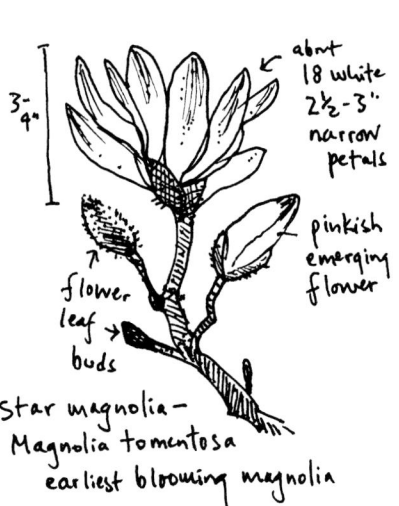

side view

or

front

about 18 white 2½–3" narrow petals

pinkish emerging flower

flower leaf → buds

3–4"

Star magnolia —
Magnolia tomentosa
earliest blooming magnolia

March 10 - Cambridge
neighbor's orange crocuses
in 1" of snow

Drawing Landscapes

In your nature journal, do not try to make a great drawing of a landscape. You are documenting a particular habitat — woods, field, ocean, coast, mountains. Landscapes give you the big-picture view of the area you are journaling in. There are some basic rules to follow in planning a landscape drawing and achieving a suitable sense of perspective. Because you have a flat piece of paper you must create the illusions of depth, distance, and space. Notice the differing angles of lines and strokes used on the next page to create the sense of mountains, rock faces, trees, and water. For more specific exercises on drawing trees, see pages 76, 99, and 100.

Keep your early landscapes small, no more than 5 x 7"

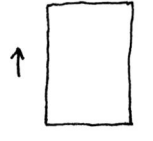
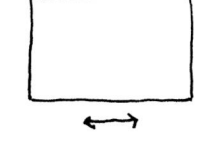

Which shape do you want? Draw one of these shapes on your paper. Then set up your landscape inside, like a picture _in_ a frame.

Suggested divisions:

2.

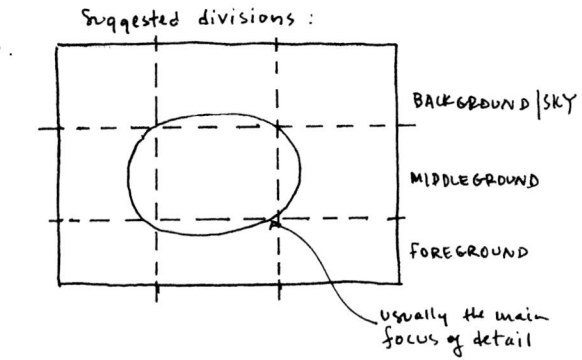

BACKGROUND/SKY

MIDDLEGROUND

FOREGROUND

usually the main focus of detail

A.

B.

3. If visually confused by a landscape, choose your four edges of your frame and do a CONTOUR DRAWING. Laugh, but look hard at the shapes in front of you, going from Foreground, to Middleground, to Background, or the reverse:

4. Remember, objects get smaller in the distance and roads, streams, rivers seem to converge:

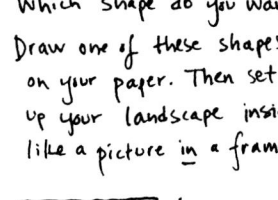

Background

Middleground

Foreground

perspective angle

not △ or △

sky lines drawn in at angles to suggest loft of the sky — an arching dome not flat

SHRUBS.

DECIDUOUS

EVERGREEN

1. Vegetation is drawn by symbols =

2. water must show symbols for movement =
   flat
   flowing
   reflections
   falling
   etc.

3. rocks have lines going in direction of planes.

Appalachian Mtn. Club
Lost Pond NH.
Nov. 20

Drawing the Weather

Weather surrounds us, so take the time to study and record rain, snow, sleet, fog, wind, and storms.

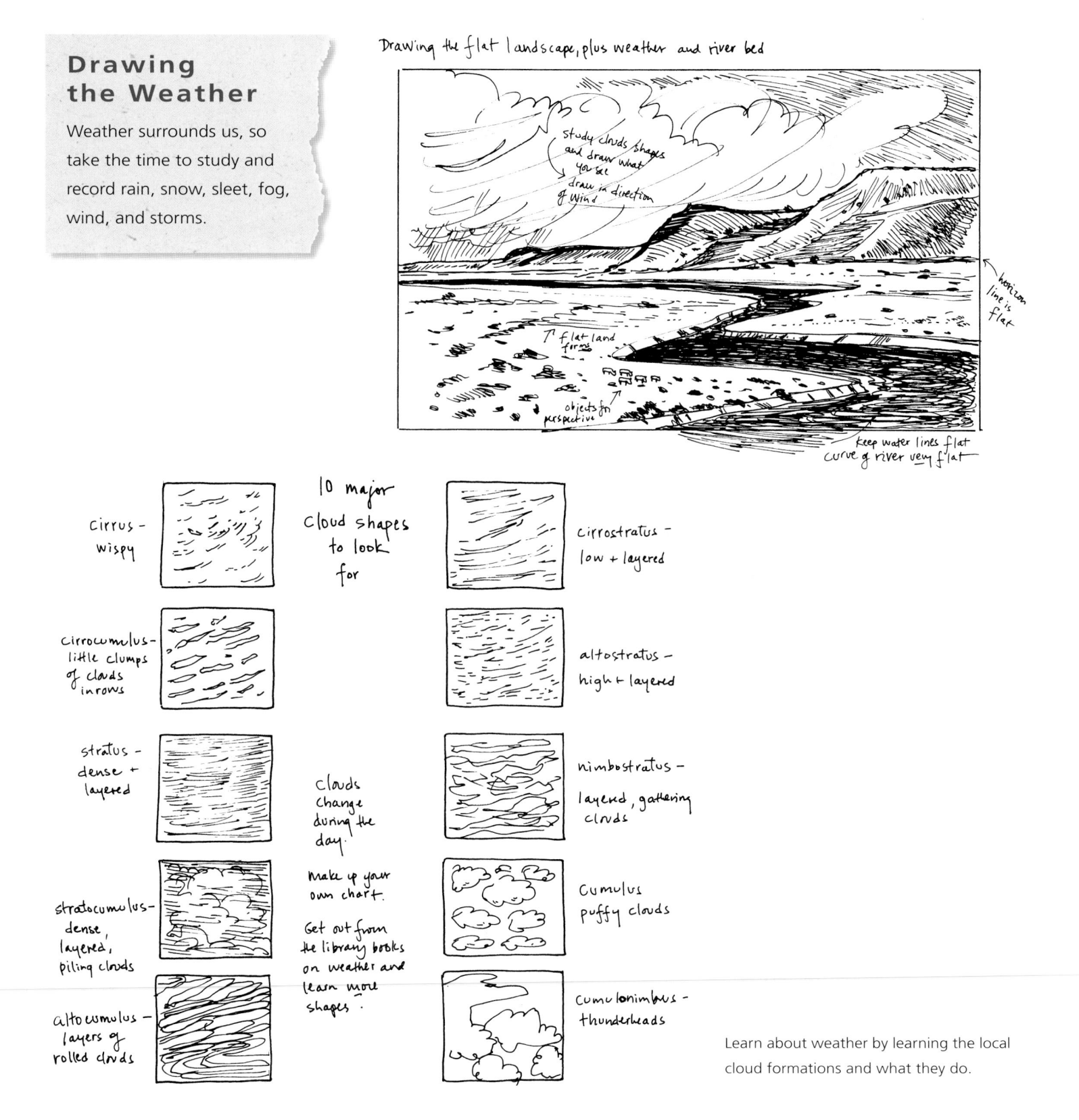

Drawing the flat landscape, plus weather and river bed

study clouds shapes and draw what you see draw in direction of wind

horizon line is flat

flat land forms

objects for perspective

keep water lines flat curve of river very flat

10 major cloud shapes to look for

cirrus - wispy

cirrostratus - low + layered

cirrocumulus - little clumps of clouds in rows

altostratus - high + layered

stratus - dense + layered

Clouds change during the day.

nimbostratus - layered, gathering clouds

Make up your own chart.

Get out from the library books on weather and learn more shapes.

stratocumulus - dense, layered, piling clouds

cumulus puffy clouds

altocumulus - layers of rolled clouds

cumulonimbus - thunderheads

Learn about weather by learning the local cloud formations and what they do.

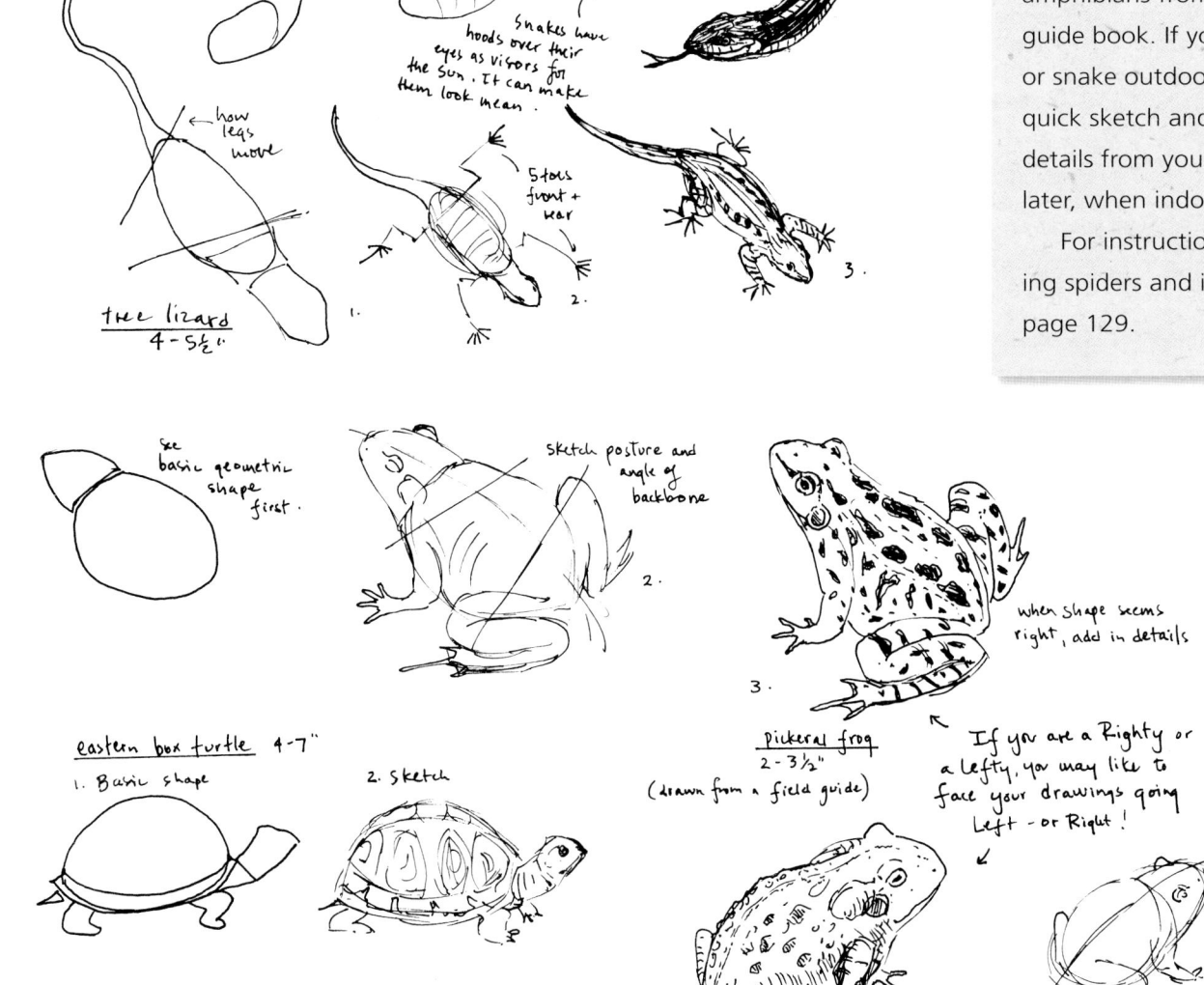

common garter snake 16-51"

1.

practice thin to thick width

2.

3.

follow pattern of scales

Snakes have hoods over their eyes as visors for the sun. It can make them look mean.

how legs move

5 toes front + rear

1.

2.

3.

tree lizard 4-5½"

Drawing Amphibians and Reptiles

It is easier to begin your dreaing of reptiles and amphibians from a field guide book. If you see a frog or snake outdoors, make a quick sketch and work in the details from your guide book later, when indoors.

For instruction on drawing spiders and insects, see page 129.

See basic geometric shape first.

Sketch posture and angle of backbone

2.

when shape seems right, add in details

3.

Pickeral frog 2-3½"
(drawn from a field guide)

eastern box turtle 4-7"

1. Basic shape

2. Sketch

3. Finished drawing

If you are a Righty or a Lefty, you may like to face your drawings going Left - or Right!

American toad 2-4"

3.

1.

2.

salamander

5 toes

all amphibians have: 4 toes

draw along spine and leg axis

Drawing Birds

Birds live all around us and make great subjects. They are easier to draw if you learn their basic anatomy and something about the kind of bird you are working with. Incidentally, most bird guides identify groups of bird species from the least evolved (most ancient) to the most evolved (most recent). First listed are loons, then grebes, fulmars, pelicans, ducks and geese, hawks, grouse, herons, cranes, shorebirds and gulls, doves, owls, parrots, woodpeckers, and last, all the little songbirds.

In drawing birds, start with the basic egg shape, then add other geometric forms to build the fundamental structure of the species. Feathers are arranged in groupings, whether on the tail, wing, back, or head. Carefully note the shape of the eye, bill, feet, and other specific features characteristic to the particular bird you are drawing.

See page 111 for more technique suggestions on birds.

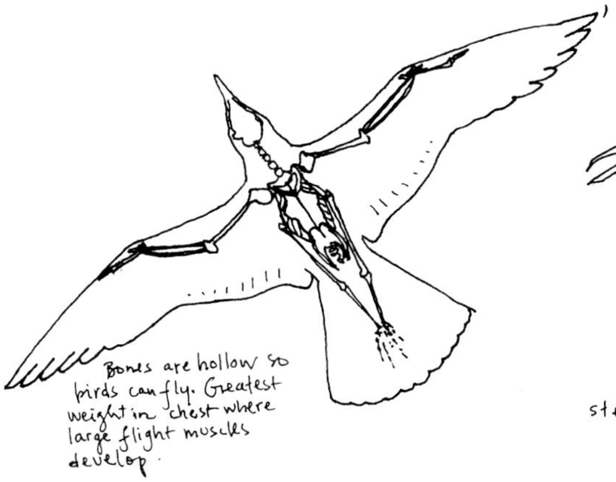

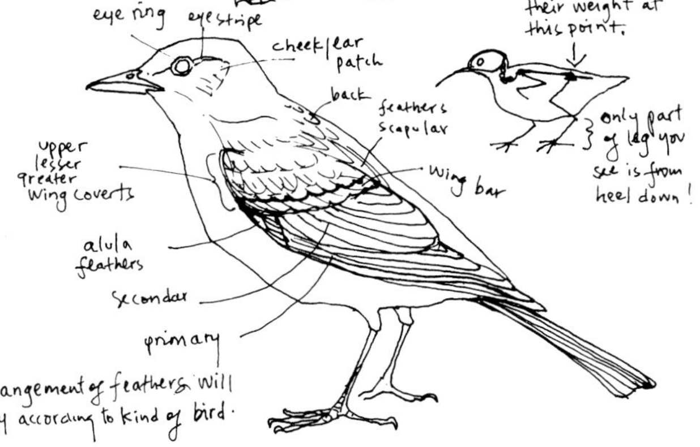

Bones are hollow so birds can fly. Greatest weight in chest where large flight muscles develop.

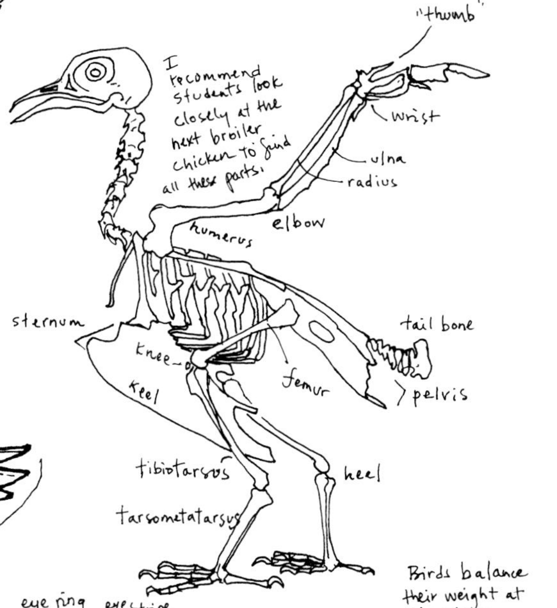

I recommend students look closely at the next broiler chicken to find all these parts.

"thumb"
wrist
ulna
radius
elbow
humerus
sternum
tail bone
knee
femur
pelvis
keel
tibiotarsus
heel
tarsometatarsus

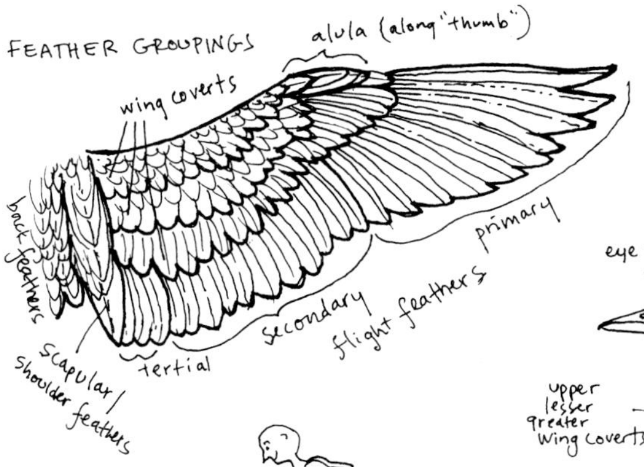

FEATHER GROUPINGS

alula (along "thumb")
wing coverts
back feathers
scapular/shoulder feathers
tertial
secondary
flight feathers
primary

Try walking like a bird!

Birds balance their weight at this point.

Only part of legs you see is from heel down!

eye ring   eyestripe
cheek/ear patch
back feathers
scapular
wing bar
upper lesser greater wing coverts
alula feathers
secondar
primary

Arrangement of feathers will vary according to kind of bird.

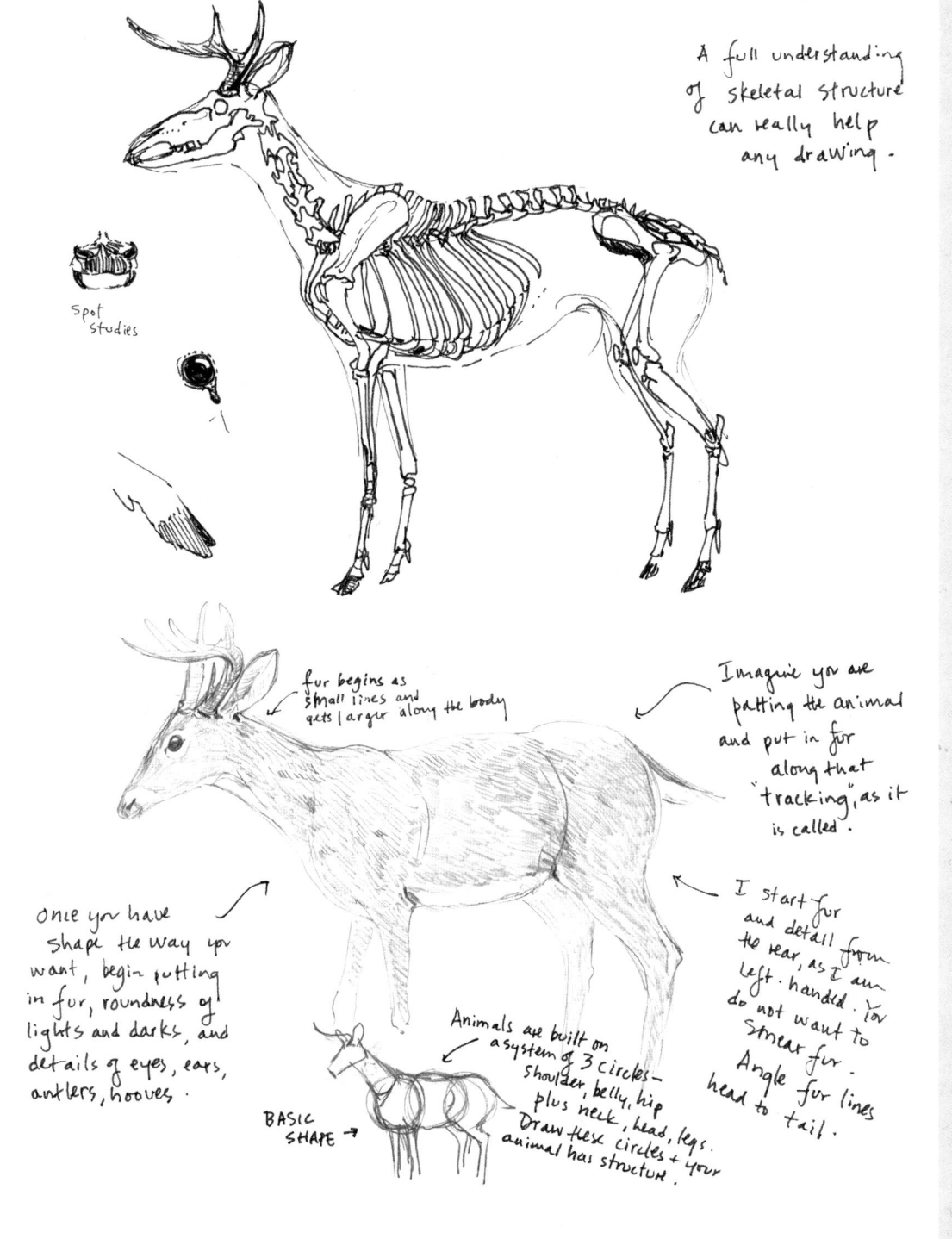

A full understanding of skeletal structure can really help any drawing.

Spot studies

fur begins as small lines and gets larger along the body

Imagine you are patting the animal and put in fur along that "tracking", as it is called.

Once you have shape the way you want, begin putting in fur, roundness of lights and darks, and details of eyes, ears, antlers, hooves.

I start fur and detail from the rear, as I am left-handed. You do not want to smear fur. Angle fur lines head to tail.

BASIC SHAPE →

Animals are built on a system of 3 circles— shoulder, belly, hip plus neck, head, legs. Draw these circles + your animal has structure.

Deer Anatomy

It can be very useful to draw from field guide photographs and illustrations; just remember that shadows, camera distortion, and quality of image can affect what you are seeing and thus the accuracy of your drawing. It is best to draw an animal first in full profile and with as little shadowing as possible. This way you can see all the parts clearly delineated and not confuse shadow with color pattern, or tall grass with a missing leg. Once you know the parts of the animal and its basic shape, then you can foreshorten it, draw it moving, or portray it lying down in the grass..

If you don't have access to pet cats or dogs, take your sketchbook and visit a local zoo, nearby farm, or even a pet store. Drawing live animals helps you really see how an animal "works." Science and natural history museums often have habitat dioramas with well-mounted examples of animals living in those areas. These animals are also helpful to practice on as they are in natural poses *and* do not move!

October 16 · 1988
Antioch / New England
          Graduate School
Keene N.H.

11:05
65°
overcast -
drizzle imminent

Behind Antioch:
  crickets
  feet walking on
  wet asphalt
  Goldfinch (?) in
  Willow

(...with my
father dying,
this is a time
of intense
need to
focus for
me.)

Doing a
contour
drawing

CHAPTER 10

Teaching Journaling to Groups of All Ages

Nature journaling is a great activity for informal groups of both children and adults in nonschool settings, from family outings to outdoor adventure programs, field study trips, home-school, Elderhostel, youth groups, and environmental studies programs. Fostering nature journaling involves stimulating curiousity about the world around. No matter what their age, race, language, or culture, anyone using a nature journal can find a place through which to discover a connection, a relationship with, the environment that surrounds us all. Once you notice something, stop to watch how it works, and learn something about it, a relationship has begun.

And, when you relate to something in this way, you feel differently about it. Caring fosters responsibility, and responsibility leads to action. As we both say, "If we are to help preseve what we still have, we must know what we are preserving."

While nature journaling, we can open a window, even if briefly, onto that expanse where we and it are one with, as the Chinese say, "the ten thousand things" around us. Watching people process this connection is a profound experience for the observer. Journalists slow down, stop fidgeting, soften face muscles, and drop shoulders. Silence and concentration reign — for perhaps five minutes. But we never forget these moments and

The native peoples who inhabited these lands long before us worshipped the Earth; they were educated by it. They didn't require schools and churches — their whole world was one.

MICHAEL ABLEMAN, ORGANIC FARMER,
GOLETA, CALFORNIA

Simply going out-of-doors has helped others shed socially assigned roles and discover an untamed, authentic self.

LORRAINE ANDERSON, *SISTERS OF THE EARTH*

Nature Journaling in pairs encourages later discussion to compare observations.

will be able to return to them. We owe ourselves these moments of connection, reflection, understanding, and calm. Nature is there for all of us to experience no matter where we live, no matter how joyous or distressed we may be — the sky overhead, the trees out our window, the bird that flies, the rain that falls.

Activities for Jump-Starting the Journaling Process

When you're doing group journaling with people of any age, try to limit the time devoted to each drawing or each written description. Probably about five minutes for each piece is about right for all ages. Detailed drawings and lengthier written pieces can be done later, or when the individual is working on his own. Carefully detailed and enriched drawings and refined writings can also be done when the journalists are reflecting on their journal pages at a later date. Following are several useful exercises for getting groups going.

The Living Camera

This is a combination observation and trust activity. Pair up

participants before going out. Take them to a site and individually have them roam it for about five minutes, searching for something that excites them and upon which they want to focus, such as an insect on bark, a colorful plant, a fallen seed, or an interesting leaf shape. Allow each participant to sit for five minutes and describe the selected object in his or her journal.

Now break off into pairs. Have partner number one wear a blindfold or close her eyes while partner number two guides her carefully to the object that he chose for his journal study. Partner number one then stands, kneels, or assumes whatever position is needed so that when she is allowed to look, she will be focused on the object.

She is then told to remove her blindfold or to open her eyes and observe. She should try to remember everything she sees. No talking about what is seen. The two people then reverse roles.

When both participants have seen the other's special object, ask both to add descriptions of this new observation to their journals. When the exercise is completed, either outside or back in the classroom, have the pair exchange journal entries and compare what each saw and described.

The Observers' Circle

Take the group to a site. Hold hands to form a large circle. Drop hands, turn around, and ask everyone to take ten paces straight ahead (as much as possible). Have everyone sit down and, for the next fifteen to twenty minutes, record everything they can see, hear, smell, and feel in that site. No talking with neighbors! The observations in their journals may include words, drawings, or both. After the observation period, invite the group to share the diversity of experiences.

As a leader/mentor you can help each student grow in his ability to express himself in the journal, whether by word or sketch or both. When reviewing his journal with him, ask probing, provocative questions that may expand the range or detail of things that he's attending to at the time. You can also make supportive or congratulatory comments on what he has perceived, drawn, or written.

Journaling with Children

At a public lecture, the renowned evolutionary biologist Ernst Mayr was asked by a high school biology teacher what he could do to teach his students the most important things they needed to know. Without hesitation Dr. Mayr replied, "The most important thing we can teach our young people is to observe well." That is what nature journaling is designed to do. As adults, taking up nature journaling with the children in our families and communities is one way we can help teach them about the world, and experience the world fully, with them. We have much to learn if we are to protect our home, Earth. (The word "ecology," comes from the Greek word *oikos*, meaning *house*. Ecology is the study of our home. We can live nowhere else!) Teaching an appreciation for nature may save a marsh, a river, a beach, a town, a child!

Teach your children what we have taught our children —
that the earth is our mother.
Whatever befalls the earth befalls the sons and daughters of the earth.
If men spit upon the ground, they spit upon themselves.

This we know. The earth does not belong to us, we belong to the earth.
This we know. All things are connected like the blood which unites one family. All things are connected.

Whatever befalls the earth befalls the sons and daughters of the earth.
We did not weave the web of life, we are merely a strand in it.
Whatever we
do to the web we do to ourselves.

— ATTRIBUTED TO CHIEF SEATTLE

Exploring Together

Discovering nature with children is an adventure. A committed, involved parent, teacher, or other adult can generate enthusiasm among the students. On this day, I journaled along with a fourth-grade class and their teacher. The ladyslippers were magical — and real. We all wanted to get in close and draw them more carefully. The heron egg still puzzles me. The child who found it was so excited. Four or five of us drew it carefully so we would be able to identify it accurately later.

We stood and drew for forty-five minutes. The children were so involved, they were ready to continue doing it all day. Later in the day, after I had left, the teacher took the children out again to see if the owl was still in the tree. She continued to guide the students in nature journaling projects throughout the year, helping them to identify what they found and develop new confidence in drawing outdoors.

Nature journaling lends itself to intergenerational activity. Parents can keep journals with their children. Grandparents can do nature journaling with their grandchildren. Keeping and sharing nature journals with members of our immediate or extended families helps all of us develop our observational skills, and is fun as well. It offers a chance to learn about each other's perspectives, values, and interests. For children, this process is a great way to develop a wide range of skills, since journaling is truly multidisciplinary. Keeping a nature journal over time will reveal the young journalist's gradual learning and skills development.

"It spits leaves out of the top of the blossom"

beautiful pink lady slippers in the woods

"I never knew there was so much nature in the woods."
Stephanie Fish 2nd grade

"I had so much fun."
"I didn't. There were too many bugs."

mockingbird
northern oriole
titmouse
crow
? warbler

April 20
Sanborn elementary
4th grade
Andover. MA.
sunny 60°'s
perfect spring day

we found numerous feathers — owl hawk crow

We dissected an owl pellet - baby rabbit?

we think we saw silhouette of an owl in pine tree

2½"

turquoise w/ no spots
? egg

large!
found by one little boy
2" egg broken

Encouraging Ongoing Journal Keeping

There is no magic way to getting your kids in the journaling habit, but the following tips may be helpful:

- Keep a journal along with the kids. You are a mentor and if you find and take the time to overtly maintain your journal, the kids are more likely to as well.

- Use the journals regularly as learning aids. The more you have kids turn to their journals both to record and reflect, the more they will see the need to keep them going.

- Help kids see that setting up nature journals ties them to a long tradition of science and history study — a way of learning that is still of value today. Other types of journaling are also widely used in various professions — ship captains, pilots, and explorers keep detailed logbooks of their activities; artists keep detailed sketchbooks to refer to; scientists keep journals of their observations and experiments; writers keep journals of their observations and feelings about people and places, which they draw upon in their work.

- Encourage kids to have a private corner of their journals, a section they might call Inside ME.

Here they can write down their innermost feelings in safety. The Inside ME section is never to be reviewed by a leader. It is that quiet, safe place reserved to them alone. This section will help the youngster strengthen the notion that "nature is part of me; I am part of nature."

Involving Adults in Journaling

Engaging a group of adults in nature journaling is often more challenging than working with young people. Adults have generally developed more reserve and have unwarranted expectations of themselves. They don't want to seem ignorant or unskilled, even when they're doing something totally new to them.

Adults may also bring negative remembrances of school and previous art classes into a group with them, even though they have enrolled in your workshop. As a leader/mentor, you invest the time to develop a real rapport with the group members. Help them see that you are not out to embarrass them or criticize their efforts. You will need to show them your own

Teachers and students enjoy interacting over a journal.

Journaling with a group helps build confidence in individual styles.

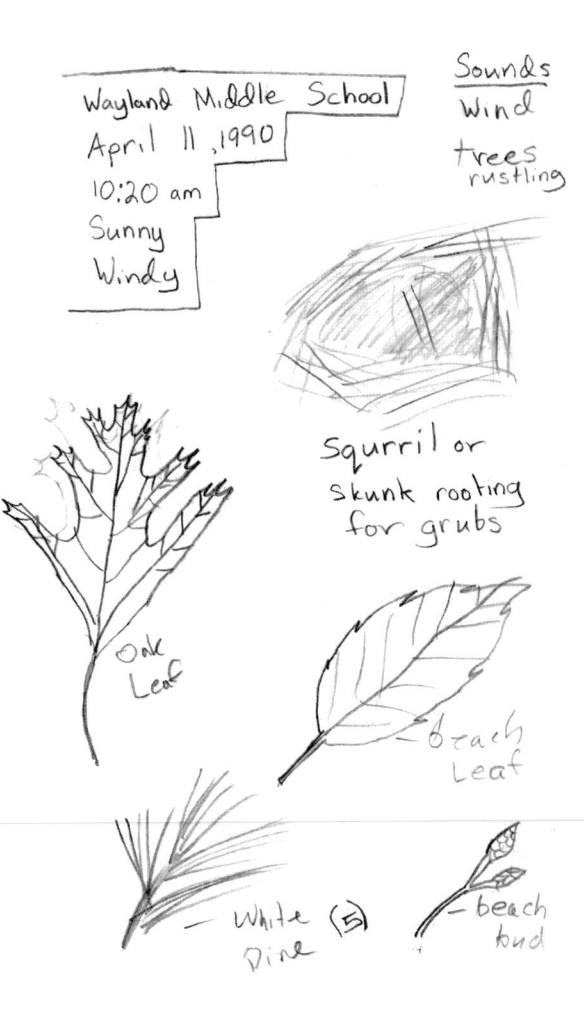

Wayland Middle School
April 11, 1990
10:20 am
Sunny
Windy

Sounds
Wind
trees rustling

squrril or skunk rooting for grubs

Oak Leaf

beach Leaf

White (5) Pine

beach bud

telling, point out the great diversity of things people were attending to, even though they were all in the same area.

Ask how many were drawing their observations; how many were writing and how many were combining writing and drawing. Ask if any were using a different method of recording their observations. Affirm that all these ways are valid, and that just as people were attending to different things in their environment, they were also using a variety of means to record what they were sensing.

The key is to help people feel comfortable in their individuality and present skill levels. If you repeat this exercise several times during the first few sessions, you will generally see a relaxing of tensions in the group and more and more people settling into their journaling with joy and abandon.

Establishing Individual Study Plots

Having students choose their own individual places to observe in detail over a period of days, weeks, or months can not only increase their sense of belonging to a natural place, but also encourage greater awareness of the subtleties of change within a

enthusiasm and joy in doing nature journaling, and share with them your roughest as well as your most polished efforts. Confirm their efforts from the beginning; reaffirm their work continually.

Softening the Barriers

Try taking the group to several spots that are of broad interest. Get the group to cluster in the area and find a place they want to stay in for ten or fifteen minutes. Have them make journal entries there. When the time is up, ask the group to gather around, and have each person briefly describe what caught her attention. This should not involve direct presentation of journal entries at this point. When all have finished small area. Have each student select and define a 5-foot by 7-foot, 15-foot by 20-foot, or 25-foot by 30-foot plot to observe. Then ask them to draw and write their observations on a regular basis, in the early morning, late afternoon, after dark, and at any other regular intervals, noting weather changes, tree species, diverse plant species, animal evidence, and activity, and any human evidence and activity in that plot. Ask each student to draw/write from different positions in his plot: north, south, east, and west. Have him draw/write lying down, sitting, crawling like an animal, standing, hiding like a prey hiding from a predator. Ask him to draw a map of the plot.

Blending Individual and Group

At each session, set aside some time for individuals to share their observations and journal entries with the rest of the group. No one should be forced to share. At first, sharing from you as a leader may be all the sharing you get. As time passes, however, more and more members of the group will be willing to share what they are observing, and the group will find much enjoyment and learning in the sessions. Expect that there will be some people in every group who are shy or withdrawn and want to keep their observations and journals strictly private. Honor this!

Help the people in the group understand that you are only the nominal leader of the group. The only thing that truly sets you apart from them is that you may have been keeping a nature journal for a longer period of time. In truth the group is a peer learning group — everyone learns from all the others. One may be skilled in visual perception, while another's talent may be in auditory perception. Some group members will shine at spotting fine details, while others are quick to see the broader context that the detailer may miss. Each member of the group will grow in his own way while gaining from the insights of the others.

Something about this January has been different from my first two winters in Williamstown and I don't think it's the weather. I think it's my eyes . . . Carrying my journal with me around campus and looking closely at the shape of branches, needles, and the patterns of prints in the snow, I started to realize that life was still out there in winter, we just had to look at it differently.

TIM STODDARD, WILLIAMS COLLEGE JUNIOR

Little Miracles Happen

The Caryl School in Dover, Massachusetts, has a nearby outdoor classroom. The four fourth-grade classes study it all year long with short but frequent visits. For eight years, Clare has worked with the students and their teachers to help them become better observers of what can be found in the wooded area between a firehouse and the busy street.

This class had drawn the usual plants, trees, mushrooms, and occasional salamanders. The children, as is usually the case, had through their drawing become very attuned to the woods. It was the teacher who said "shhhh,"

and there, just beside her, in a honeysuckle bush had landed a small, dark bird. It flicked its tail, balanced confidently on the slender branch, and eyed us curiously.

Thinking it would fly right off, Clare whispered, "draw!" Silently all twenty-four children peered around to draw the tiny bit of wildness. "Why might it be here? Where is it headed? What key features do you need to draw to identify it?" Clare asked softly. For a good ten minutes, they had eye contact with the bird, and with nature untamed.

written down as the students spoke spontaneously =

"We are on a roll!"

"I feel so happy"

"Let's stay out all day"

"This is so fun"

← red berries mice eat all winter

long veins

Canada Mayflower

6"

veins like a hand

red maple

hole beside tree trunk base — Chipmunk

October 3 Caryl School Dover MA

1½"

write/draw key ID features →

Indoors we identify the bird from a field guide — a fall plumage phoebe

black

no eye ring

3' away — around 5"

yellow

gray

loose feather wounded?

bobs

black feet

notch

A small gray bird lands on honeysuckle just 5' away from us and stays almost 10 minutes. We draw, try to identify and get very excited to be this close to a wild bird.

Journaling with School Groups

Nature journaling is a powerful tool for breaking the bonds of viewing our world through isolated and separate disciplines. Instead, it incorporates sciences, local social and natural history, math, language, art, and physical education into one, integrated practice. The developmental sequence in journaling usually begins with recording simple objects and events; in time it progresses to putting these objects and events into contexts that stress connections among objects and events. The accomplished journalist comes to focus on whole systems and their meaning to her life. Journaling can become a personal journey into development of a real sense of place and a holistic vision of life.

We have observed hundreds of students exploring the outdoors, paper and pencil in hand, carrying abundant energy and varying degrees of curiosity, then finding a squirrel or leaf or spider to attach their attention to. The connection is made and the students are amazed at how good their drawings can be. There is no such thing as a child who does not love nature; all kids simply need to be taught ways to connect.

We must draw our standards from our natural world. . . . We must honor with the humility of the wise the bounds of that natural world and the mystery which lies beyond them, admitting that there is something in the order of being which evidently exceeds all our competence.

— VACLAV HAVEL, *LIVING IN TRUTH*
(LONDON: FABER & FABER, 1989)

Enthusiastic grade school students surround Clare as she demonstrates a technique.

At this change of millenia, schools are in another cycle of reform, of trying to be sure that they teach young people what they really need to know to lead worthwhile lives. The long-time industrialized approach, the so-called factory model of school-ing, has failed many; some of the new reforms still focus primarily on developing more efficient, productive workers for a new century. The better reforms focus on developing healthy, holistic learners who can meet the challenges of creating truly sustainable societies and economies on what has become a somewhat diminished planet. Nature journaling, by helping learners become observant or immersed in, and reflective on, the world around them, sets the stage for life-long self-learning from primary sources.

This "curriculum web" shows one way of understanding the interconnected topics, skills, and traditionally defined disciplines that nature journaling links together. This reflects Barnstable, Massachusetts teacher Susan Stranz's under-standing of the process; you may develop your own web.

Yew

mapl LF

Kari

A Curriculum Web for Nature Journaling

EARTH SCIENCE

- Plants
- Insects
- Birds
- Other animals
- Trees and shrubs
- Habitats and seasons

- Weather
- Observing
- Identifying
- Measuring
- Comparing
- Listing

SOCIAL STUDIES

- Local history
- Natural and human communities
- Environmental health in history
- Mapmaking

Nature Journaling

PHYSICAL EDUCATION

- Walking and exploring
- Outdoor activity
- Hiking

LANGUAGE ARTS

- Written: poetry, prose, fiction, nonfiction
- Oral: description, problem solving, communication
- Listening: group communication, group sharing, oral learning

MATH

- Measurements
- Charts
- Graphs
- Mapmaking
- Computation

ART

- Hand-eye skills
- Self-confidence and social skills
- Learning to compose work supportively

- Observational drawing versus imaginative drawing
- Different forms of art expression
- Mapmaking

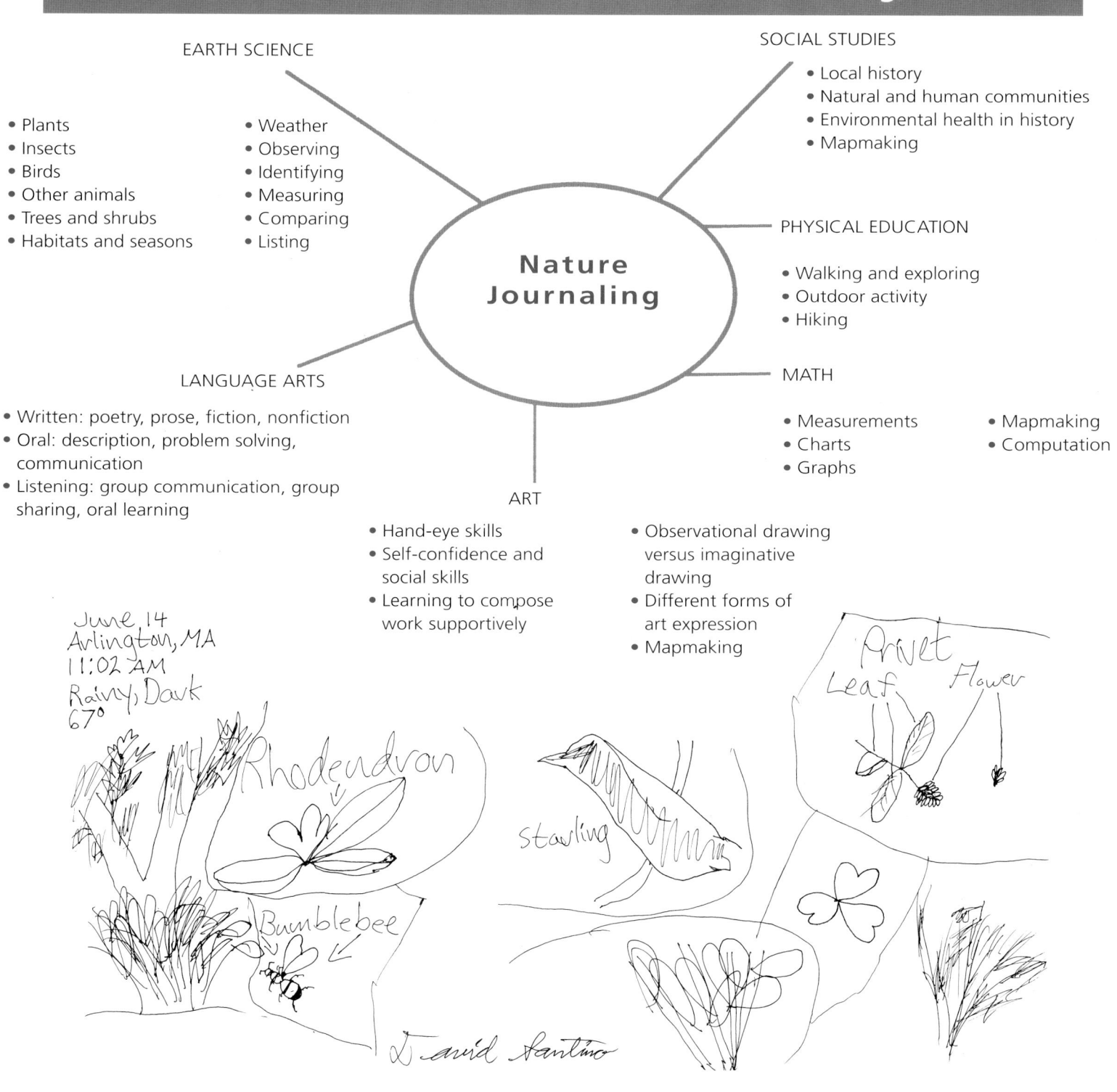

June 14
Arlington, MA
11:02 AM
Rainy, Dark
67°

Rhododendron

Bumblebee

Starling

Privet
Leaf

Flower

David Santino

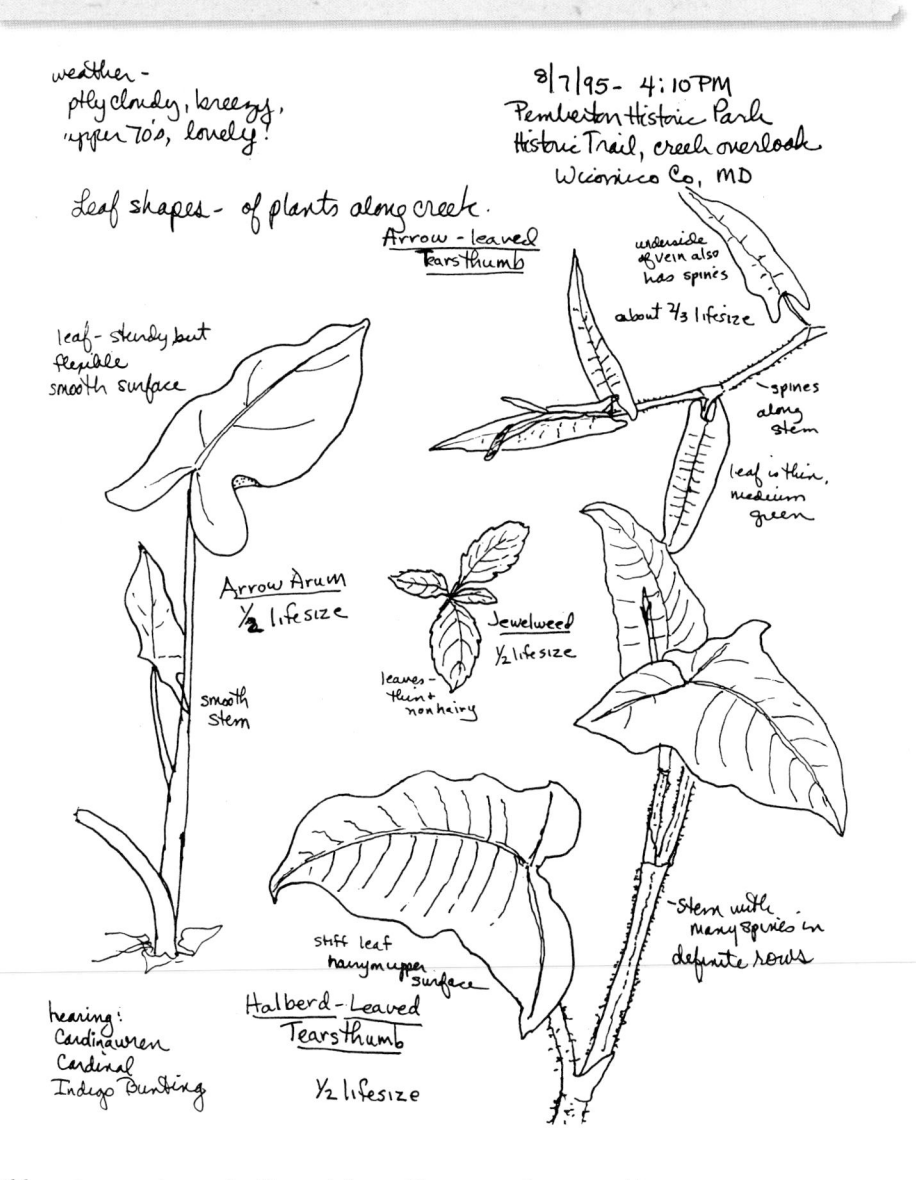

The Teacher/Leader Role

As a teacher or leader, you need to create learning situations that stimulate learners to begin writing or drawing in a journal. As time passes, start asking students what connections they see between recorded objects and the rest of the world around them. Stimulate them to record the broader context for each object and event they're attending to. Finally, urge them to record how they feel about what they are observing, and what meaning the observations have in their lives.

It is important for you to journal along with your students. This demonstrates to them that journaling is an important activity, not just another directed student task. It also helps them see that learning is an ongoing, lifelong activity — particularly if you share some of the things you learned during the journaling session.

If you are using nature journaling in a classroom and wish to assess the individual journalist's progress, it is wise not to try and assess all aspects of her development at once. Choose only one or two aspects at a time. You might proceed as follows:

- Write down the changes observed as you read through the journal.
- With the journal keeper, work through a list of criteria that will give some indication of the degree of improvement. Criteria can include specifics about the skills and activities noted above. (See page 177 for suggestions on assessing journaling activities.)
- The actual evaluation using the agreed-upon criteria can then be done by the journalist, or with her consent; or it can be done by another journalist who, in turn, shares his journal with the group.

There are great benefits for the journal keeper who engages in assessing her journaling skills. There is the satisfaction in seeing tangible evidence that she is truly learning something, whatever her age. This recognition motivates the journal keeper to continue the effort.

Creating Windows Into Perception

Looking at the journals of other people can give you insight into how they see their world, interact with it, respond to it, challenge it, and accept it. The best way to encourage your students to see and observe is through careful

Eyes to the Sky

A good example of journaling as part of a school program is the For Spacious Skies project founded by Jack Borden. Writer Elizabeth Levitan Spaid described this program in the *Christian Science Monitor*:

"On an overcast spring day, Elaine Messia's fifth-graders at the Mitchell Elementary School in Needham, Mass., file out their classroom door clutching chairs, notebooks, and pens. In a grassy yard they scatter like wildflowers across a meadow, as they plop their chairs down in different spots. Soon, the chattering stops as they begin what has become a ritual: observing the sky and writing what they see in their 'sky journals.'

"After 15 to 20 minutes of pensive silence, they return to the classroom to share their poems and verse.

"'The clouds look like a white sheet on a bed,' Melissa Volpe says. 'There are gray spots on the sheet. When the gray clouds fade away, it's like a sheet that has been washed.'

"'It's like a gray arena, motionless, lifeless,' one boy writes.

"For these children, looking up is an integral part of their curriculum. Whether it is creating cloud charts for science, finding sky references in literature, or observing the kind of skies that provide background in Van Gogh or Monet paintings, the sky is woven into nearly every activity or lesson.

"This particular writing exercise 'gives students time to really reflect on their own, to be still,' says Mrs. Messias, who has integrated the sky in her teaching for the past 10 years."

In 1985 and 1986 researchers at the Harvard University Graduate School of Education tested elementary students in Needham who had participated in the For Spacious Skies program against those who had not. They concluded that kids who were exposed to the program scored 37 percent higher in music appreciation, 13 percent higher in literary skills, and 5 percent higher n visual arts skills. For more information contact Jack Borden, For Spacious Skies, 54 Webb St., Lexington, MA 02173.

Journaling extends the classroom into the natural world around the school.

questioning, rather than critical commentary. The developing journalists need to develop the confidence and trust to honestly record *their own* observations, thoughts, questions, and insights. Journals are not the copying of the observations and thoughts of others; they are an individual's direct responses to physical, social, and internal environments. In essence, a journal is a hands-on, minds-on activity, with hands-off input from you.

Journaling as Part of an Interdisciplinary, Hands-On Curriculum

The direction of change in education today is toward interdisciplinary study, hands-on, minds-on direct experiencing, critical and creative reasoning, and a mix of group and individual activity. Nature journaling meets all of these reform goals. Journaling activity can take place both in class and out, thus providing both class- and homework. The journal becomes a database from which the learners can mine material for creative writing, art, and science projects. Keeping the journal fosters a variety of skills including

observational skills, critical and creative reasoning, communication skills, and drawing skills.

Moreover, the journal provides an ongoing record of the learners' progress in developing these skills. Comparison of journal pages over time helps track the progress of each learner. It also helps the learners perceive changes that are going on about them all the time; they can see for themselves just what they are learning. Furthermore, the firsthand experiences and observations of nature journaling foster valuable personal qualities such as caring, understanding, and responsible action.

Prompting the Process

Particularly with beginning young journalists, offering prompts may help them focus their observations. These suggestions can help guide the journaling activity, leading to growth in all areas — awareness, understanding, concern, and action. The prompts should be rather open-ended questions — specific enough to help learners focus observations and ideas, but not so specific that they severely restrict what the learners can respond to in the immediate area.

Written prompts can be provided on a separate sheet of directions for each day's activities, or you may want to create small loose-leaf journal booklets, with prompts for each small project written at the top of each journal page. (See pages 68–69 for some examples.)

Projects to Encourage Learning and Reflection

Make sure your student journalists reread journal entries regularly and reflect on what they have observed, and what they may have missed. Encourage them to return to a particular journaling site again and again, on different days of the week and at different times of the day, to see what has changed or what they may have missed before.

As a group activity in a classroom or club setting, journaling may be seen as merely another form of busy work. With your guidance, the students may find that journaling can be a joy when exercised as a form of self-expression, creativity, and discovery. You can instruct them in *ways to use* the journal, as well *as how to keep* it in the first place.

A Reflection Page

Provide your students with a page every week or two that asks them to review what they have put in the journal, and to summarize on those pages what they think are the most important things they have observed or learned. They may put their thoughts into prose, poetry, or a detailed drawing that summarizes their experiences.

REFLECTION PAGE

Read your journal pages. Think about the questions below and write or draw your thoughts about the questions.

What were the most interesting things I observed over the time period we have been keeping this set of journal entries?

What are the big ideas that I have learned from this set of journal entries?

What skills do I plan to improve upon over the next set of entries?

Which of my observations and comments would I most like to share with others?

From the Journal of: _____

Date: _____ Time: _____
Location: _____
Temp: _____ Humidity: _____
Pressure: _____
Percent cloud cover: _____

Session task: Look around for things that are in the process of changing. Describe the object or event and indicate how it is changing.

Once in his life man ought to concentrate his (or her) mind upon the remembered earth, I believe. He (she) ought to give himself up to a particular landscape in his experience, to look upon it from as many angles as he can, to wonder about it, to dwell upon it. He ought to imagine that he touches it with his hands at every season and listens to the sounds that are made upon it. He ought to imagine the creatures there and all the faintest motions of the wind. He ought to recollect the glare of noon and all the colors of the dawn and dusk.

N. SCOTT MOMADAY, *THE WAY TO RAINY MOUNTAIN*

Journaling is a year-round activity — so dress for the weather.

Give an Open-Journal Pop Quiz

Based on questions you create while observing the group journaling at a site, give a pop quiz later in the week or marking period. Let enough time pass that their short-term memory of the activity will have faded. Tell the learners they can use their journals to research answers to the quiz. This will help them see how journaling supports and builds memory.

A Writing Project

Give the learners a creative writing challenge that relates in some way to journaling activities you have provided for them. This may be an essay, short story, haiku, or other poem. Encourage them to use material in their journals as inspiration for the writing challenge. Ask them to include a note at the end of the writing assignment indicating what materials from their journals they used. Ask them to indicate what they couldn't find in their journals that they wished they had noted when journaling.

You can also challenge the students to create a place in their journals for their own poetry, personal responses to things observed, or quotations they like from writers on nature.

Teenagers and young adults especially are seeking answers often found in the writing of others such as Rainer Marie Rilke, Henry David Thoreau, Rachel Carson, Robert Frost, or Haiku poets like Basho. *Earth Prayers from around the World*, edited by Elizabeth Roberts and Elias Amidon, contains works of many good writers to expose students to.

Then ask them to try one or more of the following tasks in their journals:
- Write a poem about fall: colors, smells, sounds, feelings.
- Write about a little experience you just had while being outdoors — playing soccer, bicycling, noticing the moon, or sitting by water that is reflecting the fall colors, for example.
- Describe in poetry or prose a flower still blooming near you.
- Copy into your journal poems or prose that you like and that speak to the season or your feelings.

An Art Project

Ask the learners to create a detailed drawing or painting based on sketches and notes they created in their journals. Ask them to indicate what they couldn't find in their journals that they wished they had noted when journaling.

A Science Project

Have the students create a science research project based on observations and questions they recorded in their journals. They should indicate the question they want to explore, the observation strategy or research activities they plan to follow in doing so, and the kinds of data they expect to record in their journals as they proceed.

A History Project

Have learners select a particular area — school site, vacant lot, farm, housing development, or industrial park — and then find out what the area was like before its present use. What was there before? What did people do there? What other things lived there? If students perceive problems in the current land use, have them determine how the problem came about. Who were the players involved? What was going on in society that led to the decisions that caused the problems?

Check out such things as stone walls, glacial boulders, or giant trees on the site. Are any of these mentioned in property deeds? How did the walls and boulders get there? Can you find foundations of old buildings on the site? Are there plants like lilac, apple trees, or lily-of-the-valley that are clues that homesteads once occupied the site?

A Math Project

Have your students choose a local area, and then locate old maps of that spot. What system of measurements was used? Investigate such terms as *rod, chain, acre, mile*. What are the relationships among such measures? How do the measurements on the map translate into metric system? How can you measure objects you find without a standard ruler? Develop a measuring system using your own body parts. Figure out your own pace and stride. Translate these field measurements into standard units.

A Music Project

Record all the sounds you can hear from a particular observation point. Do the same at several other observation places. Can you develop a picture of a place based solely on the soundscape? Develop landscape drawings based on the soundscape. Create a song based on a particular soundscape, adding musical sounds that evoke that soundscape.

You cannot heal the Earth's suffering unless you feel it too. You cannot heal the Earth's joy unless you feel it too.

— JOANNA MACY,
COUNCIL OF ALL BEINGS WORKSHOP, 1990

Clare's daughter Anna finds opportunities to journal wherever she goes.

Suggested Reading

Many of the older, and very good, books on nature are out of print today. And newer books may be put out by small specialty publishers and therefore become hard to find on the shelves of high-volume bookstores. If you look for a book we recommend in your library and cannot find it, ask the librarian if the book may be available on interlibrary loan from a central library organization or special library. Use whatever information networks you have available — schools, nature centers, colleges, or local residents interested in your natural history topic, be it trees, birds, ecology, rocky coasts, stars, or weather. You can also try networking on the Internet.

Most of the naturalists we know are largely self-taught. Consider the following books and resource ideas suggestions for your own study.

Natural History

Comstock, Anna B. *Handbook of Nature Study*. Ithaca, NY: Comstock Publishing Company, 1916 (reprinted by Cornell University Press, 1986).

Durrell, Gerald. *The Amateur Naturalist*. New York: McKay/Random House, 1989.

Finch, Robert and John Elder, *Norton Book of Nature Writing*. New York: W.W. Norton & Company, 1990.

Gould, Stephen Jay. *Eight Little Piggies: Reflections on Natural History*. New York: W. W. Norton, 1994.

Halfpenny, James C., and Roy Douglas Ozanne. *Winter: An Ecological Handbook*. Boulder, CO: Jackson Books, 1989.

Hunken, Jorie. *Ecology for All Ages*. Saybrook, CT: Globe Pequot Press, 1994.

Johnson, Cathy. *The Naturalist's Path: Beginning the Study of Nature*. New York: Walker & Co., 1991.

Lawlor, Elizabeth. *Discover Nature Close to Home*. Harrisburg, PA: Stackpole Books, 1993.

Leopold, Aldo. *A Sand County Almanac*. New York: Oxford University Press, 1966.

Mitchell, John. *The Curious Naturalist*. Dubuque, IA: Kendall/Hunt Publishing Co., 1996 (reprint of a 1977 edition).

National Geographic Society, *The Curious Naturalist*. Washington, D.C.: National Geographic, 1991.

Orr, David W. *Earth in Mind: On Education, Environment and the Human Prospect*. Washington, D.C.: Island Press, 1994.

Palmer, E. Lawrence, and J. Seymour Fowler. *Fieldbook of Natural History*. New York: McGraw-Hill, 1977. Another classic that provides information on a wide range of natural history items, from plants to insects, birds, mammals, shells, rocks, and minerals.

Reader's Digest. *Joy of Nature*. Pleasantville, NY The Reader's Digest Association, Inc., 1977. A large photo essay on habitats.

Reader's Digest. *North American Wildlife: An Illustrated Guide to 2,000 Plants and Animals*. Pleasantville, NY: Reader's Digest, 1982.

Sierra Club Naturalist's Guides. San Francisco: Sierra Club Books. A very useful series to explore before visiting new areas of the country: *The North Atlantic Coast; Southern New England; The Piedmont; The Northwoods; The Sierra Nevada; The Deserts of the Southwest; The Middle Atlantic Coast*.

Silver, Donald. *One Small Square: Backyard*. New York: W. H.Freeman and Co., 1993. A novel way to study a small area of nature; highly illustrated.

Trimble, Stephen, ed. *Words from the Land: Encounters with Natural History Writing*. Salt Lake City: Gibbs M. Smith, Inc., Peregrine Smith Books,1988.

Wilson, Edward O. *Naturalist*. Cambridge, MA: Harvard University Press, 1994.

— — — . *Biophilia*. New York: Island Press, 1984.

Nature Observation

Brainerd, John. *The Nature Observer's Handbook*. Chester, CT.: The Globe Pequot Press, 1986.

Boot, Kelvin. *The Nocturnal Naturalist*. London: David & Charles, 1985.

Fadala, Sam. *Basic Projects in Wildlife Watching*. Harrisburg, PA: Stackpole Books, 1989.

Hanendrat, Frank T. *Wildlife Watcher's Handbook*. New York: Winchester Press, 1977.

Rezendes, Paul. *Tracking and the Art of Seeing: How to Read Animal Tracks and Signs*. Charlotte, VT: Camden House Publishing Co., 1992.

Roth, Charles E. *The Wildlife Observer's Guidebook*. Englewood Cliffs, NJ: Prentice-Hall, 1982.

―――. *The Plant Observer's Guidebook*. Englewood Cliffs, NJ: Prentice-Hall, 1984.

―――. *The Sky Observer's Guidebook*. New York: Prentice-Hall Press, 1986.

―――. *The Amateur Naturalist*. New York: Franklin Watts, 1993.

Smith, Richard P. *Animal Tracks and Signs of North America: Recognize and Interpret Wildlife Clues*. Harrisburg, PA: Stackpole Books, 1982.

Walton, Richard K., and Robert W. Lawson. *Birding by Ear*. Boston: Houghton Mifflin, 1989.

Field Guides

Arnett, Ross H., and Dr. Richard L. Jacques. *Guide to Insects*. New York: Simon and Schuster, 1981.

The Audubon Society Nature Guides. New York: Alfred A Knopf. A series on deserts, grasslands, the Pacific Coast, the Atlantic and Gulf Coasts, eastern forests, western forests, deserts, and wetlands.

Brown, Lauren. *Grasses: An Identification Guide*. Boston: Houghton Mifflin, 1979.

―――. *Weeds In Winter*. New York: W. W. Norton & Co., 1976.

Chambers, Kenneth A. *A Country-Lover's Guide to Wildlife*. New York: New American Library, 1979.

Chartrand, Mark R. III. *Sky Guide — A Field Guide for Amateurs*. New York: Golden Press, 1982.

Covell, Charles V. Jr. *A Field Guide to the Moths of Eastern North America*. Boston: Houghton Mifflin, 1984.

Farrand, John Jr. *An Audubon Handbook: How to Identify Birds*. New York: McGraw-Hill, 1988.

Field Guide to the Birds of North America. Washington, D.C.: National Geographic Society, 1983.

Harrison, Hal H. *A Field Guide to Birds' Nests*. Boston: Houghton Mifflin, 1975.

LaChapelle, Edward R. *Field Guide to Snow Crystals*. Seattle: University of Washington Press, 1969.

Linhoff, Gary H. *Simon & Schuster's Guide to Mushrooms*. New York: Simon & Schuster, 1981.

Meinkoth, Norman A. *The Audubon Society Field Guide to Seashore Creatures*. New York: Alfred A. Knopf, 1981.

Menzel, Donald H., and Jay M. Paschoff. *A Field Guide to the Stars and Planets*. Boston: Houghton Mifflin, 1983.

Montgomery, F. H. *Weeds of Northern United States and Canada*. New York: Frederick Warne & Company, Inc., 1964.

Murie, Olaus J. *A Field Guide to Animal Tracks*. Boston: Houghton Mifflin, 1975.

Peterson, Roger Tory, and Margaret McKenney. *A Field Guide to Wildflowers of Northeastern and North-Central North America*. Boston: Houghton Mifflin, 1974.

Pyle, Robert Michael. *The Audubon Society Field Guide to North American Butterflies*. New York: Alfred A. Knopf, 1981.

Reddington, Charles B. *Plants in Wetlands*. Dubuque, IA: Kendall/Hunt Publishing Company, 1994.

Robbins, Chandler S., Bertel Bruun, and Herbert S. Zim. *Birds of North America*. New York: Golden Press, 1966.

Shaefer, Vincent J., and John A. Day. *A Field Guide to the Atmosphere*. Boston: Houghton Mifflin, 1981.

Smith, Hobart M. *A Golden Guide to Field Identification: Amphibians of North America*. New York: Golden Press, 1978.

Smith, Hobart M., and Edmund D. Brodie Jr. *A Golden Guide to Field Identification: Reptiles of North America*. New York: Golden Press, 1982.

Stokes, Donald W. *A Guide to Nature in Winter*. Boston: Little, Brown & Co., 1976.

―――. *A Guide to the Behavior of Common Birds*. Boston: Little, Brown & Co., 1979.

Symonds, George W. D. *The Tree Identification Book*. New York: William Morrow & Co., 1958.

―――. *The Shrub Identification Book*. New York: William Morrow & Co., 1963.

Whitaker, John O. Jr. *The Audubon Society Field Guide to North American Mammals*. New York: Alfred A. Knopf, 1980.

Zim, Herbert S. *A Golden Guide: Botany*. New York: Golden Press, 1970. (*See also* the other useful and inexpensive Golden Guide Series: *Insects, Weeds, Nonflowering Plants, Pond Life, Weather, Butterflies, Spiders, Stars,* and *Zoology*.)

Working with Kids in Nature

Carson, Rachel. *The Sense of Wonder*. New York: Harper and Row, Publishers, 1984.

Cornell, Joseph. *Sharing Nature with Children: A Parent's and Teacher's Nature and Awareness Guidebook*. Nevada City, CA: Dawn Publications, 1998.

Herman, Marina L., and Joseph F. Passineau. *Teaching Kids to Love the Earth*. Duluth, MN: Pfeifer-Hamilton Publishers, 1991.

Leslie, Clare Walker. *Nature All Year Long*. New York: Greenwillow Books, 1991.

Nabham, Gary. *The Geography of Childhood*. Boston: Beacon Press, 1994.

Russell, Helen Ross. *Ten Minute Field Trips*. Washington, D.C.: National Science Teachers Association, 1990. Developed by a master teacher-naturalist who finds nature in the most urban of school grounds.

Sisson, Edith. *Nature with Children of All Ages*. New York: Simon & Schuster, 1982.

Simon, Seymour. *Science in a Vacant Lot*. New York: Viking Press, 1970.

Sobel, David. *Children's Special Places*. Tuscon: Zephyr Press, 1993.

Drawing Nature

Appellof, Marian E., ed. *Everything You Ever Wanted to Know about Watercolor*. New York: Watson-Guptill Publications, 1992.

Barlowe, Dorothea, and Sy Barlowe. *Illustrating Nature: How to Paint and Draw Plants and Animals*. New York: Portland House, 1987.

Borgeson, Bet. *The Colored Pencil*. New York: Watson-Guptill Publications, 1983.

Cameron, Julia. *The Artist's Way*. New York: J. P. Tarcher/Putnam, 1992.

Franck, Frederick. *The Zen of Seeing: Seeing/Drawing As Meditation*. New York: Vintage Books/Random House, 1975.

Goldberg, Natalie. *Writing Down the Bones*. Boston: Shambala Publications, 1986.

Guptill, Arthur L. *Rendering in Pen and Ink*. New York: Watson-Guptill Publications, 1947.

Hodges, Elaine R. S., ed. *The Guild Book of Scientific Illustration*. New York: Van Nostrand Reinhold, 1989.

Johnson, Cathy. *First Steps in Drawing*. Cincinnati, OH: North Light Books, 1995.

———. *Sketching In Nature*. San Francisco: Sierra Club Books, 1990.

———. *Painting Watercolors: First Step Series*. Cincinnati, OH: North Light Books, 1995.

Knight, Charles R. *Animal Drawing: Anatomy and Action for Artists*. New York: Dover Publications, 1947. A classic book by one of this century's early masters of wildlife art.

Leslie, Clare Walker. *Nature Drawing: A Tool for Learning*. Dubuque, IA: Kendall/Hunt Publishing Company, 1995.

———. *The Art of Field Sketching*. Dubuque, IA: Kendall/Hunt Publishing Company, 1995 (republication of the 1984 edition).

Nice, Claudia. *Sketching Your Favorite Subjects in Pen and Ink*. Cincinnati, OH: North Light Books, 1993.

Nicolaides, Kimon. *The Natural Way to Draw*. Boston: Houghton Mifflin, 1941.

Seslar, Patrick. *Wildlife Painting: Step by Step*. Cincinnati, OH: North Light Books, 1995.

West, Keith. *How to Draw Plants: The Techniques of Botanical Illustration*. New York: Watson-Guptill Publications, 1983.

Nature Journals

Hinchman, Hannah. *A Life in Hand*. Salt Lake City: Peregrine Smith Books, 1991.

———. *A Trail through Leaves: The Journal as a Path to Place*. New York: W. W. Norton, 1997.

Holden, Edith. *The Country Diary of an Edwardian Lady*. New York: Holt, Rinehart, and Winston, 1977.

Johnson, Cathy. *One Square Mile: An Artist's Journal of America's Heartland*. New York: Walker and Company, 1993.

Leslie, Clare Walker. *A Naturalist's Sketchbook: Pages from the Seasons of a Year*. New York: Dodd, Mead and Co., 1987.

Midda, Sara. *Sara Midda's South of France: A Sketchbook*. New York: Workman Publishing, 1990.

Poortvliet, Rien. *Noah's Ark*. New York: Harry N. Abrams, Inc., Publishers, 1985.

The Natural History in America

Barber, Lynn. *The Heyday of Natural History*. Garden City, NY: Doubleday and Company, Inc., 1980.

Bonta, Marcia Meyers, ed. *Women in the Field: America's Pioneering Women Naturalists*. College Station, TX: A&M University Press, 1991.

Cronon, William. *Changes in the Land: Indians, Colonists, and the Ecology of New England*. New York: Hill and Wang, a division of Farrar Straus Giroux, 1983.

Hanley, Wayne. *Natural History in America*. New York: Quadrangle Books, 1977.

Huth, Hans. *Nature and the American Mind*. Lincoln, NE: University of Nebraska Press, 1975.

Kastner, Joseph. *A World of Watchers*. San Francisco: Sierra Club Books, 1993. A book on the history of bird-watching in this country.

Shepard, Paul. *Man in the Landscape: A Historic View of the Esthetics of Nature*. New York: Alfred A. Knopf, 1967.

Resources

Sources of Personal Guidance on Natural History

To find people of similar interests who may even be involved in their own nature journaling, you can turn to a variety of local and regional organizations. Some of the organizations that are accessible in or near most communities across the country include:

• The local public library and its regional affiliate
• Nature centers or science museums
• Community colleges and state colleges and universities
• Sportsmen's clubs
• State fish and wildlife agencies, many of which now operate watchable wildlife programs
• Local conservation commissions and land trusts
• Some Internet Web pages
• Local Audubon clubs
• National park staff members, particularly ranger-naturalists.

Places to Go Journaling Outside Your Neighborhood

• Town-owned conservation areas (most town offices will have simple maps of the locations of these areas, as will town libraries)
• Lands owned by local land trusts
• Nature center lands
• Wildlife management areas (ask the state fish and wildlife agencies for directions to these)
• National wildlife refuges
• National forests
• National recreation areas
• State parks
• Abandoned railroad rights-of way
• Cemeteries (many have quiet wooded groves and ponds)
• Farms (get landowner permission first)

Bookstores often carry local books on short walks for specific areas. Organizations such as the Appalachian Mountain Club and the Sierra Club have detailed maps and descriptions of interstate trails. Birding clubs also may have books on locations of hot birding spots in their area. Two books that are of use in locating natural areas to visit are:

Perry, John, and Jane Greverus Perry. *The Random House Guide to Natural Areas of the Eastern United States.* New York: Random House, 1980.

Riley, Laura, and William Riley. *Guide to the National Wildlife Refuges: How to Get There; What to See and Do.* Garden City, N.Y.: Anchor Press/Doubleday, 1979.

Organizations Devoted to Nature Activities

Appalachian Mountain Club
5 Joy Street, Boston, MA 02108
(Publishes *AMC Outdoors,* which announces events and workshops.)

National Audubon Society
950 Third Avenue, New York, NY 10022
(Publishes *Audubon,* full of articles, photos, and information on special places. The organization also runs several natural history camps around the country.)

National Wildlife Federation
1400 Sixteenth Street, N.W., Washington, D.C. 20077-9964
(Publishes *National Wildlife, International Wildlife, Ranger Rick,* and *Your Big Backyard.*

The organization also sponsors several Summits — family outdoor activities — each summer at selected locations around the country.)

The Sierra Club
730 Polk Street, San Francisco, CA 94109
(Noted for its outstanding nature book publication program. Local clubs also sponsor a variety of hiking trips.)

The National Parks and Conservation Association
1776 Massachusetts Avenue, N.W., Washington, D.C. 20036
(Publishes *National Parks* with lots of information on places you may want to visit and problems that face our parks.)

The American Museum of Natural History
Central Park West at Seventy-Ninth Street, New York, NY 10024
(America's premier natural history museum and publisher of *Natural History,* one of the best sources of natural history articles. The regular feature "This Land" is useful in pointing out some unique but accessible natural history sites you might want to visit.)

Consider also the following organizations and their publications for information on nature writing and nature art:

The Orion Society and the Myrin Institute
195 Main Street, Great Barrington, MA 01230
(Publishes *Orion* magazine, which focuses on the relationships between people and environment. It is the most literate source of information about contemporary nature writers and their works.)

Wildlife Art News
P.O. Box 430
Elk River, MN 55330-0430

Naturalist-Journalists to Know and Read

Among the earliest nature journalists known to our Western culture was **Aristotle**, the Greek scholar who wrote *Historia Animalia* around A.D. 335. This book cataloged three hundred different kinds of animals with backbones. He was followed by the Roman **Pliny the Elder,** who in A.D. 75 produced the thirty-seven volumes of *Historia Naturalis,* which illustrated and described for the first time typhoons and earthquakes, along with exotic sea serpents and a wide variety of odd-looking birds and animals.

Leonardo da Vinci, living in Italy between 1452 and 1519, was a talented and creative artist who became one of the first to record in journals his studies of waterfalls, cyclones, lilies, trees, and human anatomy, along with a host of inventions.

Gilbert White (1720–1793) author of *A Naturalist at Selburne*, kept a journal of his observations of his British countryside, which he referred to in developing his book.

Throughout the nineteenth century in Europe and America it was quite popular to be a naturalist, collect natural history specimens from around the world, and keep nature diaries. (Even **Queen Victoria** kept a nature diary.) It was also common for schoolchildren and young women to keep nature diaries of their villages through the seasons. Nature study was an integral subject in the British school system, and still is in many regions today. **Edith Holden's** *Diary of an Edwardian Lady* has become quite popular in recent years due to a recent reprint and is a good example of the nature diaries of that period.

Charles Darwin (1809–1882) was also a nature journalist who recorded his thoughts and observations over the years, particularly during his long voyage on the HMS *Beagle*. It was later reflections on these journals that led Darwin to see the basis for his theory of evolution. Darwin is known to have commented that his "greatest regret was not knowing how to draw better" so as to help his observations.

Other European nature journalists of accomplishment and fame in the nineteenth century included the great Swiss geologist and naturalist **Louis Agassiz**, who gave us the watch phrase "Study nature, not books," and the great French student of insect behavior, **Jean Henri Fabre**.

In America, most early naturalists had to be skilled at drawing and writing as well as observation. They had to paint their specimens in the swamps of Florida or the dense woods of the Smokies, or before the cold took over their fingers on the prairies of the Dakotas. The paintings, sketches, and written observations are invaluable today, for they depict a land and its occupants that have in large measure vanished.

Mark Catesby observed and painted everything from bison to frogs during his travels in America from England between 1712 and 1726.

William Bartram (1739–1823) recorded in words and paintings the flowers, alligators, and many birds he encountered during his travels through the southern states from the 1740s to the 1770s.

John James Audubon (1785–1851) explored America looking for bird life, recording all he saw in great life-size paintings. He also kept extensive journals of his observations of the American frontier. Eventually he published his journals, and turned his watercolor paintings into colored engravings with the help of the great engraver Havell.

Our great travel journalists were **Meriwether Lewis** and **William Clark.** Their detailed descriptions, sketches, and collected specimens from their expedition across the American west from 1802 to 1805 helped Americans learn more of what we had actually acquired through the great Louisiana Purchase. Both explorers were chosen by **President Thomas Jefferson**, himself an accomplished journalist and naturalist, because they could keep accurate and detailed journals.

Henry David Thoreau faithfully kept journals of his ramblings, whether through his hometown of Concord, Massachusetts, or his visits to Cape Cod and Maine. Thoreau's journals were the database upon which he drew to create his masterpiece, *Walden*, and his other books.

Margaret Morse Nice was a housewife who, between her household chores, kept notes in her journal on the song sparrows that shared her yard. Over the years she added more and more detailed notes on this species, and when her children grew older she became a full-time ornithologist. Her journals gave her the detailed information she needed to write the most complete life history of this bird that had ever been done.

Ernest Thompson Seton (1860–1946) was an artist and naturalist who kept detailed journals over the years full of drawings and words. He used these journals as the basis of popular books such as *Wild Animals I Have Known*. Some people challenged his knowledge, and called him a nature faker. At the urging of President Theodore Roosevelt, he turned his journal notes into a multivolume scientific book called *Lives of Game Animals*, which is used as a reference to this day.

Suggested Scale for Teachers to Assess Nature Journaling Skills

Teachers often ask, "How can we create a scale to assess these journals, and how can we convert this to a grade if expected to?" Journals are not about marks or grades, although schools often demand them. The key is to have the learners get great satisfaction from the observations and their recording, and to use their journals as a source for other activities. Assessment should be used to help foster satisfaction in the efforts made and the material learned. Wherever possible, assessment should be positive and reassuring.

A 4-point scale is useful for teachers to use in assessing student journals. You can set up criteria on a grid similar to what follows, and use it to determine how well each student is progressing.

Vocabulary

0 = No new entries made from determined start date
1 = Few new words used and several used incorrectly
2 = Few new words used but all are used correctly
3 = Several new words are used and most are used correctly
4 = Many new words used and all used correctly

Sketching Ability

0 = no sketches used
1 = Some crude sketches attempted but they are unclear in their representation
2 = Some sketches made that clearly represent what was observed
3 = Most sketches are clear and indicate understanding of the shape and structure of the objects drawn
4 = All sketches are clear and show understanding of basic concepts of rendering form and shading

General Assessment

Similar ranked criteria can be established for all categories and can be used either for self-assessment by the learner or for assessment by the teacher/leader. It is usually helpful to have the learners help set the criteria for each level so that they are always aware of what they are striving for. For the classroom teacher who is bound to give a letter or numerical grade for everything, the 4-point scale can be used as a basis for creating grades. For example:

0 = F or a number 59 or below
1 = D or a number between 60 and 69
2 = C or a number between 70 and 79
3 = B or a number between 80 and 89
4 = A or a number between 90 and 100

Portfolio Review

Portfolios are an assessment form that is growing in popularity in schools. A portfolio is a collection of samples of a student's work over a period of time. In many ways a journal is a de facto portfolio and can be used by itself or combined with other documents to provide evidence of a student's progress.

Index

Other Storey Titles You Will Enjoy

The Backyard Bird-Lover's Guide, by Jan Mahnken. Covers feeding, territory, courtship, nesting, laying, and parenting characteristics of a variety of birds. 320 pages. Paperback. ISBN 0-88266-927-3.

Hand-Feeding Backyard Birds, by Hugh Wiberg. Learn to feed wild birds right from your hand! Wiberg reveals the best foods, weather conditions, and time of year to hand-feed birds. 160 pages. Paperback. ISBN 1-58017-181-8.

Making Bentwood Trellises, Arbors, Gates, and Fences, by Jim Long. Learn how to collect limbs from a wide variety of native trees and craft them into dozens of trellis, gate, arbor, and fence designs. Includes full-color photographs of all projects and suggestions for growing vining plants on your trellises and arbors. 128 pages. Paperback. ISBN 1-58017-051-X.

Nature Printing, by Laura Donnelly Bethmann. Step-by-step instructions for applying paint and ink directly to plants and flowers to press images onto stationery, fabrics, furniture, and more. 96 pages. Paperback. ISBN 1-58017-376-4.

Papermaking with Plants: Creative Recipes and Projects Using Herbs, Flowers, Grasses, and Leaves, by Helen Hiebert. Learn how to collect wild and cultivated plant material, set up a studio, and make paper, vegetable papyrus, and natural dyes. 112 pages. Hardcover. ISBN 1-58017-087-0.

Rustic Birdhouses and Feeders: Unique Thatched-Roof Projects Designed to Audubon Society Specifications, by Colin McGhee with Tracy Breyfogle. Get advice on designing, selecting natureal materials for, assembling, and detailing functional and fun feeders and housing for bluebirds, chickadees, wrens, and more. 144 pages. Paperback. ISBN 1-58017-137-0.

Year-Round Gardening Projects, from *Horticulture Magazine*'s Monthly "Step-by-Step" Column, with drawings by Elayne Sears. 86 how-to articles arranged seasonally with accurate, detailed line drawings. 224 pages. Paperback. ISBN 1-58017-039-0.

These books and other Storey books are available at your bookstore, farm store, garden center, or directly from Storey Books, 210 MASS MoCA Way, North Adams, MA 01247, or by calling 1-800-441-5700. Or visit our Web site at www.storey.com.